Flying
SCOTSMAN

Graeme Obree

Flying

SCOTSMAN

Foreword by
Francesco Moser

Birlinn

First published in Great Britain in 2003 by

Birlinn Ltd
West Newington House
10 Newington Road
Edinburgh EH9 1QS

www.birlinn.co.uk

reprinted in 2003

ISBN 1 84158 283 2

British Library Cataloguing-in-Publication Data
A catalogue record is available on request from the British Library

Typeset by Palimpsest Book Production, Polmont, Stirlingshire
Printed and bound in Great Britain by
Creative Print & Design, Ebbw Vale, Wales

contents

foreword

There is a little madness in all of us, the men who dared defy the Hour. One must be a little crazy to undertake such a torture: can you remember what Merckx said after getting off the bike in Mexico city? He talked about pure suffering; it is difficult to deny it.

So Graeme is crazy, like all of us . . . Maybe a little more crazy than us, a kind of peculiarity, like an artist. Yes, Mr Obree is unique: an artist of the pedal, able to make his brain, his heart and his legs function with the same effectiveness. A strange animal, a very rare thoroughbred, and for this reason very delicate just like a crystal. I like him, as does everyone else who loves cycling. I like him because he is different from everyone else, always showing devotion and rigour. I like him and that's why I shout today like on 17 July '93 and on 27 April '94 'Forza Graeme!'

Francesco Moser
July 2003

one: my early years

My childhood is far more influential in my present than a childhood ought to be, so that is where my story begins.

I was born in Nuneaton, Warwickshire on September 11, 1965 and came to Scotland shortly afterwards. My parents, John and Marcie, came from Scotland – Ayrshire to be more accurate – and were in Warwickshire because of my father's posting as a police officer. I was their second son and there were only 15 months between Gordon and me.

My father's posting in Scotland was in Prestwick, Ayrshire and it is there that I have my earliest memories. We moved from Prestwick to Kilmarnock when I was four years old. It was there that I first felt different from the other children – we were police. I cannot remember very much because I was so young, but our bogie was set on fire and our tortoise got the chop too.

I have clear memories of Kilmarnock in incidents. My first introduction to the school system was in the form of punishment for a window broken by a stone which left my brother's hand. It was not a deliberate act but an accident in the playground, which was just by our house. It annoyed me that the punishment could not be joint and my first impression of school was, for me, the correct one, as time would prove.

I also quite vividly remember the day my brother and I learned to ride our bikes at the same moment. It was Uncle Stuart who pushed us off at the top of the brae, side-by-side, with the prophetic words 'Mind the corner at the bottom!' It was white-knuckle stuff and we might have been scuffed a bit, but from that moment on we could ride.

We were not there long before we moved to Newmilns, which was a small town set in a valley, but there the story was no different. Newmilns was parochial enough to single you out, but large enough to be nasty with it, to compound matters we were not only 'police', we were also newcomers.

It was a terrible combination and from day one at school we were 'the filth'. Part of the problem was the fact that my father's posting was in the valley itself, so the enmity towards him was passed down to the local children from their parents and from them to us. We were outsiders the entire time we were there, which was eleven years.

The enmity towards us manifested itself in three ways – name calling, ostracism and violence. Even my sister Yvonne, five years my junior, was not excluded from the party but the violence was mainly reserved for Gordon and me. It seemed that rarely a week would go by without my being strapped for fights I never asked to be in. In fact I was doing my utmost to avoid them, but seeing as I was a common denominator, I was seen as a troublemaker by Mr Gillespie, the headmaster.

This set the pattern for my whole school life and clowning around became habitual as a means of trying to be accepted. When I think back on my school days I can only remember feeling sadness and loneliness. The violence does not stand out so much, although there was plenty of it and some of it quite extreme. Being head-butted from the crowd or roughed up was common enough to lose its shock factor and, apart from the worst incidents, I do not think that the violence itself left a large impression on me emotionally.

Avoiding violence, and the fear of violence, there were worse forms of victimisation: those that were intangible. When it came to physical violence though, I thought of it and perceived it as two different sensations after a while. Being kicked about the head was so different from being kicked about the body.

Ironic as it may seem, in the midst of it, violence has a beauty and excitement that nothing else can generate. Sometimes, even though it was nothing more than extreme physical harm, I could almost be disappointed when it ended. At times the most extreme violence, especially to the head, brought an orgasm of fear, excitement, panic and adrenaline.

Nonetheless, I always slipped back to my mode of violence avoidance.

For me there was also a much, much more hurtful thing called social exclusion. Because of being the 'newcomer' and 'the filth' as well as feeling I was the odd one out in the family, I was desperate to be accepted into the periphery of my peer group. I was the tag-along child on a good day, but when I was seven an event happened that mired what hope I had into the ground.

My memory of it starts at the point of arrival at school, where there were three double-decker buses decked with streamers and balloons sitting in the schoolyard on a beautiful, sunny, summer morning. The engines are turning over and all the children are getting on board – the whole of primary three are going to Millport, a small town on a small island a mile or two off the Ayrshire coast. It is a beautiful scene, except for one problem – I'm not going.

I cannot recall the given reason for my non-participation, but it made no difference to the material fact that I was there beside Mrs Jamieson and Mr Gillespie, waving goodbye to my peer group. It was the 'belt first and ask questions later' headmaster, Mr Gillespie, who cruelly made me stand and wave at the laughing and pointing classmates at the back windows of the departing buses.

Next I was escorted to another class by Mrs Jamieson, who only seemed to teach the three 'D's – Discipline, Discipline, Discipline. I was taken to a fourth-year class, where I was placed at the front of the class like a prize example of unworthiness. I don't mean in the front row, but at the very front like a pulpit to a congregation. There I sat, in my own island of abject sorrow, staring at the blue sky through the side window. Every second of every minute I could feel the mockery of sixty eyes burn into the back of me as I shielded my face from its glare, and every second of every minute I felt the weight of tears bursting behind my eyes. I refused to cry – I could not cry – because I knew that the wolves behind me would devour my emotions and leave me as good as dead inside.

At the end of the next day I had to endure the sight of my tormentors' return; I felt dead inside anyhow. At that point I felt like 'the other boy' at home, and at school as I was 'the filth', but now I knew I was worthless and detestable. It was not until the next morning, when my tormentors started teasing and laughing at me, that the full impact struck my seven-year-old head to such effect that it inspired my childhood dream that everything I knew would be annihilated by a nuclear holocaust. For others it was the great fear of the era, but for me it became a day-to-day hope to cling onto.

I can remember the exact spot where I stood when the blow came and at that moment the world ended for me. It was of my doing. I could not live and be part of the world around me any more – it was too sad and painful. From that moment I was no longer here, and I was no longer that little boy. No, I was merely an observer behind his eyes and anything that hurt the little boy did not hurt me, because I only witnessed what happened to the boy.

These are truly the saddest days of my life by a long way and I lived in my self-imposed protective prison for more or less most of my school life. Beyond that my childhood left me with an isolationist and insular personality as well as a real and subconscious fear of social situations.

One other incident that stands out, though, in my memory from childhood is my brother and me being taken at knifepoint when we were nine and ten. We were walking down a backstreet in the town when we were set upon by three older boys and taken at knifepoint into a derelict house. There my brother was urinated on while I could do nothing to help. We were taken into the basement, where other things happened. One of those was being made to touch each other's genitals at knifepoint while being threatened that they'd hurt the other brother if we refused to do it and vice versa.

The incident was taken to the authorities and when it came up in court I was too young to give evidence, and my brother fainted in the dock. In the end, it made no difference as the assailants were effectively let off.

What scant regard Gordon and I had for 'justice' was gone and nothing else of this kind in the future would ever be reported.

Gordon and I never spoke about the matter to other people or to each other from then on and it was consigned to history and our memories.

As far as my primary school years are concerned it was a teacher called Myrtle McKay who gave me a lifeline, by letting me be part of something. She taught music.

She ran a recorder class in her own time after school hours, and she encouraged me to get involved. I was interested in music, but at the start I was more interested in walking home on a near-deserted footpath after school time.

My initial motive never waned, but my interest in the recorder soon overcame it. After a while I had a small part in the band, but more importantly Mrs McKay took time – her own time – to speak to me like a person. I will always remember her as a kind and warm-hearted person who provided an oasis of hope in a desert of despair.

One incident I should mention, as I am famous for cycling, is my first serious bike accident when I was about nine or ten. Gordon and I were racing down the main street when we touched wheels. I went straight over the handlebars and ended up with my front tooth totally embedded in my bottom lip. The remaining stump had to be removed and now I only have one front tooth. Luckily, the other teeth moved round and closed the gap so that only the keenest of eye can spot the deficit. Strangely, the whole thing was remarkably painless, despite the broken tooth and copious amounts of blood.

Gordon and I did a lot of cycling about as boys. It always seemed a safer way to travel than on foot, and it gave us freedom to go wherever we wanted. We would go to the far end of town on bike, but very rarely on foot. In fact, there was a shop at the far end of town which I never realised was there until I was about eleven.

Newmilns is basically a one-street town with a few sidestreets branching off, so it was long and narrow, following the course of the river Irvine that runs through the valley. Because it is in a valley, there is no avoiding hills if you cycle anywhere but the main road. You can climb to about a thousand feet on either side, which we often did and we would seem to take it in turns to fall off on the descents.

We started venturing further and further, and by our early teens, we could cover up to 60 miles in a day. We were not cyclists by any manner of means – we were just boys on bikes, clothed in padded jackets and trainers. The funny thing was that Gordon always seemed hardier than me in terms of his endurance of adversity, especially cold and wet weather. I can honestly say that I have no recollection of him complaining about anything ever, and I suppose in our daily lives we were used to adversity.

Cycling trips were not really my brother's thing – just something to do. He was a radio amateur and buried himself in electronics from a very young age, so the more involved he got in that the less cycling he was into. I had also gotten into cycling through forests and on rough paths, which my bike wasn't really built for. In the '70s, it was seen as a bit immature for a boy of my age to romp along dirt paths on bikes – but it was fun. The forests nearby had good drop-offs, and I always liked to challenge myself to see how big a slope I could handle without spilling it. I always felt much safer by bike because I could easily cycle away rather than be set upon. I would rarely go to the forest by foot, as I would have to run the gauntlet of the open street first.

I always preferred rainy days, as almost nobody would be out and about. Sometimes, though, during the summer holidays, I would brave the 200 yards along the main road to a stream which ran underneath the road. I could cross the road through the tunnel, and this led to a field that led uphill to the open and deserted countryside. I would simply hide there and come back in time for dinner. That way, I would avoid my parents' comments about being a couch potato and that I should go out and play – which is the impression I gave when I returned.

I used to love climbing trees, especially really hard ones with no branches at the bottom. I always felt safe in trees. There were a couple of trees which I climbed all the time and they were two of my favourite places. One was so high above ground that I could see right down the valley all the way to the coast, which was about 17 miles away, and I would spend hours up there, just watching the world go by. It seems a strange thing to talk about trees in an autobiography, but they were a bigger part of my life than friends, and I was quite dismayed when one of them was chopped down.

At secondary school, I had no real interest in academic achievement, although my best subjects were maths and physics. Mrs Monaghan asked me if I would represent the school in a maths competition, but I instantly refused, as I had spent most of my life either being invisible or a clown to other kids. I did not actually think why I refused at the time – I just refused.

Ironically, my worst subjects at secondary school were metalwork and physical education (sports). This might seem strange, as I built my own bike and won the world championships a few years later, but the truth of the matter is that metalwork was the ultimate place of physical danger. Not only were my fellow pupils armed with lumps of metal and sharp tools, we were usually completely unsupervised for entire classes.

I used to dread metalwork so much that it seemed to me like going into the gladiators' arena. I believe I spent most of these classes with my back to a workbench and a sharp implement at hand. In four years of metalwork, I produced a grand total of a trowel and half of a plant-holder bracket. I could have knocked out the same in my father's shed in half a day.

In sport I also liked to keep out of the way, but, to be honest, I really was pretty poor at most sports except climbing and the long jump. I was always last or nearly last to be picked. Team sports were the worst. We almost always ended up with football and it was always, without deviation, the same select group of boys who were given the honour of selecting teams and deciding who plays where. If it was football, then

I knew the routine off pat – I would get picked last or second-last, and I would play in defence. In four years, there was no exception to this. Not once. At least I was not the worst, as the boy whom I competed with for last-picking spent his entire secondary school years in goals for the crime of being effeminate.

As I went through secondary school at Loudoun Academy, the situation improved slightly as the rowdier element tended to be in lower-grade classes. Loudoun Academy is situated about a mile from Galston, which is about the same size as Newmilns, at about 5,000 population, and is two miles further down the valley towards the coast. It was common practice for the majority of the school population to stream down to Galston during lunch break.

I would never indulge in this practice for the sake of avoiding trouble, but a mate from class persuaded me to visit his house on the lunch break. After a couple of times, an incident happened which changed my mind. Three thugs recognised me and must have been waiting for my return. One of them had an axe, with which he threatened me and my friend, so my friend had no choice but to stand aside while the other two kicked the absolute crap out of me. I can remember the physical struggle to make it back to school. The beating was noticeable enough that one teacher did ask me what had happened, and after I told him, he pointed out that I should have hit them back. This further undermined my faith in authority and establishment, and even my parents will be unaware of this incident until they read the brief for this book.

I think I became even more withdrawn at secondary school, to the extent that I never had a single friend at my house for the time that I was there. I had already been taken to a child psychologist at primary school, but it was at secondary school that suicide seemed like a tempting idea. The language lab window was the biggest drop, and onto concrete, and at these times it was that window which seemed to be the passage to freedom. Ironically, having the 'big get-out' in the back of my mind gave me the flippancy to carry on regardless.

Luckily, cycling at that time was becoming more and more a vehicle of freedom and escapism for me, and it was a classmate, Gordon Graham, who suggested I come along to Wallacehill Cycling Club in Kilmarnock, the main town in the area. It is a town of about 50,000 people and is seven miles from our old house in Newmilns.

It was January or February of 1981, and I'm not sure if Gordon actually believed I would show on a cold winter's night. Gordon was a member already, as was his father, Gus. I was completely apprehensive about walking into a club of strange people. I went for it anyway, but I was right to be apprehensive. As soon as I opened the door and walked in, there was complete silence from what had been busy chitchat. Everyone turned around and stared for a moment, and I froze and panicked at the same time. It was Jimmy Train who broke the silence, and said to come in. I remember being relieved that Gordon was there that night, as it meant I was not completely among strangers.

I was clad in black boots, jeans and a parka jacket. My bike was a racing-style bike with five gears, that my brother and I both had bought for us by our parents. It became apparent quite quickly that, in real cycling terms, I was a complete amateur. I met a few members of the club that night, but it was obvious that Jimmy Train was the leader. He seemed to be the stereotypical opposite of what one would expect as the elder statesman of a cycling club. He was dressed in old jeans and a jacket, smoked almost continuously, and he instantly reminded me of Popeye. Despite his idiosyncrasies, it did not take me long to realise that Jimmy Train was not only a source of wisdom – most of it moulded from a previous era – but also an honest and straight-to-the-point type of person.

The journey home was a taster of the way that beginners are treated in cycling clubs – or certainly at that time in Britain. There were three other boys who lived in the valley – my classmate Gordon, Tony Williamson and Alex Currie. The whole idea was to humble the beginner and test him out by trying to drop him. I might have been a complete amateur, but I had learned enough by cycling with my brother to know that the easiest place to be is right behind someone else's back wheel. So when the pace went up and up, I was glued to the last wheel by the skin of my teeth. I bid them goodnight as we passed my house in a way that would hide my exhaustion, and then crawled slowly into the house.

My metamorphosis from rank amateur to champion would be driven along by many rides of this nature, where trying to outdo each other was par for the course. The starting point was the club run on Sundays. Beginner or not, it was obligatory to become part of the through-and-off system, where side-by-side, two riders would take it in turns to provide the slipstreaming at the front of the group for the others behind.

At the start, I was physically unable to ride very far at the pace before being 'dropped', but every week I would cycle back alone and pretty soon my fitness and staying power grew to the point where I could hack it. Also, I was starting to use better clothing and footwear, and I managed to improve my bike slightly with toe clips and the like.

The winter rides were dying out in March, as a lot of the riders were either riding competitively or helping others to organise events. As luck would have it, I had become friendly with Gordon Stead and John Stewart. Gordon was a year older than me, and had been in 'proper' cycling a lot longer. John was in his early twenties, but was not as fit as Gordon or me. We started going rides together while most of the club was involved in racing, and sometimes we covered remarkable distances.

This suited me fine because my original reason for joining a club was the idea that I could get involved in touring trips, and Gordon and John were both into that, especially youth hostelling. Gordon had also introduced me to a guy called Alistair Gow, who lived on the opposite side of Glasgow, about 30 miles away. To me, at that time, Alistair Gow was an absolute guru in cycling terms. His whole house was steeped in cycling and the attic was nothing short of an Aladdin's cave to someone like me.

Alistair was into long-distance, high-speed touring and some of those rides were like races. I was only fifteen, Gordon sixteen, and sometimes we would cycle to Alistair's, before setting off on a long ride and on our return his dear old mum would make us onion soup and dinner and then, after a bit of cycling gossip, we would set about the 30 miles back home. One time, I remember drinking a can of cold baked beans and being so exhausted I had to walk part of the moor road to Newmilns, reaching home at about 1 a.m., with school the next day.

It wasn't long, though, before I had been talked into riding a time trial. I think it was about May of that year, and I had managed to persuade my parents that my sixteenth birthday had come early, and they bought me a proper racing bike with alloy wheels and components and state-of-the-art twelve-speed gears. It was a Peugeot from Billy Bilsland's shop in Glasgow. It rode like a dream compared to my other bike, and I suppose I was curious to see what I could do, but nervous at the same time.

My first race was a 10-mile time trial on the open road, and I made a bit of a gaffe with the timekeepers. I thought the finish was directly opposite the start. I was halfway through getting changed, when someone told me the finish timekeeper was 200 yards down the road, and my

official time for my first race was 32 minutes and a handful of seconds
– second last. My team mate, John Stewart, saved me from last place.

I did not ride many races that year. Touring and long rides were still
what I wanted to do. As luck would have it though, on one ride through
Glasgow, Gordon Stead and I met a boy who tried to sell an old frame
to us. We followed him to the backstreets and it turned out to be an
old Cinelli pre-war track frame. It needed a lot of work and there were
no forks, but it was a classic, so I settled on a price of £8. It needed
components as well as work, but Gordon gave me a pair of 1950s track
wheels that were badly buckled. It took me ages to get them straight,
but it was a good lesson in wheel mechanics that would get me started
in bigger things.

Gordon Stead and I had also gone to the Girvan three-day race at
Easter, which the Wallacehill CC used to organise, and we camped down
the coast. We got up early – long before the race start time, so that we
could hang about the team mechanics at work preparing the bikes for
the top riders. Many of our heroes that we had only read about in the
magazines were riding with the professional teams, and we had the good
fortune to bump into the late Len Malvern, who was delighted to let
us watch him at work, and even answered our every naïve question.

Len was working for the KP Crisps team, which included Tony Doyle,
Dudley Hayton and Phil Bayton (The Engine). He said he would see
us the next morning, and he didn't have to ask us twice. The next
morning, our lesson in the art continued, and we could not believe our
luck as we got to watch and ask questions of one of the country's top
mechanics.

All in all, my knowledge was increasing at an amazing rate, and I
soon mastered the art of building wheels from scratch – a skill that most
cyclists simply do not need to possess. The result was a lot of customising
of my racing bike, and the Cinelli track bike was starting to take shape
with old and second-hand components.

The few races that I rode that year were on the pre-war Cinelli.
There was not much point in riding gears in time trials as a juvenile,
because the gear restriction meant that even with gears, the biggest
available is the one I would use all the time anyway. The problem I had
was tyres, or, more specifically, tubular tyres. The track wheels were for
tubular tyres, and decent ones were quite expensive, at a time when I
had bottomed out on cash.

Luckily, a few riders in the club used them, and when they inevitably punctured the effort needed to repair them meant that I could have the old ones if I thought I could do anything with them. Tubular tyres have a bonded base tape, followed by tight stitching, followed by a light inner lining. One has to unpick all this without damaging the tyre, patch the super-thin tube, and then sew it all back up and re-bond the base tape. The effort I put in, in relation to the money saved, made it worth it and it allowed me to race on the Cinelli.

I mainly rode in the club's own confined events which were 10 miles, and I could see my times getting quicker and quicker. Only a few times in the season did I ride open 10- and 25-mile Time Trials, but the aggregate of the best times at those distances was enough to win the Ayrshire schoolboy championship. It was one of my appearances at a club '10' that caused me to gain the reputation of a bit of a grubber. Gordon Stead and I had gone out to do some 'rough stuff' as it was known before mountain bikes were invented. We had headed over the moors from Rankinson to Dalmellington, which is a barely rideable dirt path. It was quite a long round trip, and when we got back both we and our bikes were filthy. Gordon was starving and tired and decided to miss the club '10', but I still had a handful of food in my back pocket and decided to go directly to the '10'.

It was old Jimmy Train who told me off about not having respect for my best equipment, and pointed out that if this had been an open event, I would have been disqualified from starting, as well as bringing down the reputation of the club. I had already known by then why Jimmy was so respected – he always gave his honest opinion, irrespective of how it might be received. Not only that, but Jimmy organised and timed the club events, and he would be there, whatever the weather. I suppose that was one reason I was keen to show up every time.

The club '10's were the only specific training I did for racing. I still considered long rides and touring to be what cycling was all about, and one popular destination that I had been initiated into was Wanlockhead Youth Hostel. It was high in the Leadhills, and the village sat at over 1,400 feet, so any ride there would culminate in the seven-mile climb of the Mennock Pass. The hostel itself was very basic, in that there were no showers, central heating or hot running water. The dorms were cold and damp for the same reason. This was a perfect situation, as it meant that general public types did not come very often. In those days it was a cycling youth hostel and the only place of warmth was in the kitchen with the huge wood-burning stove giving out such heat that you could peel off your damp clothes and dry out. Such was the popularity of Wanlockhead to cyclists that it was rare to go there and not meet other cyclists that you knew already and the kitchen was the centre of activity.

Mrs Young was the warden and had outlived her name by several decades. She would always moan to us about people sneaking in way past the 11 o'clock deadline and we would always sympathise with her. All the while, we knew the kitchen window had a broken latch and that after a good session at the British Legion Club just 200 yards away there would be a port of entry even if the door was locked – which it always was by the wee small hours, our normal arrival time.

At fifteen, drinking seemed to come to me naturally. Wanlockhead about April or May that year was my initiation to alcohol and from the first pint I felt an inner compulsion to drink more and more until complete intoxication was achieved – and then I usually wanted to argue with everybody.

Mrs Young was no walkover, though, and when it came to doing a duty in the morning, as was youth hostelling tradition, she usually reserved the best ones for the worst offenders. One time I had to weed and rake the driveway and car park, which took me about two hours with a hangover. Most of the guys wouldn't mind doing physical stuff because Mrs Young was about 80 and she looked after the hostel on her own. Some folk even stayed more than one night and did woodwork and the like – but no one ever sorted the kitchen window!

With so many other trips and racing, the Wanlockhead experience was not a regular feature, thankfully, but I was lucky to have experienced it as part of Scottish cycling culture at that time. Still being at school and sitting my O-grade exams meant that I did not have much spare time after cycling.

The summer holidays were coming up and then I would have loads of time to tour and race, but I had to decide whether to leave school or stay on for Highers. I did not have any job lined up and as unemployment had risen to three million the hopelessness and futility of job seeking was common knowledge. Not only that, but I was fifteen and on paper it seemed more sensible to stay on for fifth year as I would only be sixteen when I left. I was always the youngest in the class because of the intake birthday cut-off system.

I absolutely hated school for all the reasons I mentioned earlier, but things were not as bad as before as the scum were leaving at the first opportunity. I decided that it was the only real option and it would give me a better chance of a job or college. I did not have any real vision at all of what I might want to do, and really I was just drifting along with the tide.

During the summer holidays I did loads of cycling with Gordon Stead and John Stewart. We even went a two-week tour of Scotland, but had to come back after a week, when John could not hack it any more. We were camping and roughing it all the way. I also had the great opportunity to go along with the Scottish Health Race, which was being organised by George Miller, an organising member of the Wallacehill CC. It was not a free ride – I had to help route and de-route the race with direction arrows – but it was a good insight into the involvement of running a large event.

A lot of the season was spent either going to distant youth hostels or doing long rides. Meeting up with Alistair was common practice and when this happened we would have both pace and distance to deal with. Sometimes there would be a good group of us, if some of the guys from the Glasgow area came along. It was better if there was a group because it meant that there were more bodies to put some effort into a head wind and it also meant that there was always a good wheel to hang on to during a bad patch.

If there was a group then it also opened up the possibility of pranks taking place. My favourite was the 'tin trick': it was an almost certainty that in a group of cyclists there would exist at least one tin of Ambrosia Creamed Rice. I used to get a tin myself and swap labels with a tin of chopped tomatoes, and switch them whenever I found a victim. The look of disgust made it all worthwhile.

This was not a one-sided affair, and on one occasion I went to mount my bike only to discover that my cranks were at 90 degrees to each other. This requires a special tool, and everybody flatly denied having such a thing in their possession.

On another occasion, I was last to leave Wanlockhead Youth Hostel after a particularly long duty to find my bike sitting ready for me. I jumped straight on it, and it was only when I arrived home exhausted after a 90-mile round trip that I discovered a huge boulder in my saddlebag.

That season went on though, and in the end I won Ayrshire schoolboy best all-rounder on the strength of two reasonable rides, one of them on the day before my sixteenth birthday. I probably would have tied it up earlier in a 25-mile time trial if I had not glanced across the road and seen Alex Currie riding in a knotted handkerchief instead of a crash helmet. I never recovered from the loss of seriousness and finished with a slower time than I had hoped for.

There were time trials on the road, and there is not much to say about them, but the race that stands out in my memory that season was not a TT and was anything but ordinary.

It was the Three Peaks Cycle Cross, held in Derbyshire. Gordon Stead suggested riding it, and having a wild and adventurous (probably best described as reckless) streak, I instantly thought it was a radically good idea. He explained from the start that it was the world's longest and toughest cyclo-cross (29 miles and three of England's highest peaks), and that we would have to prepare for it a bit.

The rules were quite clear that only experienced riders of over sixteen were allowed to compete. I was lucky on this score, as my sixteenth birthday was a week or so before the event. All competitors were obliged to carry a survival bag and a proper whistle.

Obviously I had to make sure my bike was up to the job as well. We had to think about gearing, and how to get them low enough to climb the steepest parts of tracks before losing traction. And that was another problem point too. The tyres would have to be the knobbly sort to get the best grip. This might seem a bit obvious to some readers from the perspective of the twenty-first century but, at that time, it was all 'niche'. Even knobbly tyres were hard to get hold of, and were quite expensive because they were only made for cyclo-cross.

We had to think about carrying food and drinks on ourselves and our bikes as the length of the race meant that most riders just could not complete the event without sustenance. I obtained an ancient handlebar-mounted wire bottle-cage, which could hold a water bottle, from my grandfather John, who had cycled quite a bit in his younger days. If you see an old picture from the 1950s Tour de France riders, you will see the sort of thing I am talking about.

We would put sugar and glucose into our drinks, as well as carrying food in our pockets for the sake of energy on the day. We had every single angle covered, even punctures, as we each had pumps and a spare inner tube with us. I reckoned that loads of dextrose tablets and Kendal Mint Cake would be just the thing on the day. We had the whole thing organised like the D-Day landings. We even used the compulsory survival bags to make a shoulder pad on the inside of the frame triangle to stop the top bar digging right into our backs when shouldering the bike on mountain slopes. Everything was ready. We had received our entries for the race, and we booked up the local youth hostel for the night before, so that we could look at some of the course the evening before the race.

I had seen some pictures of Gordon's race the previous year in beautiful sunshine and on country tracks. Gordon had said that the pictures were a little bit misleading as most of the race was over real mountains, and that when you turn off the track after a couple of miles in the race, a huge mountain just appears in front of you and is so steep that you have to grab lumps of grass in front of you with your bike on your back.

As it turned out, this year's race would not be bathed in sunshine. In fact, it was the worst weekend on record for the race and was one of the worst weekends on record at the Met Office for rainfall. It was flooded everywhere, and not just in Yorkshire. Our local river burst its banks and washed away the bowling green, and when we were driving down with Gordon's father Tom, we saw flooding all around. It just did not stop raining.

We gave the pre-race recce a miss, and the next morning it was still pouring down. We were late leaving the youth hostel and, as I remember it, the reason was a last-minute mechanical problem with one of the bikes. The result was that we were a little short of preparation time at the next race start, and some of the riders were starting to line up as we got into the changing room. It was a mad dash to get ready.

We decided we would go as we were – shorts, T-shirt and short-sleeved cycling jersey over the top and a skipped hat over our cycling hats (the old strap type). We slapped 'Red Hot' massage cream on our legs, as was the tradition (and still is in cycling) in cold weather events. It doesn't actually keep you warm – all it does is irritate the skin and gives the impression of warmth. I grabbed handfuls of dextrose tablets and a large mint cake and put them into my pockets, and put my number on. Once we got into it, we would be warm. We were ready. But what we missed whilst being late in the changing room, was a severe weather warning of driving sleet or snow on the higher ground.

We joined the back of the assembled throng (about 200 riders) just in time to start. It started incredibly fast, along narrow tarmac roads. It was still lashing down with rain and all the wheels around me were spraying up muddy water, so I was racing along, just squinting out of screwed-up eyes so as not to be blinded by the spray.

I was racing well and was starting to move up the field, when I was treated to my first experience of bad sportsmanship. We were on an uphill section of road, when a hand came across and flicked my bar-end gear lever. I went straight into top gear and came to a standstill. The thing that shocked me most was that the perpetrator had 'RAF CC' on his jersey – a club I would have least expected to have members like this.

I got going again pretty quickly, and was warming up nicely when I turned a corner and saw a huge mountain in front of me. It was like a stairway to heaven, with distant figures disappearing into the low cloud. As soon as I bounced across the cattle grid onto rough track, my water bottle bounced out of my '50s holder. I stopped to pick it up and it happened again within yards. In the heat of the race, and not wanting to lose valuable time, I just left it there.

When I put my bike on my back and started to climb the first mountain, I almost caught up with Gordon ahead of me. Less than halfway up, I was starting to get really tired, my output was going down and down and I was really starting to suffer. At this point, I saw a figure coming down the mountainside through the mist. As he got closer, we realised it was Jim Frew, now a good friend of mine, from our own club. I have rarely heard Jim swear, either before or since, but on this occasion, he was cursing the race and its insanity. After a bit of shouting and teasing, we convinced him to turn around and carry on.

Gordon and Jim disappeared into the mist as I got slower and slower and colder and colder. At the top half of the mountain, it was more sleet than rain, and windy with it. Almost the entire field had passed me now, and it was the best I could do to carry on, as I was shivering with cold. Just as I thought it couldn't get any worse, my skip hat blew off from my crash hat, off the edge of the mountain, and disappeared into the low cloud.

Things were getting worse as I reached the summit of the first mountain. Mountain rescue members were at the checkpoint on the summit, and I made a point of trying to look warm and not shiver as I passed, so that I would not be withdrawn from the race. It seemed as though I heated up a little on the descent of the mountain, which was just a trail of mud, knee-deep in places. All I could think about was getting warmer.

As I approached the second mountain, my body was almost numb and I was so weak I could hardly turn a pedal or lift my bike. I had to hold the bike in the bend of my elbow because my hands were now so numb I could not hold it tight enough to lift it. As I started to climb,

I couldn't take normal steps, so I just started edging my bike up the mountain. I reached for my food in my back pockets, but all that remained of it was a line of syrupy sludge at the bottom. I carried on at a snail's pace, upwards into the mist, but I only got so far when I just could not continue. I felt numb and almost drunk with exhaustion and cold, and I could only see in black and white and in tunnel vision. I looked around and couldn't see anything except wilderness in the mist – not even the path I was supposed to be on. At this point, I thought, 'I am going to die. I must carry on.'

It was very misty now, and with the driving sleet I was starting to think about survival. I had seen an advert on TV depicting a man staggering through deep snow with hypothermia, and a voice booming something about, 'He wants to stop but he must go on.' I was way past shivering, and I really thought I might die.

I was starting to think of my other option of climbing into my orange survival bag – if I could remove it with my numb hands – and blowing my whistle. I had overcome both pride and the voice saying that I must go on, and decided that I had to use my survival bag.

Just as I was trying in vain to dislodge my survival bag, I saw the outline of a figure in the mist. I left the bike and stumbled towards the figure as quickly as I could manage, which was painfully slow. When I got there, I could not believe my luck. It was a race helper, and he had a flask in his hand. I was so hungry and cold that the first thing I tried to do was ask for a drink of whatever it contained, but my lips were as frozen as my hands, and it came out like a drunken mumble. He gave me a woolly hat and sent me off the mountain. He explained that I was only a few miles from the race HQ, and from here, it was mostly downhill.

I can remember standing on top of my clothes in the shower block for hours, trying to heat up. I went back through the shivers again, and that was when I really started to feel cold again. On the journey home, I had excruciating leg and arm cramps as a reward for my efforts. At the time, rather than put the whole effort down as a waste of time, its usefulness was embodied by my peer group as 'character-building'. The annoying thing about it was that I did not even get a certificate for completing the course in less than five hours.

That was the end of my season, in terms of racing, but now it was time to get involved in club rides and trips to youth hostels. I had just turned sixteen, and was back at school with no sense of direction or ambition. One thing that was certain was that cycling had become a way of life, and I had learned so much in just one season – most of it the hard way. I kept myself in reasonably good shape over the winter, with youth hostel trips and club rides, so when spring came, I was still pretty fit and ready to go.

two: coming of age

Like most sports, cycling is divided into age categories, and in the season of 1982, when I was competing as a junior, this meant I could use a bigger gear than I could as a schoolboy. Even so, this was pretty small by modern standards, and juniors would have to pedal pretty fast to achieve good results. I was still more of a 'pleasure and touring' cyclist than an out-and-out racer, but I was keen to have a go at time trials and also some road racing. Being a junior meant that I could compete in bunch races on the road, as opposed to parks or industrial estates. Other than the ill-fated Three Peaks cyclo-cross the September before, I had not ridden any bunch races, so I was keen to get involved, and the racing machine my parents had bought me for my birthday was ideal for the job.

I used this bike in the first team trial I rode that season. It was an evening 25-miler, and the weather was fine. I still did not train specifically for racing, but I was reasonably fit. I never took events as seriously as I might have done, until on this one I was passed by a veteran (over forty), before the turn in the out-and-back course. Jim Cameron was his name, and he was favourite to win the race. When he passed, I let him gain a considerable distance, and, keeping him in sight, I tried to ride at his pace. Having found my legs, I decided to lay on my pace, and eventually passed him again. He caught me again and I dropped back an appropriate distance. It wasn't as hard as I thought, but my presence some way behind seemed to annoy him, and he kept looking round. He complained to the commissionaire (cycling's equivalent of an umpire) and I was told to slow and let an even bigger gap open, which I did. I finished with a personal-best time and was in line for a prize. At the readout, I was accused of cheating by Tommy Bruce the commissionaire. He said he knew that I could not go that fast on my own, and that I was disqualified. I was really brassed off with the time trial scene after that, and I did not enter any for a long time after this injustice. However my love of cycling prevented me from being lost to the sport at that time, as well as a few times in the future.

I was still at school at this time, studying for my Highers. Cycling seemed so much more important and I never took school as seriously as I should have. Before I left school, my father and I had visited Commercial Components in Newmilns, and we arranged for me to begin an apprenticeship in tool-making as soon as my Highers were finished. The results of the Highers were of no importance to the boss, and this was another major factor in my losing interest in them. While I was studying I was still doing quite a lot of mileage, and I still planned to compete when I could.

From a young age, I was always made to feel – perhaps not intentionally – that I was stupid and Gordon was clever. It never occurred to me to go to college or university, and by this time (after the 'outcast' childhood, the ostracism and the friendless isolation), it was not a matter of 'Can I?' It was simply a fact in my mind that I was not cut out for it. In other words, academic study was just that – academic.

I started at Commercial Components the day after I left school, but one race I did ride that year, despite the constraints of weekend work, was a junior race at Bellahouston Park in Glasgow. I cannot remember if it was before or after the time trial debacle, but it certainly got me into trouble and this time it was all of my own doing. It was a circuit race with tight corners and narrow park lanes. In preparing my bike for the event, I had to change the rear tyre. I had left it until the night before, and the tyres I was using were tubulars (tyres that have the inner tubes sewn on directly and have to be glued onto the rim of the wheel). As it turned out, I had no glue left and Gordon Stead had none either. Tubular glue never really hardens, and Gordon reckoned that the old layers of glue would maybe be enough to glue it on, but it would be taking a chance. I reckoned if I pumped the tyre up really hard, it would be fine. In junior races, the bikes have to be checked for gear size and general mechanical safety.

On inspection of my bike, I was told that my rear tyre was not glued on sufficiently and that I would have to get a replacement. I had signed on and had my race number, but I was unable to borrow a replacement wheel. I didn't know what to do and then another competitor said I should just join the line-up, start the race and nobody would notice. In an error of judgement, that is exactly what I did. Half of the race went fine, but then my foot started pulling out of the pedal on the climb, and I was losing distance. Each time, I was catching up before the end of the lap, but on one of the laps, the gap was especially large. I thought that if I took the bottom corner really fast, I would be back in the pack before the climb again. My rear tyre rolled and I slid across the deck and let out an un-sportsmanlike mouthful of foul language, as my skin was being ripped off. As chance would have it, that was the corner where the organiser was standing, and I was in big trouble, not only for foul language, but for riding without official sanction. I was close to losing my racing licence, but good old Jimmy Train from the club appealed on the grounds of my youth and inexperience. I apologised and was let off lightly. It was another harsh lesson in my cycling apprenticeship, not that I thought of cycling as a possible future career. I thought that I was doing an apprenticeship of the normal kind in an engineering workshop in Newmilns.

I started at the firm the very next day after my last exam, at the end of May. It was an unhappy experience from the start. The boss was verbally abusive, and foul-mouthed with it. Almost my whole time there was spent pulling swarf from the machines while the workers were machining, and sweeping swarf from the floor. Cleaning sumps by hand was the job I hated most. It was certainly an eye-opener for me. On one occasion, an 18-inch chuck flew off one of the huge lathes and hit the operator square in the chest, and laid him out flat. The boss came along, smoking a fat cigar, stepped over the worker and said, 'Is the job all right?'

The hours were very long – usually 8 a.m. to 8 p.m. – and overtime was more or less compulsory. The pay wasn't very good either – 62 pence an hour, flat rate. I was lucky I could cycle there and back from Kilmarnock, where we had just moved, otherwise I could not have afforded public transport. Sometimes weekends had to be worked as well, at the same rate of pay, and it really knocked a hole in my cycling activities.

After six months, I just cracked and walked out, after a particularly distasteful diatribe from the cigar-smoking boss. I can still remember his prophetic utterance about 'what would I do because of the high unemployment?' and that I would never make a living from cycling.

I felt guilty about leaving an apprenticeship but, on thinking back to the time, I remembered that I was asked to sign forms with all but the signature area covered by plain paper. So I always wondered whether

I was on a job creation scheme or a training programme. Either way, I would never have been able to carry on at that place. I wasn't alone anyway, as the throughput of youths was like a conveyor belt.

Despite the time restraints that summer, I still managed a few weekends away, as well as a few races. A common destination was, of course, Wanlockhead Youth Hostel.

It is possible to take the old miners' roads through the mountains, but normally we would ride up the Mennock Pass, with its seven miles of constant climbing.

The whole thing was sociable, especially at night. The local pub was the only entertainment in the village, and at the weekend I think it usually turned into a private party, as closing time was usually 'whenever'. Many a good night was enjoyed there, but unfortunately, the venue has gone right downhill in recent times, from the perspective of our cycling club. Central heating and hot showers have taken their toll, not to mention the removal of the wood stove. People often arrive by car, such is the current state of affairs.

Besides Wanlockhead weekends, I also enjoyed some truly epic journeys, with Gordon and Alistair Gow. Usually we would venture north or west after meeting Alistair, and sometimes we would cover up to 120 miles in a day. I can remember one occasion when Gordon and I were so tired and hungry while returning to Kilmarnock late at night, that we were down to walking pace in places, just to make it back. It was almost a matter of survival. It's very hard to explain to the un-athletic how hungry and desperate for food a cyclist can become.

On a couple of occasions, I have been unfortunate enough to get, what they call in cycling talk, 'the bonk'. This is a situation where the cyclist has absolutely no food energy left and, without food, can only continue at a snail's pace and in terrible suffering. On one occasion, my mother Marcie got mixed up with this word, and told someone she had met in a supermarket that I had gone away for a weekend cycling, and had ended up getting the clap!

My dad had also become acquainted with the 'please rescue us' phone call, sometimes as a result of mechanical problems and sometimes sheer exhaustion.

I can see now that it was a wonderful era in cycling terms, as it was possible at that time to do all that I did, and the structure of cycling at club level was still based on a model from past generations. There wasn't the fear of violence there is now, and traffic levels were not as high. It seems a strange thing to say about the world less than two decades ago, but things have changed pretty rapidly since then, especially in terms of what parents would allow their offspring to do in the modern world.

Even the junior races quite often had a full field, and there was real competition that kept the standards high. Nowadays, entries are very low, and it is rare to see a juvenile or junior race with a reasonable number of competitors. The club scene was very vibrant too, and at Wallacehill CC club night, it would mean a pile of bikes at the doorway. Things are different now, unfortunately, and you'll be lucky to find a single bike.

One trip I did go on that year that was very worthwhile was with the whole club to Meadowbank Velodrome. There were track bikes at the velodrome that the club could use, but I decided to use my Cinelli track machine. There is no freewheel on a fixed-wheel bike, and I took the front brake off as no brakes are allowed on the track.

The first ride around a velodrome is a weird experience. No-one in the club had ridden on the track before, and most of us thought it was either exhilarating or downright frightening. Some of the members never even made it onto the track proper, but just cycled round the flat skirting instead. I remember phrases like 'wall of death' being used. Personally, I thought it was wonderful. You could sweep down from the high banking and get some good speed up, and you could feel the centrifugal force on the banking. I remember there was a big stack-up that day behind the 'derny' (the motorbike-type thingy for high-speed training). About five of us came down, and two or three of the borrowed bikes were badly damaged. I was laid out flat and badly winded, but luckily, my own bike was one that survived undamaged. It was inevitable that there would be a stack-up, and Gordon and I saw it coming in slow motion as we were at the back of the line-out. Gordon was behind me and just managed to get round. It was a good taster in an aspect of cycling that few from Ayrshire had ever got involved in. It seemed like a venture into the unknown, and track racing seemed to be its own culture – a sort of sport within a sport. This was made worse by the fact that Meadowbank is about 70 miles from Ayrshire, and outdoors - if a shower dampens the track (which is open), then it is unrideable until it dries. There was also the East-versus-West implied rivalry, and crazy as it seems, there was a slight implication of hostile territory in the East at that time. All in all, if I was going to break into track racing, with its own culture, possibly clique, and definitely its own traditions (which most in Ayrshire know nothing about), then I would have to do it alone.

I had no thought about that at that time anyway, and I was too busy enjoying mainstream cycling to get involved in the alien culture of track racing. I wasn't serious enough anyway – I was still mainly an all-round cyclist enjoying touring trips whenever possible.

It sounds, perhaps, like a dousing of nostalgia, but the point I am really trying to make is that had I been just a racing cyclist, then I am pretty sure I would never have become World Champion.

Such was the availability of youngsters and the interest and vibrancy of the scene that a new club was being formed. Billy McFarlane, who lived up the valley, reckoned it was time to start a new club there. Loudoun Road Club it was called, and shortly after its formation late that year, I decided to join. It attracted loads of new members and, on the winter rides, there was usually a good-sized bunch. It was quite usual for riders to be dropped alone at their riding pace. It was more-over a touring-based club and that was good because it meant that new members could start out the way that I had done at Wallacehill CC.

It was Billy McFarlane, a local 'fast man' in racing circles, who encouraged me to take racing more seriously. There were five or six of us who were motivated and taking it seriously, and we would congre-gate at Billy and Morag's house twice a week for roller training. This involved taking turns at doing 20 or 30 minutes of intensive effort on a static rolling road in Billy's outbuilding in the garden. The efforts were gasping from start to finish. We waited around until we were all finished and then we all cycled home – it was rare for any of us to arrive by car.

James Evans was one of the faithful, and he also lived the farthest away – 14 miles away. He was fourteen or fifteen years old and he would cycle there, train and then cycle back. He was incredibly strong for his age and Jim and I would sometimes go on fast rides together at the weekends, on winter days that were harsh enough to make all others stay indoors. It would pay off in the end, as we would both be Scottish Champions the following season.

An influence on Billy then was Gordon Johnson, a cycling coach from Dumfries, who was up on the latest thinking and training tech-niques. He himself would acquire his knowledge from Harold Nelson who was based in Manchester. The 'in thing' at the time in England was interval training, which involved going at it well beyond your limit for two to three minutes, and then recovering before doing the next interval. This would be repeated five or six times before warming down for the end of the training session.

Gordon visited that winter, and his catchphrase seemed to be 'get your hat on – you'll catch a cold'. The strange thing was, as we would realise in time, is that he would say the same thing on warmest summer days. Gordon's input did not have a direct bearing on us at the time, but it certainly got me thinking about specific training for specific events. We alternated between the traditional efforts and interval training after this, in the hope that we would be better riders in the season to come.

Billy was a great motivator, and I can remember him shouting towards the end of each interval, when I thought I could not finish the three-minute effort. He would shout things like, 'You can do it! Come on – just 40 seconds to go! Keep going! One last dig! Sprint to the finish!' He would never accept submission before exhaustion, and the sessions we were doing really did improve us as cyclists. It was Billy who first brought out the winning instinct in me, I suppose. I developed a sense of wanting to win and a willingness to respect others but fear none.

With Billy's motivation, we could not wait for the racing season to begin. We trained without fail, and we were all gung-ho to get torn into it. Driving snow would be no obstacle, usually to the extreme concern of my parents, who would try in vain to dissuade me.

I was unemployed by this stage, and there was absolutely no impediment to me training and cycling as much as I needed or desired. Almost every day I was on my bike. If I was active from a training session the day before, I would still go out, but I would just meander and enjoy the open countryside. Ayrshire being what it is, there are many country roads that you can ride on, meeting very little traffic.

So it was that winter and spring that I was undergoing a change in attitude, and was training to win as a result of Billy's influence. I was still looking for a job, but there wasn't much going at that time. It would be true to say that I became a bit cynical about the job-seeking system. I got in the way of just going to the Jobcentre now and again, merely going through the motions of job applications and rejections. The unemployment backdrop of over 3 million in the UK, combined with a lack of positions coming on-stream made the whole situation seem quite futile. I also had no direction, so I was never enthusiastic about any one career, which probably showed in the few interviews that I got. The year ended this way, with roller training and club nights taking up most of the week in terms of social activity.

Basically, I was training hard and waiting quite impatiently for the season to begin in an almost obsessive way. Things did not change at all during the spring, and I would get my chance to race at last.

My entire life was taken up by cycling. It filled the void that should have been filled by work and social engagements. I would describe my lifestyle in 1983 as insular, narrow-minded and lonely. I had no social network at all and no outside contact other than cycling.

When I left school, I left with almost nothing. There was not a single friend, not even a contact number. All I had to show was a single Higher in physics, and a gut-load of cynicism about human nature.

It was Billy who kept my hopes alive with his belief that I could be something with my cycling. He showed such belief that it was impossible to believe that anything other than success was what we would experience in the season to come. That winter we trained like we had never trained before. The sessions at Billy's outhouse, combined with the rides at weekends with James – and sometimes Alistair – meant that we would both enter the season with a fitness level unusual for that period in time.

There were training rides that Jim and I went on, that most others in the world of cycling would have thought were crazy. Sometimes we would set off in conditions that were already considered to be 'blizzard'. Jim was always my junior in terms that he was fifteen and I was seventeen, and as such I always felt responsible for his safety.

Many a time we would both have to huddle under our touring capes (a poncho-type thing that was completely weather-proof), before continuing on our way to completing our mileage, which could be 80 miles or more. I remember one incident where I was cycling with Jim to Loch Ard Youth Hostel, and because I had the only reliable lighting on my bike, I was obliged to take the lead on the ride when it became pitch black. Jim had no choice but to follow my tail light, so for a laugh I turned off all of my lights, and the screams of fear from Jim, who was riding feet from the water's edge in total blindness made the journey a little more interesting. I was riding in total blindness too, but just for the sheer hell of it.

Most of my memories of that year were of snow, or winter adversity, and Jim was there for most of it.

By the time that March came around we were both ready for the season to come. We and the other participants in Billy's shed were ready for the season to come, with good preparation behind us.

The biggest gift that Billy gave us was a sense of arrogance that we could do anything we set our minds to. Billy was a fantastic motivator in that he could keep us believing that there was nothing achieved by anyone before that could not be bettered by us now. There was nothing that we did not possess that would prevent us from being champions.

When I started the season in 1983 I was ready, and my target was to be the best in Scotland. Road racing was not really my scene, so it was time trials where I hoped to win a championship. The best average of the average speeds between 25- and 50-mile TTs was the deciding factor in the Scottish 'Best All Rounder' championship (BAR), so this was my aim at the start of the season.

I could not have been much better prepared than I was, both motivationally and physically. I was in good shape at the end of the winter, and I had good attitude, and belief in my cycling ability as a result of Billy's input. Socially I had nothing in my life to speak of, except my involvement in cycling and racing.

Not only that, but my father was on hand to be a willing early morning chauffeur to the best races – often having to rearrange shift patterns on a weekly basis. There was no sign of employment, and as things stood in the spring of 1983, it would not have been possible to be more full-on than I was at that time, and with hindsight I can see that success was almost inevitable.

Being in Loudon Road Club was good, because there were loads of young riders that had joined the club. The winter scene wasn't just hard rides and training, as sometimes groups of us would descend on nearby youth hostels at the weekend.

There were the 'old timers' like Bob Gebbie who were able to pass on the art of 'drumming up'. Bob and his generation would carry a 'tinny' on the side of their saddlebags. This consisted of a smoke-blackened bean can with an old spoke that could be handled with a stick onto a carefully built fire. There were known 'drumming up' spots in various places, and on long journeys the 'drum up' spot would be the rallying area for heat, tea and food.

There was, of course, a chain of command, and it was quite usual for the youngest to collect the most wood. Drum-ups could last for hours. You see, cycling in this form is not about arriving, but about the journey itself.

The hard part about drum-ups was getting moving after being stopped for so long, especially in midwinter. There was also an unwritten code that no rubbish was to be left behind, and everything must be set in order as it was. These sites were communal, and it would be quite common for a completely separate group of cyclists to join us at a drum-up. There were no maps, but cyclists knew where these spots were, in the same way that elephants know where water holes are – passed down by group-knowledge.

Drum-ups were a rarity once the season of '83 got underway. I can still remember the excitement and nervousness at the start of my first race as a properly trained cyclist. The race was the 18-mile time trial from Ayr to Girvan. It was only 20 miles to the start, so Gordon and I cycled there. I was using fixed-wheel, which was my old Cinelli track bike. Bob Addy was on holiday from England. He was an ex-Tour de France rider and favourite to win it. I was more concerned about beating Ian Campbell for the junior prize. He set off two minutes in front of me, but I would not have thought it possible to catch him in such a short distance. I rode my heart out from start to finish, and as it turned out I caught my quarry on the line, and won the event outright by just three seconds, from Bob Addy. I had done the unbelievable, and won the senior race outright, and was grinning from ear to ear, all the way home. It was not long, though, before the buzz and sense of excitement started to fade and my mind started working on where I could get another win. I did not have to wait long because Billy suggested we enter a 50-mile time trial in Fife. It was about 100 miles away, but we would go up in his car and stay at a cheap B&B. On the morning, Billy felt guilty about finishing his fry-up, but because he forgot to bring his own food, he had no choice. I only picked at mine, and was glad of that after hearing Billy's after-race account of re-tasting the sausages throughout most of his effort.

This time, the taste of victory was just as sweet, and the result was even better. I had won the race outright, by a considerable margin, and I broke the course record in the process. On the journey home, Billy told me something with complete sincerity that I have never forgotten. He simply stated that I was the greatest rider he'd ever known. Of course, I turned this compliment away as a matter of instinct, but his words stuck with me, because I knew he had meant it, and Billy's not the type to roll platitudes out for the sake of it.

The season had just opened, and my aim of winning the junior BAR was looking good. I started entering TTs all over the place. When they were local I would just cycle out to the start, but when they were further away my father would be conscripted to drive me. The usual destination was Stirling, which hosted 25-mile TTs on the Kippen Flats. Fifty-mile TTs were less common on the calendar, but Stirling was still the best course.

It was 50 miles or so from our house, and we would normally set off at about 7 a.m. for a 9 a.m. start. I would always check out the wind speed before anything. If it was dead calm, then I could look forward to the opportunity to break my own personal-best times, but if it was windy, then I would just ride for the win. I won quite a few races outright, but my personal-best times hovered about the same mark for most of the season.

My father was cool. He never put any pressure on me at all, and, during the event and the readout of results, he would read a book and, as we were driving off, he would ask how I got on. If it was a bad ride, he would say, 'Never mind,' and if I'd had a good ride, he'd say, 'That's fine.' Other sons would get all sorts of pressure from their fathers, to the point where they were nervous wrecks, and would have parental pressure to do better. I was self-motivated and did not need any of that.

If I'd known that the first few good rides would tie up the BAR, then I would have concentrated on road-racing, or even track, rather than having tunnel vision about TTs. I did ride the Junior Scottish Championship for road that year, although I'd gained almost no experience at road racing, because of my obsession with TTs. The race was stop-go most of the way, and any time I tried to break clear, I was marked down right away. Drew Wilson of Johnstone Wheelers was the favourite, and I knew I had to break clear, in order to avoid a sprint finish, which was my weak point.

I had been trying all afternoon to get clear, but it was not until a few miles to go that I succeeded. It was not a huge gap – maybe 150 yards or so – but it was enough that I could have gone into TT mode for the finish. Just then, there was a van blocking my progress. I had to apply the brakes, and I tried to pass but could not. When the pack caught up and the van pulled clear, I noticed it was the Johnstone Wheelers' van. The race finished as a sprint finish after all, and I ended up fourth on the line. I was shocked and seething about the incident, but it was only me and my father who were there, and we knew nothing about complaint procedures. By the time we found out what to do about complaints, the one-hour window of opportunity for complaint had lapsed.

That was my last road race as a junior, and the rest of the season was spent coursing up and down dual carriageways against the stop-watch. Despite this, I still managed to squeeze in a few touring rides. One of my weekend trips was the same weekend as the 50-mile TT Championship.

Alistair arrived out of the blue at about 10 a.m. on the Saturday morning, and said, 'I'm off to Tighnabruich Youth Hostel if you want to join me.' It was a glorious warm summer's day, and my immediate gut feeling was to say yes. It did not take long to overcome my sense of duty about the '50' in which I was one of the favourites for the title, and I packed my saddlebag even quicker. In the end, I got more mileage in the press for my unorthodox non-appearance than I would have got if I had ridden the race.

The season was effectively over by early September, and Wanlockhead would obviously feature once again. During that off season, as well as drunken youth hostel trips, I also took on cyclo-cross races, and, as I remember, I won three out of three in the races that I rode. These were nothing like the Three Peaks event. These were normal races, with 'x' number of laps round a park of forest area, and normally lasted about an hour. Cyclo-crosses are tough, because you have to cycle and run, so any weaknesses are exposed. I used my track bike in all of them, except I fitted a single freewheel. On one race in Glasgow, organised by Glenmarnock CC, obstacles kept appearing round corners that were not there on previous laps. One such obstacle caused me to shear off my front, and only, brake. At the downhill finish to the race, I had to scream and wave my arms to make an opening in the crowd to fly through.

At the end of the year, there is the Scottish Cyclists Union dinner dance and prize presentation. Gordon Stead was there, and it was at this dinner that he suggested we could open a cycle shop together as a partnership. Gordon had not been doing much cycling in recent times, because he was working full-time in a cycle shop in Irvine. He had gained a lot of knowledge and wanted to have a cycle shop of his own. It was a simple 50/50 deal, where we would be equal partners. Gordon had gathered names and addresses of vital suppliers, and had worked out that Kilmarnock would be the ideal catchment area.

I thought about the lack of employment or opportunity, and, when it came to wheel-building or repairs, we could both out-compete anyone. Gordon and I had been messing around with oxyacetylene bottles and old frame tubes, and we'd become quite good at it. We had even built a track frame with Reynolds tubing that I was trying out, and we were confident we could do frame repairs as well. All in all, I thought it was a good idea, and we shook hands on it.

All we had to do was find finance, premises, suppliers and customers. In the beginning of 1984, I was eighteen years old, I was Scottish Champion, and I was starting to arrange my own business, which would be called Cosmos Cycles.

three:cosmos cycles era

From January '84, Gordon Stead and I were trying to get into business. From the very start it was a complete run-around, considering it was such a simple, straightforward and conventional small business. The hardest and longest-running problem was getting finance to set up. The banks were our first port of call, and that is where we first met the request for detailed business plans.

Our next port of call was the enterprise people, who could help us prepare our plans, and if we could receive some sort of grant, then we could make our financial projections look so much better for the bank. Problem number one was that Gordon would have to be unemployed for six weeks prior to applying for a grant, in order to be eligible, and the second problem was that the bank would not look at it until we had premises sorted out.

After a lot of constant running around, we eventually found a small shop premises that would do us fine, so now we could fill in the missing pieces of our plan. A major problem, too, was that the banks do not give out unsecured business loans to teenagers on the strength of mythical sales predictions and profit margins. Gordon's knowledge of sales figures from Tony's shop in Irvine helped a little in convincing them that we were in the ball park with our projections, but in the end, there was nothing we could do but ask our fathers if they would underwrite our loan so that we could secure the finance to move on with the business of being in business. That they did. If I remember rightly, our start-up fund was not huge at something in the order of £3,000. We would have to spend low and wisely.

Between running around in circles with finance, grants, premises and gathering up second-hand shop equipment, like tills and counters, I was still trying to train hard, with an eye on riding the Girvan Three-Day race at Easter. This was the race that Gordon and I had looked at in awe just three years earlier. I would be riding for the Ayrshire and Dumfriesshire Cycling Association as part of a team of four riders, and we would have no expectations put on us, other than to do our best and provide local representation.

At the time of riding the Girvan Three-Day, we were almost ready to launch our new venture. The ride itself was pretty poor – I was absolutely destroyed every day, and if I remember rightly, I finished in 49th place out of about 100 riders. The race goes up and down all the hills it can, on the narrow roads of Carrick, and there is rarely any respite for tired legs, so I more or less collapsed in a stupor after the final stage – wondering what I did it for. It was Billy who pointed out that the English road-racing season starts earlier, and by the time Easter comes round, they have got good racing form, whereas the Scots riders have no races behind them at all – just winter training. So, with that, I put my disappointment behind me.

My first priority now was business, and our opening was now imminent. We had an accountant lined up in advance, and since the end of the tax year was approaching, we would start at the beginning of a new tax year. Our start was delayed by the enterprise grants people, who said we could not trade before a certain date. That day came soon enough, and I can remember the mixture of apprehension, excitement and pride on that first moment when we opened the door of our emporium to the public. I was eighteen years old and I was a businessman.

The first days were nerve-racking, willing passers-by to come in and browse around our limited, but well-chosen, range of stock, but as time passed and summer got closer, there was no shortage of custom. We could not have opened at a better time than we did. The BMX craze was on the way up, and after a while most of our stock was BMX bikes and components. Our turnover was increasing rapidly, and by midsummer, we had taken on a youth trainee. With the turnover rate, we managed to keep increasing our stock and our range of bikes. We were so short of space that we decided to reclaim the cellar. There was no hatch and everything had been covered over by floorboards. We cut a hole in the floor, and as we looked down into the darkness with torches, we could see that there was, indeed, a good-sized cellar.

I shimmied down first, with Gordon on his way behind. I could not believe my eyes. I shouted to Gordon, 'I can't believe it! It's full of fridges and cookers and stuff!' I was about to walk forward, when Gordon pulled me hard by the back of the shirt, and said, 'We're in Comet's storeroom!' He had noticed the red security beam just in time. A couple of yards further over, we did indeed find our own cellar, and it took some digging out. It was capable of storing 30 or 40 flat-packed bikes, and not just that – it had a skylight at pavement level right next to our front window, so we could eavesdrop on what the kids really thought about the prices and the stock etc.

Things just got busier, and we had to have space. As luck would have it, the old theatre upstairs was empty, and it was also owned by our landlord, so for an extra £20 per week, we had a space big enough for two or three tennis courts. It was divided into two rooms, and we used the small one (about the size of a primary school gym hall) to display our full range of BMX bikes. By this time, it was coming up to the time of year when people start thinking about putting a bike away for Christmas, and this storage area was just perfect.

Business was way above our predictions, but the approach of Christmas saw the start of our troubles. The common practice for bike shops was to have a Christmas club, where people would choose a bike, put 10 per cent deposit down, and would then collect and pay for the bike just before Christmas.

We had the full range of BMX bikes in most of the top brands, as well as the lower-priced models. The expensive bikes were amazingly popular, and we had loads away for Christmas in our storeroom by the end of October. We had managed to get credit accounts with the major suppliers, which was a lifeline, as our borrowing capacity at the bank was pitifully low for the size of the business we now had.

As well as the entire overheads of the rent and improvements, we also needed a van to ship bikes to customers and to get stock from warehouses, or so Gordon convinced me. It wasn't long before the van had alloy wheels, which one of Gordon's friends 'acquired' for him. It was not long before other wheels started appearing in the storeroom. I knew what was going on but I turned a blind eye.

All the while, I was still trying to keep fit by training early in the mornings and on Sundays when I could. I had not raced much that year but one day in the shop an opportunity came along that I sometimes still wonder about. An American in his mid-forties came to the shop with the intention of finding me, because he'd read a bit about me in the press. He was the dean of Santa Barbara University, and he was here visiting family.

What he was suggesting was that if I could get over there, I could take up a sports scholarship at the university. I did think about it for a while, but with the business and everything else, I decided I would just stay. With the business going so well, there seemed to be so much opportunity at home, but it was still tempting for a while.

With Christmas getting closer, our sales were escalating so quickly that we had to order unprecedented amounts of bikes. Most of them were ending up in the Christmas club store, which was now numbering hundreds of bikes. When December came, we realised we had a slight cash flow problem as a result of the money tied up in sold bikes with 10% deposits. We had to pay our creditors for those bikes as well as the unsold stock.

It was then that we started to realise that although the business was doing exceptionally well, our cash turnover had dropped considerably to the point where we were struggling to stay within our agreed over-draft limit. As more and more bikes were being put by on the Christmas club, then more of our capital was locked until Christmas Day. It reached the point where we could not service our accounts to our suppliers, who insisted that the bicycles remain their property until the 30-day invoice was cleared. We were well beyond that to several suppliers, and they were threatening to come and repossess their bikes, even if they were in a Christmas club.

The situation was getting much more tense, as our Christmas club exceeded 400 bikes. We approached the bank for a temporary extension of our borrowing capacity, but the answer was a firm no. We saw our accountant Ronnie Gilmour, who said we would have to sell anything we could in any way to get cash sales. He kept telling us of the absolute seriousness of the situation. We would have to clear these accounts or face bankruptcy. We stayed open late every night, to help bring in regular cash-paying trade, but most people wanted a bike on the Christmas club. We did anything we could to generate straight cash, to service the cost of the 400-plus bikes stored away, but that had to be paid for imme-diately or dire consequences would follow.

We met the bank again, and explained that the huge volume of money that would come in on Christmas week would pay for everything and more. The bank was unbending and said that we'd found ourselves in an overtrading situation. The only possible solution was to go back to our parents and ask for even more underwriting so we could pay our creditors, stay in business and rake in the profits from our Christmas club bikes. Neither Gordon nor I were willing to do so, as each of us was being questioned at home after leaving the business most nights, being told how anxious our parents were that the business was okay. I also had regular reminders from my mum about how the house was at risk with the underwriting. For that reason, neither of us felt that we could approach our parents for even more underwriting.

A final plea to the bank failed, and we were warned that any cheques we sent now would be bounced. A visit to our accountant made us panic even more. Ronnie forcefully emphasised the absolutely perilous situation we were in, and said that if we could not get money from anywhere, then we would be bankrupt and would never get into business again.

At this point, we were really panicking and were looking at all our options. From nowhere, a crazy idea emerged. If we were broken into and most of the stock bikes stolen, the insurance would be enough for us to pay for the Christmas club bikes and everything would be just fine!

In our desperation, the crazy idea was being put into action straight away. We figured that the burglars would burst open the door at the back of the block, climb up the stairs past the Christmas club bikes, and knock a large hole in the wall, to break into out shop directly, to steal the pre-picked, top of the range bikes held in the cellar.

The hole-in-the-wall project was started right away, and it did not take long for us to discover that the wall was three-feet thick and made of stone. It took us a week to knock a hole in the wall that would take the burglars one evening when the disco was on next door. The dust was flying round the shop for a week while the work progressed, and even customers noticed it.

The bikes that were supposed to be missing would have to be missing when the police arrived. Gordon arranged this through re-jigging a lot of paperwork, and any sales of bikes direct were dialled off the stock of the Christmas club, so that invisible bikes existed on paper.

Things were getting so tense in terms of legal problems with our suppliers that we had to act or be forced into involuntary bankruptcy. We couldn't write cheques for anything, but we sent a cheque to the main creditor with the envelope folded slightly wrongly so that the sticky part of the lip of the envelope stuck to the signature, so that cheque could not be cashed. That bought us a few days.

We delayed our creditors as much as we could, while trying to sell as much stock as we could, but the pressure was really mounting from the bank, the accountant and the creditor's lawyers. At eighteen and nineteen years old, we panicked and tripped our plan into action.

We smashed the place up a bit, shoved the broken pieces of stone down into the shop from the hole, and set about opening up the back entrance. We had previously had to remove two huge beams securing the door, so that it could be broken in from the outside, but for all our efforts, we could not make it open more than 12 inches at most. The genuine Christmas club bikes were locked in a separate part of the building and would be overlooked by the thieves. The whole thing was a complete amateur bungle from the start, and when the CID arrived the next morning, they were obviously sceptical from the start. The first thing they said was that it must have been a very thin burglar, having seen the gap at the back entrance. They asked a whole lot of questions about everything. A lot of things seemed strange to them, like, 'Why did they not burst open the till,' or, 'Why is the rear entrance covered only in your footprints?'

The police eventually went away and took some of our paperwork with them. Time passed and nothing happened. The incident was even featured on Crimewatch UK. As more time passed, we became less worried, but when the insurance assessor arrived and started asking very awkward questions, Gordon and I both felt more scared than we had done in a long time. Eventually he seemed to accept the loss and we were paid over £6,000, which saved out bacon with the suppliers.

Really, the business did not need money as such, because the final sale of Christmas club bikes unlocked all the money and profit in the business – all it ever needed was temporary extended borrowing.

Things were all right for several weeks, and then, out of the blue, the police came into the shop and told Gordon and me that we were under arrest for fraud and resetting stolen goods. We were handcuffed and led away into the back of a police car, then taken directly to the cells, where we were searched and deprived of shoelaces and belts. It was down to the youth trainee to lock up the shop.

At the cells, Gordon and I were separated and questioned independently. Gordon cracked early and admitted everything, and because Gordon had given a statement, then I had to as well. I believe we were released on bail to appear before court to declare a plea at a date soon afterwards.

In a matter of hours, both my life and Gordon Stead's life had changed for the much, much worse. I believe it was a week after this that we were on trial at the High Court. Our solicitor was quite clear that we would be going down for a good stretch on this one, without doubt. The only hope of leniency would be on the grounds that we were young, had no previous convictions, and we had a viable business. This, though, would take months to prove.

The Social Work Department came round to make a social background report, which involved asking a lot of quite intimate questions with the whole family present, looking as decent and cohesive as possible. By now, it was April.

I would love to be able to write about my feelings at that time, but I cannot recall having any at all. I was totally emotionless as far as I know, and it was as if it was happening to someone else while I was hiding in my head, as I always had done at school. If I had emotions, then I could not touch them.

The time passed quickly, and pretty soon I was on the eve of my nemesis. The lawyer had told us we would go down for sure, so this was my last night of freedom. I spent it like any other – it was club night at Loudoun Road Club, so I cycled there and I told Billy what had happened, and that I would be gone for a long time.

By this time, I was still emotionless, but depressed, with a feeling of pointlessness and a strong desire to be dead. I left the club and cycled into the complete darkness, and to add to the effect, I put my dark sunglasses on. It was a tailwind back home, and I punted on the pace into the near blindness. I enjoyed the danger, but nothing happened – not until I got to Hurlford.

It is a downhill run to the start of Hurlford, and I flew down there at top speed. I did not see a parked car until the last minute, when I half-swerved to sort of miss it. It was a huge impact, and as luck would have it, I managed to break my thighbone. I flew right over the car and landed near a bus shelter, where a couple of people came over to see if I was all right. I knew what I had achieved, and I told them that there was nothing to worry about – I had only broken a leg!

The ambulance men could not understand how I could be so calm about it, but little did they know I was content with the situation.

In the mid-'80s, the remedy for a broken femur was traction (lying in bed on your back, with weights pulling the bone into place). The whole process would take at least twelve weeks. The trial and sentencing was postponed, and a new date would be somewhere around October or November. My recklessness had paid off and, for now, we were free.

In the meantime, Gordon was left to run the business. If he could show that the business was viable in its own right, even after paying back the £6,000 from the insurance, and was capable of possible employment for others, then things would look so much better for us when the day of judgement did come. As it turned out, the business paid the insurance back, and also covered all the expenses incurred by them in investigating the claim. To make matters even better, Gordon had a young employee to be considered when it came to summing up.

We were lucky it was a thighbone and not an arm or lower leg I had broken, because if you can make it to court in a wheelchair, then you will be taken. While I was in hospital, I knew Gordon was working hard to make good, but I also knew that if we were to have any hope of freedom, I had to do what I had to do.

The longer I was there on my back, the more depressed I became. I used to look at the thermometer and try to work out the toxicity of mercury, and other times I would not think anything at all. Sometimes I would stare from my bed, out to Barnweil Monument about 10 miles away. I would remember the times I'd cycled up past there with nothing to bother me but the past. I said to myself, 'When I get on a bike again, then that is the first place I'll cycle to.'

At the start, I was told I would probably be in traction for about twelve weeks and a brace for as long again, but now that the trial date was set, then I was free to heal as quickly as I liked.

I was out of traction in six or seven weeks, partly due to youth and good health, and partly due to standing almost upright on the bed, in order to stress the joint and cause it to heal more quickly. Once I got the full-length brace on, I was able to walk on two crutches. This lasted for another six weeks, but towards the end, I was able to come to the shop now and then.

At the shop there was a huge punch bag, and if I balanced myself, I could do a really good aerobic workout with my arms, while balancing on the spot, and I could do some strength exercises on my good leg too. I was hoping that some day soon, when I got my cast off, I could actually go for a short ride – to Barnweil Monument.

During that summer of '85, we worked away as if nothing was wrong, but at the back of our minds we knew that there was a gavel hanging over our heads. It was still the height of the summer when I finally got my cast off, and I still remember the intense disbelief as I looked down at my good leg, and what looked like a length of rope with a knot in for the other.

Unfortunately, I could not cycle right away, because my left knee could only bend to a partial angle. I worked and worked at taking it far enough for a pedal stroke, and as soon as I was there, my brother Gordon and I headed out across the Ayrshire countryside and made our way towards Barnweil Monument.

It is a fond memory during a dark era. It was a beautiful sunny day and we were in no rush to get there. It looked even more strange on the bike to have one leg half the width of the other. It was just as strange to have to put safety pins on my lycra shorts to hold them tight. It was not long before my brother had to help shove me up the climbs. We never really talked about the trial or the accident that had happened twelve hours before sentencing – he just accepted me as I was, his brother.

From that first feeble ride with my brother, I started doing more and more as time permitted. I was amazed at how quickly I gained a lot of fitness. I persevered and I decided to ride one of the last time trials of the year. It was a 50-miler, and was being held in Ayrshire. I still had a skinny left leg, although it was getting stronger all the time.

I could not rely on strength at all, so if I was to get through, then I would have to be very careful to pace myself for the entire distance. To my surprise, I won the event in a time of just over two hours, on standard drop handlebars and fixed wheel.

The glory did not do much to offset the sense of shame I carried around with me. The day of the trial arrived soon enough, and I can remember sitting in a room with Gordon Stead and our lawyer, and Gordon asked how it would turn out. The lawyer pinned him against the wall, with a finger jabbing into his chest. He said, 'You don't under-stand – you're going to the fucking pokey!' that set the tone for us as we made our way to the dock. We were done up in our best suits, and everything seemed so surreal that I almost felt like laughing. Woody Allen could have walked in at any moment.

We stood there like statues, as everything unfolded in front of us like a play. The main mitigating factors in our favour were: our age – I was nineteen by then and Gordon the senior partner at twenty; the fact that all the defrauded money had been paid back and all peripheral expenses made good to the insurance company; and that, while I was incapacitated, Gordon had shown the business to be sound and likely to create employment.

In summing up, the judge pointed out that such a serious crime would have to carry a custodial sentence, and there could be no exception in this case. We were both sentenced to one year's custody. As the judge spoke, I felt nothing at all. Then the judge continued to say that, because of our lack of previous convictions, and the fact that we had a viable business that would possibly create employment for others, as well as the fact that we had repaid all expenses to the insurance company, then the custodial sentences would be suspended.

This meant that we were free to go, but should either of us come up before the court for any reason, then the sentence would be served. The judge went on to say that we would also be fined £1,000 each, and that Gordon Stead would be fined for the resetting of stolen goods.

As we walked out of the court, we realised that we had been lucky in comparison to what might have been. We were still criminals and, although the custodial sentences were suspended, in any official application for visas etc, we were legally obliged to disclose that we had received a custodial sentence.

The local papers made front page news of it, and the fact that our fathers were police officers was made clear. When the full impact hit me, I felt totally disgraced and that I had done a terrible thing to my family. At that time, I didn't believe I could feel any worse about myself.

To make matters worse, because we have quite an unusual surname it affected my brother and sister as well. After all that was said and done, I could not bear to be in the shop, knowing people were coming in and looking me in the face and thinking that I was a convicted criminal. It was hard enough for me to just go out of the house. I quit the shop and did a deal with Gordon, where I would walk out of the partnership with almost nothing, while he would try and rebuild the reputation of the business.

Shortly afterwards, I heard that there would be a triathlon held at Ayr seafront in October. Now, one thing I do not like is cold water, but being a condemned man, I thought, 'Why not?' The other problem, though, was that I did not know if I could run on my skinny leg – not in a straight line, anyway. Because of the trial and the shame and publicity about it, though, I just did not want to be looking anyone in the eye, and I told my brother Gordon that although I would like to ride, I could not.

It was my brother again who intimated that I might be wimping out, and persuaded me that it would be a great idea. Coming up to the event, I managed to borrow a wetsuit and I tried a bit of running too, and it seemed fine.

On the day, there was a freezing cold east wind, and the water temperature was 8 or 9°C. What I said about my brother being hardier than me must be true, because he was perfectly willing to brace the October seas in just a lycra skin suit. As I approached the water, I could sense the coldness, but I could not believe the intense cold as I waded in. As the water reached my private parts, I let out a scream and almost turned back, but I looked over to Gordon just wading in like it was the Mediterranean, in his skin suit, so I carried right on in.

Soon we were swimming in open sea for the $^1/_2$-mile swim. I started off with the back crawl – my fastest stroke. I soon had to switch to the breaststroke because I could not see in front of me, and kept on punching other competitors in the legs. After a minute or two, I felt a nudge in my arm. It was my brother Gordon, and he said, 'You can walk on the bottom!' At first I did not believe him, as we were so far out to sea, but I reached down and felt sand.

From then on, the 'swim' was easy, and as I looked about, I could see that half the field had cottoned on, and the rest were really swimming. I came out of the water two or three minutes in arrears, and stripped off straight into my bike gear. I passed almost everyone on the 22-mile bike ride, and on the 7-mile run I felt brilliant. I think my time in hospital maybe helped my running, as I had lost over a stone in weight. I won it by a good margin, and I was as surprised as anyone. The ironic thing was that I got more publicity locally for that than I had done for running all over the country to win the junior BAR two years earlier. At least it was the right kind of publicity, but it could change nothing in my life or the way I felt about myself. It certainly could not change the way I thought that other people felt about me. The trial was over, but I was only just starting my sentence in my own head.

All the hopes I had had at the end of 1983 were in ruins. Back then, I was Scottish Junior Champion with a good prospect of going much further, and I would be a partner in a good cycle business, with the idea of branching out. And all because I didn't have the heart to ask my stressed-out parents for extra underwriting, it had come to this.

At nineteen, I was a branded criminal, I had no hope of work, I was virtually house-locked by my shame and self-image, and I had no hope. In just a few days, my world had crashed around me, and now I was nothing – absolutely nothing.

four: isolation and depression

The winter of 1985 was the very lowest point I had reached in my young life. I was less than zero in my own mind, and I had nothing inside me to counter it with. All through my childhood, I was made to feel worthless and inferior by others. Now I had shown myself to be the bad egg that everyone else could see throughout my youth. Well, not everyone, because the one person who never once made me feel inferior was my brother. I think he had such low self-esteem himself that he could not make anyone else feel inferior.

At this time I was still staying with my parents, and any hope I might have had of leaving home was extinguished. There literally was no hope whatsoever of finding employment with a criminal record like mine. My parents supported me and let me stay in the house, but even though I was paying what I could towards digs, I could only imagine myself as a long-term parasite.

Luckily I had not cut myself off completely, as I would go to the cycling club every week. Gordon Stead and I had rejoined the Wallacehill CC, our first club, because Gordon had had his membership of the Loudoun Road Club terminated before our brush with the law, on account of genuinely false accusation.

Someone had informed the local council where Alistair Gow lives that Alistair was conducting some kind of business in his mother's council house. Somehow Gordon ended up with the blame, and after a kangaroo court in Gordon's absence, he was dismissed from the Loudoun Road Club. I was disgusted by the junta-type behaviour of the club, and left in sympathy, and we both rejoined our former club.

After our fall from grace, the Wallacehill CC held a meeting, under more formal conditions, to decide if we had brought the club into disrepute to the degree where we should be suspended or even lose our membership. The Wallacehill CC stood by us, despite what had transpired, and every Friday I could be accepted as part of something for an evening.

In the winter of '85, this was my only social event. I had no friends come visit, and I had no-one to telephone. Apart from visiting my brother, I lived like a hermit. I desperately wanted to change my life, but I could not, mainly because this had been the way of it since I was a child, and I didn't know any other way.

It was my old pals from starting out in cycling – Gordon Graham, Tony Williamson and Jim Frew – who would form my social group, along with some other members of the club at the Bellfield Tavern, after the club on the Friday. Sometimes we would decant to Gordon's flat for an even later night. I always thought I could put on a good front for the average eye, but as well as the company, I would look forward to alcohol to make the world a lighter shade of grey just for a little while.

I only had money from the Social Security, and all of it went on a three-way split. I wanted to pay digs of some kind to my parents, and I also had to try and pay my fine, so whatever was left – if any – would do for a Friday. If I had nothing left, then I would simply not go to the club that week.

In my situation, all I could see that I could do to get any extra finance was to race and bring in some prize money to try and pay off my fine.

I still hated being exposed to the glare of the outside world, but I had to occasionally visit the Jobcentre to be seen to be trying to gain employment, and I had to sign on every fortnight. I always tried to go when it was wet, because fewer people would be out and about, and also, I could hide under a hood. It was a lesson I learned in my childhood.

I would still go out on my bike with a mind to racing in the coming season. I didn't mind going out training because, at speed, you can whiz past people before they can recognise you. I was managing to keep pretty fit during this time of virtual non-existence, but as time went by, I got more and more introverted and I became pretty despondent.

It was about this time in the spring of '86 that I became detached, to the degree where, when I was out on my bike one time, I was so depressed that I just could not make an effort of any kind. I dragged myself up a small hill just outside Kilmarnock, and I stopped and looked out towards the coast, and it hit me like a ton of bricks that I was not part of it. Society, the world, everything – I was not part of it!

Once I saw it, it was so obvious that other people are part of a network with work, relatives, friends, hobbies, girlfriends, and neighbours. Other people are part of the infrastructure – banks, hospitals, companies, children, parties, everything out there. Not me. Now I saw it as it really was. To me, the truth was that I was the social equivalent of a human's appendix. I was so disconnected that I could not make or even meet a friend, and I never had or looked like having any likelihood of having a girlfriend. It even occurred to me that I was twenty and I had never been to a party.

The image of myself and my pathetic existence had never been as low as it was then, in the first half of '86. I was more introverted than ever. I hated myself for what I was and for being a parasite on my parents. I could not see a way out, and it got to the stage where I would stare, hour after hour, into the flames of the coal fire, day after day, getting more and more depressed. I was the only one in the house during the day, as my brother had a place and a job of his own, my sister Yvonne was still at school, and my mother had a part-time job.

One day, the depression and shame and self-hatred became so strong that I could not bear to be alive any more. I went to the garden shed and reached for the acetylene bottle. It was not a whim or a desire for me now – I had overcome those in the previous weeks. Now it was both need and compulsion.

As I attached the hose to my mouth and started it, I began to cry, but I did not know what I was crying for. The more I cried, the more I carried on. In the back of my mind, I thought I was doing the right thing for everyone. As I started to lose my life, thoughts of a lot of things that happened in the past rushed through my mind. None of them were good thoughts, except Mrs Mackay from primary school. She was the only teacher who spoke to me like a human being. The deeper I got, the more I remembered a whole lot of bad things, like the time my brother and I were forced to touch each other up, with a knife at our throats.

And then there was nothing,

The first conscious moment after that was in the garden next to the shed. My father was bouncing me about and slapping my face. I was so far gone that I could not focus and I could not get a fix on reality as the world came and went. As I gained more consciousness, my dad said he had come home from work earlier than usual, and when he found me I was already dead; he had to start me up again.

I was soaked in vomit – it was even engrained in my hair. I had defecated and urinated in my pants and I was a disgusting mess all over. My dad sent me to the shower, and now my sense of shame was so much worse than before. My brother and sister were never told about it, and it was kept between my parents and me.

My parents contacted their own GP and made an appointment for me to see him. My father came with me and we went into a huge room where I told them I was fine and it was just a one-off. Keeping my feelings hidden was something I had done since I was young enough to know that people can trample all over them. On this occasion, I felt cornered, guilty and mentally exhausted, and I knew that I would not be strong enough to face the questions that follow answers and the consequences of those answers. In other words, I hid back behind my mask, and gave the answers that I knew other people preferred to hear. My father had been so upset about it and had been in tears at one point in the house, and I just wanted to do anything that would make everyone feel a little reassured. The doctor only read the mask, and passed it off as a blip, and assured us that it would not go down on medical records.

All I wanted to do was appease and seem fine to everyone. I started to go out on my bike more, so that I could get prize money. The season soon started and I did win prizes as expected, to help pay my fine. After my suicide attempt, I never reached the depth of depression that I had felt at that time. I kept going to the club and I also had the good fortune of bumping into an American tourist – or rather, he bumped into me.

Paul and I became friendly pretty quickly. He was keen to see Scotland, which was his actual birthplace – his parents were Scots who emigrated when he was seven – and I suggested I would show him round. I told him that if we were camping, we could do it for a fiver. In reality, I was broke, and £5 was more or less all I had.

It was about April when we set off, fully loaded with tents and panniers full of cheap food. Paul was pretty hardy and, in a strange way, I was looking forward to a bit of cycling, and some hardship as a challenge. I had said we could do it for a fiver, and I was determined that I would succeed. Paul could not have appeared at a better time, when my life was pretty empty, and it could have been easy to slip back into a black hole.

Our money slipped away a little quicker than scheduled in the beginning, but then I introduced Paul to the technique of 'jamming up' with cheap bread and cheap jam. In return, Paul introduced me to the art of 'spliffing up' – something I would never have imagined myself getting involved in. But since I was only a few steps away from being willing to kill myself, my resistance to a herb that might make me feel good was virtually nil. When we were camped and Paul and I spliffed up, it did make me laugh and really chill out, with apparently no lasting after-effect. I had read about its non-addictive quality before, and curiosity combined with the fact that I was a worthless piece of shit anyway, meant that the niggling guilt in the back of my mind could not deter me.

Our money had become badly depleted way ahead of schedule, so we collected loads and loads of empty lemonade bottles over Rannoch Moor, only to be told at Glencoe that the nearest shop that would take them in exchange for cash was 20 miles away. Undeterred, we carried on, purely on 'jamming up'. The weather was so bad we had to sleep in the bus shelter at Spean Bridge, and we were woken in our sleeping bags by a crowd of taunting school kids waiting for the bus in 'their' shelter.

We went to Inverness and the weather was beautiful. We left there in the evening, heading up the Drummochter Pass to camp somewhere. A terrible storm blew up from nowhere, and all round us was just bog. As it approached darkness, Paul said we should find a farm. As soon as we saw a light to our left, we headed straight for it. Paul suggested I should ask, since I was Scottish. The rain was lashing across the yard, when a man came across. I started to mumble and bumble, 'Excuse me, sorry to bother you, but, um, well, would you know anywhere we can camp at all?' Before I could finish my 'I'm not worthy' diatribe, Paul stepped in. In his full Californian accent, and as loud as you like, 'Can we sleep in your barn?'

I was actually shocked by his directness, but the man said, 'Of course you can – follow me.' He sectioned off some of his sheep, and his wife came with blankets. She said she would bring us some supper, and without even engaging the cortex, I started to say, 'No, we're fine, honestly,' but luckily Paul got to the root of it in time, with, 'That is most kind of you.'

Paul teased me with the 'we're not worthy, we're not worthy' routine. He could not believe how humble I could be all the time. On the other hand, I was taken aback by Paul's straight-to-the-point, but polite, way of asking for what he wanted, as well as his nerve to ask at all. When I thought about it though, I knew that Paul was right – I did not think of myself as worthy.

When the farmer's wife came back with our hearty supper she stated that we would be woken at 6.30 for breakfast. Sure enough, at 6.30 sharp we got straight into our rather smelly cycling gear and followed Mrs McQueen into her farm kitchen. It was an ancient farm and she gave us some of the history. She showed us the hiding hole where the priests hid during the purges.

We seated ourselves at the table where three places had been set, with toast and jam already laid out. While Mrs McQueen was waiting for the kettle to boil I reached out to take a piece of toast. Paul kicked me hard under the table to stop me and pointed with his eyeballs to an open bible in front of us.

I immediately understood, and just then Mrs McQueen joined us at the table. 'Well, boys, who wants to say Grace'. Paul looked at me with a poker face and I looked at Paul in contained panic. The only Grace my dad had taught me was rather rude, and here was the moment my shortcoming would be exposed. There was a moment of silence across the table, and I could feel my heart racing. Just as I was about to say 'Um, well . . .' Paul broke the silence with a long and perfectly prepared Grace, but not before he'd made me sweat for it.

With an immense sense of relief, we tucked into a hearty farm breakfast, and when we had drunk our last cup of tea we thanked Mrs McQueen sincerely for the family's hospitality. We asked if there was anything we could do on the farm, or anything at all we could do. She said it was her pleasure to welcome us, but there was just one thing we could do. She handed us a bundle of leaflets, and said that if we could help spread the word of God by leaving them in a public place, she would be delighted. We promised that we would go further than that, and that we would distribute them personally.

To boot, she insisted on giving us a large bag full of rolls, bananas and other foodstuffs that would see us all the way to Glasgow. It was a beautiful, sunny day, we were on the open road, and we'd just been shown the highest order of hospitality. At that moment I really felt like I was alive, really alive and glad of it. At that moment I felt so fine that I could not understand how I could have felt so terribly bad, just a few months ago.

We were going gung-ho to pace ourselves all the way to Glasgow in one go. As the day went on I got weaker and weaker with fatigue. Food or not we were absolutely stuffed by mid-afternoon. We had made it to Aberfoyle and we stopped for another drum-up. I just could not face leaving, and I was so exhausted and yet uplifted by our tour that I could not stop laughing. A great idea came to me during my outbursts of laughter. I took my back wheel out and let the tyre down. I then turned my bike upside-down by the side of the road and stuck out my thumb. Paul had never witnessed the technique before, but in no time, we were back in the outskirts of Glasgow, in the cab of a flatbed truck. Our intention was to head to Central Station and use the last of our money for the fare to Kilmarnock.

It was at this point Paul pulled out a £20 note from his shoe, and said he had cracked. He thought he could go the distance on a fiver, but the smell of the chip shop was too much. He bought us both a fish supper and as we sat on a high wall with them, I remembered our promise to Mrs McQueen. There were all types of people passing by beneath us, and we only had a short time to uphold our pledge.

A promise is a promise. I said so to Paul, to which his reply was, 'Well, I will if you will.' Normally I would be way too introverted to even contemplate such a thing, but I was on a high and still had a touch of the giggles. I reached down with a flier to the first person who came a long – a punk – and something like, 'You too can be saved. Jesus loves you.' One for one, Paul and I continued to the last leaflet. We took the train and cycled home, and all too soon, the £5 tour was over.

Paul was staying in Kilmarnock with his aunt for a few weeks, and we cycled around quite a bit. One place we went to visit was Glasgow, to see his cousin. Paul wasn't that keen to go, but he felt obliged to because he was in Scotland. Paul knew that his cousin lived on the 'other side', and that he had a heroin habit. When I got there, I got a better picture of what Paul was not keen to see.

We went upstairs, and into a communal bed-sit, taking our bikes with us. There were several young and scruffy-looking people milling about. We went into his cousin's room and it was almost bereft of possessions. The bed was a grubby-looking mattress on the floor. In the course of the conversation, he mentioned that he had been sick on his mattress during the night. His solution was to turn the mattress over – a solution he had used several times before.

The whole group of us went into the communal living room, which was also pretty bare. Paul was dead against hard drugs, but we hung about so he could get some hash from the dealer when he came round. We did not stay long, but they invited us to an acid party that was being organised for a few days' time. While I was still digesting the offer, Paul decided for us that we would give it a miss. It was a good thing we did – it was raided by the police. Running about with Paul was sound, but it was Paul's long-term plan to cycle through Europe and catch a military flight back to California. I was hoping to join him, but pretty soon an opportunity came up that my dad had heard about. The cycle shop in Irvine was up for grabs and it would be a 'stock at trade' with a small amount for goodwill.

It was a real dilemma, because it killed off the chance of a European tour with Paul, which would have been such a gas. On the other hand, good opportunities do not come along every day, and my dad was willing to underwrite me. I think my father knew better than anyone that I could not carry on for long with no sense of purpose in my life. The only problem was that after Cosmos Cycles, I could not face another cycle shop.

I chewed over the situation with Paul, and I suppose we both knew I would have to do the responsible thing. Paul suggested, jokingly, that I could get the spare room at his cousin's bed sit on the Social. For a while, it seemed like that would be a better life. The kids in the bed-sit had hardly any money or possessions and had drug problems, yet I was jealous of them. I was desperately lonely and they were not.

Decency and responsibility won out in the end, and in no time, I was the businessman behind the counter. It took only a handful of days alone in the shop to realise that this would be a hard run. A few days after I opened, Paul came in to say his final farewell before heading off for Europe. He shook my hand with a loaded palm, and left. 'It's only enough for a couple of goes if you hit a downer,' he said, as he headed for the door.

With the abject loss of the shop and the thought of the road, it was not long before I was on one hell of a downer. It was pouring wet this particular morning. There had been no sign of customers, and the shop was dull and lonely. I searched about a drawer for Paul's magic handshake, and loaded it into a tiny pipe Paul had also left.

It did not take long for me to start feeling all right. In fact, I went straight through the all-right zone and into the giggly zone in the space of a minute. I had also gone through the whole lump that Paul had left, and when I was struggling to stop myself laughing, I realised that I had maybe overdone it a tad. I thought I ought to close the shop for an hour or so, until I regained a straight face.

Before I could laugh my way to the door, a customer came in – the first customer of the day. I scurried back to behind the counter, and as he asked for a seat-binder bolt, I realised I was completely stoned. I started searching through the stack of pull-our plastic drawers sitting on the counter, while keeping my head down to hide my uncontrollable smile.

I found it pretty quickly, and I grabbed it with my left hand and held it in the air and said, 'It's one of these you're looking for!' Whilst still holding it in my left hand, I continued to search with my right. After I had searched twice again, I stated that I did not have such a thing, but that I could get one for Monday. The customer shook his head and said he would come back later.

I realised what I had just done, and again, I laughed my way to the door, when yet another customer came in. Between bouts of laughter, I asked him what he wanted. He enquired what was so funny, and I made the excuse that I had just heard a joke on the radio. It was a tyre he wanted, so I dived straight into the huge pile of tyres suspended from the wall on a series of extended poles. I must have rumbled face-first back and forth for ages, whilst trying to compose myself. I then popped my head out, again bursting into laughter. I asked what size he was looking for. The customer just nodded his head and left. I knew I was completely stoned, and shut the shop long enough to straighten up a bit. My eyes were still bright pink when I reopened the shop, but I was back in control and it would be the last time I would ever do that. Not that it wasn't tempting, when the shop was such a depressing place for me - even when it was busy with customers. The problem was the abject loneliness, because you do not really talk to customers – you simply serve them.

I suppose the Cosmos days were quite good because the business flourished on BMX sales, a lot of those guys were sixteen or seventeen, and Gordon and I were eighteen and nineteen, and it was a really hip place to hang out. Sometimes at Cosmos Cycles, the mega-wide pavement was so jammed up with BMX bikes that people could hardly get past. It never became like that here. I think the reasons were that the small size of the shop made it impossible to 'hang out', and the heat had gone out of BMX at competition level. It was the year of waning BMX sales, just before the mountain bike would take over as king. I had imagined myself as becoming part of the community if I was there long enough, but in truth, I was just a guy who opened a shop, sat alone and closed at the end of the day. Things might have been a bit different if I had been proactive in looking to be known in the community in a social capacity. Loads of times, I tried to go to the local pub at lunchtime, which was just across the road. Something stopped me every time. Sometimes I'd put out the 'out to lunch' sign up, lock the door and just go back in again. In my mind, I imagined that when I went through the door, the place would fall silent and everyone would turn round and stare at me. I had a social phobia, and I never overcame it. I just hid in my hole and hoped the world would come to me.

My one link with the real world was the Wallacehill CC, and going out after the club, and sometimes to Gordon Graham's afterwards. I had no problem going to the Bellfield Tavern with my club mates, but I would always feel on edge until I had consumed enough alcohol. I would always be stone last when entering any establishment, as if it was a privilege for me to tag along. It is a habit I only recently realised I had, while my psychologist and I were analysing how I viewed myself in a social group. It turns out that it is not a behaviour that just became force of habit – it's the only behaviour I have ever known. As a child I would only be tolerated, if I was lucky, as a tag-along, because I was filth.

As the shop began to seem more and more lonely, I became more depressed and, even though I had my own business, I still felt detached from the world as though I had some invisible force-field around me that prevented me from being a part of it.

Sometimes the world would seem so bleak and intolerable and I felt so depressed and isolated, that I almost could not stand it. I had tried the ultimate form of escape, and realised the distress caused to others. No, in those worst days, a bottle of vodka would make the world a different shade of black with maybe a hint of grey. It was not a day-to-day occurrence, thankfully, as most of the time I was under control.

I was also very fortunate that I had found a young friend for company. Matthew Weideger, the late brother of my wife, was only fifteen, but he was really keen on bikes, and he started coming more and more – not only as a customer, but also as a person I instantly liked and wanted to hang out with. He reminded me of myself, except he had the confidence to go and put himself forward.

Matthew was like a saviour to me in my own dark hole. If I'm honest, then I would say that I was a social recluse at that time, and Matthew coming to hang out at the shop was like a bird coming to a prison window. Matthew and I became good friends and he would hang out after school and at weekends.

My dad used to help out sometimes at the weekend, as did my brother Gordon. On the approach to Christmas, they would be there more often. My dad thought it was bad business to let someone hang about on the wrong side of the counter and watch the trade, but for once in my life, I insisted it was OK. On a special moment, while I was staring into nothing with my 1,000-mile eyes, I had a great idea. I would often find myself staring at one spot unceasingly, and disappear into it until something pulled me away from it. It was during one of these moments, while staring at my Time Trial bike, that I thought it would be better if I turned the handlebars around and rode in a tuck position. With nothing better to do, I got a spanner out and, when it was finished, I closed the shop for two minutes and gave it a quick spin. It felt good to me, but the bars would need a bit of mechanical adjustment by way of cold-setting (bending). I was still keeping fit by training and cycling back and forth to the shop, and I reckoned I would ride the Christmas 10-mile time trial on it if I could come to terms with looking like a freak.

Coming up to Christmas, I had the Christmas club to think about, but this time I was wary about how many bikes I ordered to stock in the hope of selling. Everything went pretty smoothly, except I had underestimated how many cheap BMX I would sell and, by the end of November, I put a Christmas club label on my last one. I left one out on display knowing I could sell them from it, and be able to order more in plenty of time for Christmas. The sales just kept on coming, and the supplier had promised a delivery. After a lot of phone calls, they finally arrived three or four days before Christmas. Because of shortage of space, we kept them boxed until the last minute. Everything was fine, until we had built all the old stock for Christmas customers to take away. About two days before Christmas, we opened one of the new bikes for customers who had put a deposit down on the display bike, thinking they would get that actual bike. The whole lot of them were pink. Just when everything was going fine, Christmas turned into a tirade of complaint, abuse and apology.

One uplifting thing to happen that Christmas was the result of the 10-mile time trial. I endured the sniggers and jokes before the start, and just went for it – mainly to satisfy my own curiosity. In the end, I won it by about five minutes, although I was favourite to win by a large margin anyway. I had also brought some cycling bits and bobs as prizes for the marshals. On the way round, I kept an eye open for the most enthusiastic and the most friendly marshal. The riders thought this was a bit silly, but I cannot finish this book without pointing out that without voluntary organisers and helpers, then the sport – in Britain, at least – would not exist. The time trial was a nice distraction before heading back to the shop to open for the Sunday afternoon. I was glad when the middle of January came, and after-sales adjustments had died down. I was back to sitting on the throne of my empire behind the counter and waiting for Matthew to come in from school to cheer me up. Matthew's sister Anne used to come in now and again to pay a few pounds towards a Christmas club bike she'd been paying off since August or September. I never thought anything of it. She never wore socks, so I thought that, seeing as she was clearly hard up for money, then she could pay it off in her own time. Little did I know it was the fashion. My dad knew all the while that she was trying to chat me up, but I was oblivious.

I still had some contact with Gordon Stead at Cosmos Cycles and, as well as supplying me and my brother Gordon with one of the first mountain bikes (Muddy Fox Courier), he also suggested going on a two-week skiing trip in February, which was on special offer. There is very little trade in February, so I was well up for it.

The Tyrolean area of Austria was the destination, and from the start, it was a fantastic holiday. The first thing after unpacking was the glühwein party to help the 100 or so people to bond. I found the beverage most palatable, as did most of the Scots, who seemed to form a clique from the first moments. Next up was tenpin bowling. Such had been my insularity that I had neither played nor seen it played in my life. It was my luck to be first up for the first team. Having asked what to do, I was told to throw the ball as hard as I could. I had seen it done in cricket, but as the ball left my hand at ceiling height, the communal intake of breath let me know I had done something wrong.

The skiing was wonderful, and on the second day, we were tackling the black runs. I had never had a proper ski lesson in my life, but because I really did not care about crashing, it was so easy to learn. There was a group of us skiing and socialising together, and one of us was a girl whom, at the time, I was totally taken over by. I had absolutely no confidence at all within the group and especially in the company of this particular girl. I was so obsessed with not seeming boring or not fitting in and trying to cover the fact that I was inferior to everyone else, that I must have seemed like a neurotic clown. I felt so inadequate. The only thing I had in my favour was that I knew I was not stupid. I had spent so many years wishing that I was to know that I was not. I could not have normal, calm communication with her, because everything that I thought I was or was not prevented me. Her group was only staying for the first week, but at least she gave me her phone number and a peck on the cheek. On the second week, I had got on a bit of a downer one night, and said to Gordon about how I had to change my life. He offered to buy my shop over, and I was tempted to shake on it there and then, but I said I would think about it. A few weeks later, I managed to get a date with her at her university. We went to the Rocky Horror Show and on to a disco. I did not dance because I always feel like everyone is looking at me, and then I get a cold sweat and I feel like I can't breathe, then I have to dance mechanically, as if at gunpoint. Then it gets so intense that I have to leave and get another drink. My date came to nothing and soon afterwards, I asked Gordon (Stead) if his offer still stood. I had been doing a lot of thinking about myself, and my conclusion was that I was socially inadequate. I did not feel comfortable around people. I could not fit in and I did not know what to do or say to people without constantly analysing my actions. I never felt part of a group. I only ever felt like I was struggling to remain, and I had to change. That ill-fated date – my first ever – had made me think about myself and how unable I was to interact with people, and I had a plan of action that would sort both that and my feeling of inferiority. I was going to become a student and whatever I studied would provide a cover for my covert plan of self-improvement. The shop was a good enough business, and on paper, it was silly to sell up, but even with Matthew coming round and going to club nights, I was never going to be able to change into the type of person I wanted to be. I hated myself for what I was, and if I did nothing, I would never escape my black depressions. It was not long before Gordon bought over the shop on the same basis that I had bought it. There was a bit of profit in it, and when everything was settled, I decided I was going to go somewhere abroad. A couple of weeks later, I was on a flight to sunny Spain.

five: spain and beyond

Parting the warm air as I cycled away from Malaga Airport was so easy. I was dressed in shorts and a short-sleeved cycling jersey, and had chosen my racing bike, fitted with friendlier gears and a light pack. It was a frame I had built myself, with a split down-tube and short wheelbase. It was also my first experiment in reducing bottom bracket width (how far apart your feet are when pedalling).

So here I was, alone, in the south of Spain, with some money in my pocket, a warm breeze in my face on the way to the Med, and no plan whatsoever. Freedom could not come much more pure than this. My first instinct was to head south to the Mediterranean and the tourist belt of coastal towns, Torremolinos being the main one. On the approach of darkness, I looked about for cheap accommodation and found a cheap room in a hotel, and as I lay back in the ambient warmth, it hit me just how totally free I was to go where I wanted and do what I wanted at any time.

I had found that when I am with other people I always fall back to a 'whatever you think' ideology, but here I was in total control, and Irvine Cycles seemed like a thousand years ago. I decided that the trinket towns with their pink beer-belly tourists were not for me, and that I would head inland towards Cordoba. The journey took me two or three days with 'hostal' stay-overs. I discovered that 'hostales' (the Spanish hostels) were the cheapest way, and this is where I would meet the interesting people who were roughing it around Europe or even the world.

The thing about real travellers that regular folks cannot understand very easily is that we can meet, shoot the breeze about life and past experiences, hit the non-tourist night spots, then part the next day, with nothing but best wishes. There is no need for exchange of address or phone numbers – that would be a step too far in the direction of familiarity. The mutual benefits of non-judgemental company, non-domestic chat and being able to express and receive honest opinions with impunity are good enough.

In retrospect, I suppose I was trying to escape familiarity, and it was strange that I could be such an outgoing and relaxed person with a total stranger, yet at the shop, I could not cross the road to the pub. Back then, as soon as I revealed myself to be from the bike shop, I would be familiar and would have to hide behind the partial protection of a beer glass, like I usually would in social gatherings at home. Here in Spain, I had lost my feeling of people looking at me and judging me.

When I reached Cordoba, I looked round the city and I decided to go to the bullfight. I was in two minds about it. On one hand, I was hesitant to buy a ticket and support an activity that seemed, on balance, to be barbaric, but on the other hand, it was here to see, and how could I condemn something I had never seen? I managed to find a 'hostal' and I left my bike there and headed out to see the 'sport' of bullfighting. I did not meet any other travellers at the hostal, so there was no opportunity for company.

I'm glad I went because it was an education for me, and it also cleared up a couple of misconceptions that I had. The bulls were much smaller than they seemed to be in the heroic depictions of bullfighters, and the bullfight is a process of slaughter – six bulls in total, one after the other. As well as that, I also realised quite quickly that the main implement of slaughter is cunningly disguised as a solid, pointed rapier, which only just superficially wounds the animals. In fact it is a hollow tube with an internal spike mechanism that punctures the bulls' lungs. What I witnessed was six bulls suffocating to death while being goaded by a swaggering torturer. The chicken had more chance with the fox, I thought, as I left with a feeling of nausea. I must say, though, that most of the Spanish people I spoke to on my trip were opposed to the practice.

I left Cordoba and headed towards Seville, which I'd heard was well worth a visit. It was a long journey, which included an encounter with a water snake as I dangled my hot feet in a stream. It was the quickest I'd moved in a long time. If I remember rightly, I had to stay over in an 'el cheapo' hotel in a backwater shantytown, where absolutely no-one spoke English. It reminded me of the stereotypical Mexican villages you see in the old westerns, except there were no tumbleweeds. By this stage, I was getting by in Spanish, because I had spent a bit of time studying it from a book before I left, and now I was getting an ear for it, I could converse quite easily about my basic needs, about where I came from and things like that. I am quite convinced that it made a big difference to how I was received by the Spanish people, and the fact that I was travelling alone by bike seemed to give me some sort of respectability that hitchhikers did not enjoy.

When I left the town the next morning, it seemed overwhelmingly hot, but the sight of a guy cycling in a Parka jacket and a hat reminded me that it was only April. When I got to Seville in mid-afternoon, it was very busy with people, and as I bowled along I came to a huge pala-tial building. There were inordinate amounts of people milling about, so I stopped out of curiosity to find out what was going on. If there was going to be an event, then I did not want to miss it. There were loads of people sitting about on the steps of the approach to the former palace, and I noticed three guys who had a northern-European-traveller look about them. After establishing that they spoke English, they explained that it was Semana Santa (in other words, it was the Easter festivities), and tonight would be the big night. We talked for quite a while about Spain and travel, then the four of us decided to go for hamburgers at a stall at the bottom of the steps. As we spoke more, it became clear that everybody was a complete stranger to each other, and we all laughed because each one of us had thought we'd got talking to three other friends.

It was obvious that I would have a real problem getting some-where to stay, but one of the travellers, a German, was staying out of town and knew there was a spare room. He offered me a lift in his car, so I chucked the bike in and went for it. The main reason I had steered clear of a full-blown touring bike was that when it comes to alternative transport, it is a real problem. As it was, all I had to do was remove the wheels and there were no mudguards or racks to make things difficult.

The hostel was good, and it was cheap as well as being available. We had something to eat and headed back out to meet up with the guys we had met earlier. We were right on time to see the Easter procession for Semana Santa, and it was not half impressive. I had never seen a town or city as busy with revellers in my life, and the sights, sounds and vibrancy of it all was amazing. It just kept on going and going. The crowds did not start dispersing until dawn, and it was 8 a.m. before we got back to the hostel. I was almost asleep from sheer exhaustion, when another procession started right outside.

The four of us met up again later on that day, once we'd recovered a bit, and messed about on pedalos on the river, just shooting the breeze. The next day, we all had to go our separate ways, and for me, it was another good memory locked away. I was still jaded from it all, but I headed out in the direction of Granada. I wanted to see the city for the sake of the Alhambra Palace, and the whole historical feel of the city itself, but Granada is very near to one of the highest roads in Europe – Pico Velata – in the Sierra Nevada Mountains.

On the road, I met a German cycle tourist and we got talking. He was headed in the same direction, so we joined up for the journey to Granada. The journey was quite long, and Gunter suggested we could just camp halfway, as he had a tent. It sounded like a good idea to me. I did not have sleeping bag, but I could wear my trousers, extra clothes and warm jacket. I was still a bit chilly, as the night air cooled sharply, and I only slept on and off.

The next day, when we reached Granada, Gunter had the same desire as me – to conquer Pico Velata, which is over 10,000 feet above sea level. At the approach to the climb, we saw a café and headed in for some pre-climb caffeine and food. Gunter asked in good Spanish if we could leave some luggage there and collect it on the road back. There was no problem with that, and we set off with just a front bag each with extra clothes.

It was 90° at the base of the mountain, but we could see people driving up with skis on the tops of their cars, so we knew we would need more clothes as we ascended. A sign said it was 40km to the top, and after about three hours of solid climbing we reached the end of the road. Snow had blocked the last 1,000 feet or so.

The descent was fast and exhilarating and it was well worth the climb. Because there was a ski station on the top part of the mountain, the road leading up to the final turnoff for the summit was immaculate tarmac, and the super-fast twists and turns on my racing bike were partly what I was looking forward to. We descended so quickly that we could feel the temperature rising round about us.

When it was over, we looked around the city a bit and headed out towards the Med again. Gunter had not been to the Med yet and was keen to get there before he had to head back. It was not a short journey, but we made it before dark and landed up in a town called Motril, and checked into a smart but cheap hotel. We headed out to town that evening and found ourselves in a genuine flamenco club. We stood out as the only foreigners there, but we were made to feel welcome, as the women danced with castanets and the men played brilliant flamenco music.

Motril is a small town about two miles from the sea and is not normally on the tourist trail. The next morning this became apparent, as few tourists could be seen in the town square and almost no-one spoke English. Gunter and I had one last coffee before he had to head back to Germany, and as he rode out of town, I realised how much I had enjoyed his company. After he had gone, I developed a slight sense of loneliness for the first time during my trip. As I sat enjoying the sun and my anonymity in the town square, I wanted to soak up the tranquil ambience of this most Spanish of towns. The longer I sat, the more curious I became as people came and went. One man passed with a donkey-load of straw and watered his animal in the town-centre fountain. While he was waiting, he pulled out what looked like a lump of coal from his trouser pocket, picked a tiny piece off of it and put it into his pipe. If it was what I thought it was, than I admired his nerve to bring it out in the town centre, but as I lingered that afternoon, I saw many 'lumps of coal' come out of people's pockets. Not thinking much more about it, and being in a slight stupor from my total exertions, I headed back to the hostal with a desire to sleep. The room was about the size of an average bathroom, with just enough room for the single bed and my bike. This was normal for a hostal, but at least the price was right.

When I awoke from my slumber, it was still early enough to go out, and also it was the weekend, so I thought about going next door to a local bar. The old reservations and phobia I had had in the shop kicked in again, and after a while of arguing with myself, I flew out of the room and refused to lose my momentum. I could speak a bit of Spanish, but I could hide behind the language barrier if I had to, and that gave me a sense of security.

As soon as I stepped into the bar, I was destined to open a new chapter in my lone adventure. I did not even make it to the bar, when I was beckoned to make up a team on one of those twiddly-handled football games – the type where the spinning footballer kicks the ball forwards. The second question I was asked, after my name, was which football team I supported. Knowing that Dundee United had knocked Barcelona out of the European Cup, and feeling manipulative, that is the team I chose. My calculation was correct, and this being the very south of Spain, my answer was met with delight.

After more games and a couple of drinks, they invited me to join them at a nightclub that I am sure no tourist would ever find, in the backstreets, and behind the 'green door'. I had a good time there but my sense of righteousness prevented me from partaking in the use of the ubiquitous herb. One of them was called Paco, and he explained that his family was on holiday and that I could stay at the farm, rather than waste money on the hostal. We arranged to meet at the local coffee shop the next day.

Paco showed up as he said he would, and four of his other friends were there too. They were all smoking joints openly, and as they passed one on to me all my impediments seemed to melt away. Soon I was floating, and the six of us and my bike, which I had almost left at the coffee shop, headed round to Paco's Renault 4. One cylinder was blown, so one guy had to bump start us at every traffic light or junction.

I spent a few happy days at Paco's farm and while I was there I learned what 'siesta' really meant to the local farmers. Each would take a turn of being host to a wine and hash afternoon, before returning to their agricultural toil. I somehow managed to refuse all offers of the herb – probably because the approach of summer had brought out the instinctive need to get into shape for racing. One thing I had found out, though, was that the lumps of coal had come from Morocco, had been intercepted by the local police and that some sort of 'tolerance deal' had been struck.

One day at Paco's I will never forget is the day we decided to go to the local nudist beach. It was not signposted and could not be seen from the road, so only those with local knowledge would know of the beautiful sandy bay with rock faces all around. Paco said his chemist friend was coming over, so we stripped off and just sunbathed until he arrived. It was one of his friends from the nightclub, and we had met before.

The trouble started when he introduced me to his wife – a well-tanned Spanish beauty. As I looked up from my beach towel, she was standing right in front of me – stark naked. The response was immediate, involuntary and unwanted. They all went swimming, while all I could do is think of brick walls or cars or anything that might make it go away. I was desperate to go swimming, but it would be difficult to cover the 10 yards or so with a more-than-obvious erection. Just when

I thought I had it beaten, and the three of them were beckoning me to join them, I looked over, and the sight of her standing waist-deep with her long black hair dangling over her breasts pinned me face down once again. Three hours later, I had the image of a spoilsport, and sunburn on my back.

While I was with Paco at the farm, he revealed to me his heroin habit. He did not want to 'shoot up' in front of me, because he was too ashamed, but he wanted me to know, because he was convinced that, sooner or later, he would be dead from it. He said that he could see now that he was condemned as soon as he had done it the first time. What he wanted was for me to promise never to do it – not even out of curiosity – not once. It was an easy promise to make and an even easier one to keep when I heard a year or so later that he had died.

It was now time to leave Paco and his friends, and head west along the coast. He had offered me a huge lump of hash to see me through my journey, but I declined, partly because I felt good and did not feel the need for it, and partly because my thoughts were turning towards the Scottish 25-miles championship TT. I took in some good efforts on my way to Gibraltar. I had planned in my head to take in Morocco for some real 'I don't give a damn what happens to me' adventure, but Paco begged me not to go there. It was the same line I had had from my concerned parents, but with the weight of local knowledge, I heeded the advice and headed back towards Granada instead.

I had two reasons for returning to Granada – Pico Velata one last time, and a train ride to Madrid.

It was a long journey, but I still tackled Pico Velata. Unfortunately the snow was still there, blocking the route to the summit, but the rush was just as good as before. Unfortunately, the same description did not hold true for the train journey.

At that time, there were two choices of train to Madrid – the Expresso or the Rapido. Both sounded perfectly all right by my translation of the words, but the Rapido was a much cheaper ticket. Of course, I chose the Rapido, but as soon as I boarded the train, it was like stepping into a western film set, with eight people to each wooden compartment, and straight-up seats. As soon as the train set off, I reached to open the window, asking the others in Spanish if it was all right. The response was, 'Frigo, frigo!' (cold!). The Spanish had this journey sussed, and brought out large quantities of cheese and wine, which they passed about liberally for the thirteen hours the journey took. It was less than 300 miles, and I calculated that, in theory, I could have gone quicker by bike!

In Madrid, I again stayed in a hostal, but I did not meet anybody of interest. I am not really into art, but I wanted to see the Prado simply because I was there. I did that and I also succumbed to my desire to buy a good guitar and just make my way back to Scotland, with racing in mind.

The train to Paris does not allow bikes, and they said they could ship it forward. I had a deep suspicion that I would never see it again, or it would arrive ruined, after being through the system. Besides, I would need it at the other end. I resorted to an alternative plan. I rushed to the train at the last minute, with my bike as compact as possible, whilst rebuffing any complaint in my broadest Scots vernacular, in the hope that I would be more hassle than it is worth to remove. It worked, and once the train moved, I was a 'sitting tenant'.

I decided to cycle to Calais with my guitar strapped to my back. By now, it was over four weeks of travel, and I had taken in so much, but now I just wanted to get back and sharpen up for the 25-mile championship in a month's time. I was in reasonable shape, but I needed some speed in my legs. In a handful of days, I made it back home to my parents' house, where I was still staying, and my lone adventure was over.

I had rid myself of the roving desire for a little while, and now it was time to dust off my TT bike and use what little time I had to prepare for the 25-mile championship, which was being held in Ayrshire that year. I was determined to use the crouch position I had used at the Christmas '10', and the Scottish '25' championships would be my next race. I had gained a fourth place overall as a junior in the event on the old Cinelli, but this time I would like to do better.

I only had a fixed-wheel bike, and I would have to ride it come what may, so I could not believe it when it was blowing a gale on the morning of the event.

I had already chosen a gear of 85 inches (48 x 15)[1] – a smaller gear than I rode as a junior. On the outward leg, the wind was on our faces and with no alternative gear, it was lucky I had the strength to maintain a rhythm to the turn, where I was apparently 30 seconds ahead of

---

[1] 48 teeth on the front chain wheel x 15 teeth on the rear sprocket

my nearest rival – Dave Hannah. On the return leg, I was travelling at 35 to 40 mph in some parts, and I was badly revved out on the gear I had on. At some places, it was all I could do to keep up with the pedals, and in the final result, I was beaten by about half a minute.

It was not the result I wanted when the race was over, because I had a feeling it could have been different if the wind had not been so strong. On the other hand, I had a silver medal in the most important TT event, and 'what ifs' do not count, so I turned my attention towards the 10-mile championship to be held in Hawick in the Scottish Borders.

Old Jimmy Train arranged for me to stay with Tosh Scott, one of the organisers, so that I could ride round the course the night before and be totally ready on the morning of the event. Time trials are usually run on an out-and-back basis, and the 'out' leg of this 10-mile course was heavy going as it drifted uphill. Jimmy said to me that the race would be won on that section, as a deficit would have to be made up on the quicker return leg.

Realising I had a lot of leg strength, and having three weeks' extra training, I decided to raise my single fixed gear a good bit. On the morning of the event the weather was fine, and more importantly there was no strong tail wind on the fast return leg, which would have been a terrible disadvantage for a fixed wheel bike. I remember being incredibly nervous and afraid of failure. Whereas silver was acceptable in the '25', only gold would leave me feeling satisfied, because my hopes and everybody else's had been raised since then.

I remembered Jimmy's advice, and I reckoned he was right. I thrashed out to the turn like it really was the finish, and when I turned to go back, I was wrecked, but the pressure and drive to win the championship drove me on. In the end I won by just three seconds, but now I was a bona-fide Scottish Champion, winner of a senior title. The first thing I did when I got to Tosh's was to phone Jimmy, who had already found out the result from someone else.

Apart from going a couple of tours with my brother Gordon and Matthew, who had saved me from myself, and even worse, depression, at the shop and a couple of tours with Gordon on his own, not much really happened that season. Those short tours were good, but one incident, which I have recounted many times, took place on a longer tour of the Scottish Borders.

Gordon and I were well loaded up with full camping gear for a six- or seven-day tour and we were setting off from Kilmarnock. After about four days of camping we were keen to stay over at Jedburgh Youth Hostel. All the while, we had literally been living on bags of sweetened rolled oats, because we did not bother with a stove, and anyway, handfuls of oat cereal were such an ideal convenience food. We arrived at the hostel at 4 p.m., but we were an hour too early. We had time to kill, and found ourselves hanging about at the Tourist Information Office down the street.

Gordon and I were standing side-by-side as I was looking at a book, and by peripheral vision, I could see that Gordon was doing the same. At that moment, the inevitable side effect of four days of oat-eating kicked in – and how. I said to Gordon, who was still beside me, 'Do you smell that?' Well, of course he smelled it – it was like mustard gas. But he said nothing. I repeated myself but still nothing. Finally I gave him a good nudge, and said, 'Smell that!' As I looked up from my book, I realised that it was not Gordon at all but a flabbergasted stranger. I was out of there in seconds and dragged Gordon with me.

As that riding season went on, I rode as many races as I could for the sake of winning and accumulating money – mainly the latter. I was still unemployed, and I applied for as few jobs as I could, because every time, there would be a question about the applicant's criminal record. The shame of it would still hurt when it was forced to the surface by a direct question like that. It would hurt for a long time after being forced to face up to what I really was, and my sense of dissociation would return to a greater or lesser extent, depending on my mood at the time. I could not avoid this process, as I had to apply for a certain number of jobs each month in order not to get into trouble.

It did not matter though, because I would soon be studying full-time at Kilmarnock College, and I would be receiving an education grant instead. I wanted to study biology, chemistry, English and maths at Higher level, but the biology was not possible. I knew that with reasonably good grades in the other three, along with my physics from school, I would still have enough for a place at university.

Round about the end of that season, I got involved in speed-skating through meeting Craig McNicol at a local TT. I thought it was a good idea, because of the achievements of Eric Heiden, who had been speed-skating and cycling champion. Craig was no slouch on the bike either, mainly through speed-skating training. The speed-skating club was sponsored at the time by Glen Henderson, who had a large garage selling Mercedes and other top-brand cars, and we would meet there for training during the off season. He had large outhouses, which had been refurbished and set up with gym equipment, as well as improvised training equipment specific to speed-skating.

We would go out running and do special leg-strengthening exercises, which I had never seen before. The man who deserves all the credit for his energy and dedication is Albert McNicol, who spent almost all of his time helping others, including myself, for no reward other than seeing people improve in the sport. Albert would run us through the drills and at the end of it I would know I had had a good workout, as I cycled the 14 miles back home at a moderate pace. On the Saturday night, we would meet at the ice rink at the Magnum Centre in Irvine, which was only seven miles from me. We had to wait until the end of the ice disco before we could get one-and-a-bit hours on the ice, and that was all we could get for the week anywhere.

Such was the dearth of ice time, that people would drive from Stirling to use this scrap of ice time, and drive back the 50-plus miles in the early hours of the morning. Albert never failed to be there, coaching a wide range of people, from under-tens to top amateurs, which his son Craig was. He even tried to coach a cyclist with almost no natural talent for skating, by the name of Graeme Obree. I persevered for ages, but I was never able to match the control of the kids who would whizz past me when I lost it, which was pretty frequently. I think I must have resembled the pond scene from Bambi most of the time.

If they did not cut the ice clean after the disco, then I would end up soaked from rolling in the film of water that was left there. The problem is that speed skates have no hollow grind, and that means the blade must be held at an angle to the force at all times, as opposed to regular skates, which I could use easily. I suppose the reason I carried on in spite of the difficulties was that when I was on a good streak, I could feel the wind in my hair and a sense of speed that could be so much greater if I could master it. The other thing is that although I was poor at skating, the people in the club were really nice and made me feel part of it all. I can remember that it was not unusual to be invited in for coffee by the McNicol family in the early hours of a Sunday morning, before cycling home.

The Friday night after the club was still a regular fixture at this time, and I had developed an addiction to 'Risk' – the world-domination board game – and my night would not be complete without at least one game at Gordon Graham's until the early hours. I was also keeping regular hours at Kilmarnock College, as well as trying to keep a good level of fitness for the following season. A couple of times, I tried to speed-skate in the early morning on a weekday. I was allowed on when it was completely empty, which was good, but whenever someone showed up, I had to get off the ice. After a while I realised it was futile, and accepted that the Saturday night was my only chance to improve. My involvement in the sport became sporadic after a while, but I always retained my desire to take part in some sort of competitive speed-skating event when I got good enough at the craft. Sadly, in the years to follow, the help from Glen Henderson stopped, as a result of financial difficulties at the Garage, and Albert, who was a real driving force at the club, had become ill. The combined effect was a near meltdown of the sport locally.

My first sport was cycling, though, and as well as training properly for it, a real fun element had emerged as a regular fixture on the weekend calendar. There was a time when mountain bikes were relatively new, and as many as nine or ten of us would descend upon a pre-chosen wild and undulating place. My friend Matthew was into it, and Gordon, who had bought over my Irvine shop, had a van, which was quite often used as the main means of transport. A bunch of bikes and bodies would simply squeeze into the back as best as they could.

It was not always necessary to use the van, as there were plenty of steep bits and testing dirt paths within riding distance. None of us were into easy meandering trails, and we would seek out the steepest, most challenging descents we could find. We would go to mountains when we could, and the nearest biggies are Goat Fell on the island of Arran, at 2,700 feet and Ben Lomond, at 3,192 feet. The whole idea was to shoulder the bike right to the summit, and then go to it in an orgy of wholesale recklessness.

Speed was not the issue, though, and we would tackle the hardest and steepest parts one at a time, to see who could make it without 'wiping out'. By steep, I mean much steeper than the average staircase, and in the natural setting, that is pretty steep. The art was to push your body right back over the back wheel, so that the centre of gravity is behind the front tyre tread. The most common cause of 'wiping out' was hitting a root or rock with the front wheel, and being thrown forward. After a while, I developed a get-out technique of vaulting over the handlebars and landing on my feet further down the slope. It soon became adopted and nicknamed the 'Obvault'.

Sometimes we would seek out parts that were so steep that they were virtually unrideable, and a game of 'chicken' would begin. It was an elimination game that would leave the brave, the confident or the foolish at the end, as we would find steeper and steeper parts. Usually there would be me, Matthew and Alan McCall, who worked in Gordon's Kilmarnock shop at the end. Apart from gloating and honour, there were no prizes.

At that time, I started to work on bagging as many mountains as I could, and the one I had to do was the 'big one' – Ben Nevis. It was the autumn of that year as I was starting my Highers, that my brother Gordon, Matthew and I decided we would make a tour of it and, as well as bagging Nevis, we would check out part of the West Highland Way. There was no real problem at that time in mountain biking almost anywhere, because they had not become popular and a problem, like they are now. We had a touch of a hangover as we set off for the arduous climb, with Matthew and I having been the most intoxicated at the local hotel the previous night, and narrowly avoiding detection at the youth hostel. With Ben Nevis, you start your walk to the summit (4,440 feet) from sea level, so it took us several hours to reach it. It was worth it though, and after about 30 minutes of solid descending, we were damp with sweat and our hands were aching from the firm grip on the handlebars and brake levers. I felt invincible that day, and reached the bottom first, as I took on almost everything the mountain could throw at me. As I drew up at the bottom I could feel and smell the adrenaline, the same way that I did when I used to get head butted on the bridge of the nose at school.

Back at college my plan to integrate myself into society was not quite working to plan. The science classes were full of people who were just there to learn. I was there for the same thing, but I desperately wanted to feel like I was part of society more than anything. I saw everyone around me as students, but I thought of myself as some sort of fake or that I was different and the other students would be talking about me and pointing me out. If I passed a group of people standing about, I would break into a cold sweat and my breathing would become laboured. Some of the feelings I had in the classroom when I was seven would return. I could feel peoples' eyes burning into me as I would quickly hasten my stride to get away, and at these times the world was polarised into 'them and me' and 'the world and me'.

However, Dorothy Patterson's English class was good academically, by the fact that she was of the 'old school' where grammar and structure are vitally important. More importantly from my point of view, there was a great deal of social comment and group philosophising over works of poetry and prose. There were only twelve or fifteen of us in the class, but I got to know some of them well enough to hang out at lunch break.

That is as far as friendship went, but in hindsight I can now see that I was never trying to make friends. All I was capable of at that time was to follow a lead that other people would make, and even at that, I would more often dismiss it as being nice for the sake of politeness. If I tried going beyond my comfort zone of just following other people then I would suffer feelings of anxiety and panic, which would often lead to me talking to excess with a load of drivel. In my conscious and subconscious, I saw myself as inherently unlikeable, and that to keep friends I would have to say interesting or funny things, tell jokes, do something funny or even give them things in order to overcome my deficiency.

That year I got invited to a party being held by one of the guys in the English class, which made me panic from the start as I thought 'what do you do at parties?' Armed with a good carryout, I went along and made my way instinctively to the darkest corner, and with my pint glass shield I could protect my face from the glare of staring eyes, whilst seeking out the people I knew. I rarely drank spirits in company, because the glass is too small, and it goes down too quickly. At that party I did not drink as much as I could have, mainly because I panicked at the process of people taking turns to do a party song. For some reason I got a sense of paranoia, and throughout the party I was in a state of cold-sweat panic, and it seemed that everyone was staring at me as I hid behind my pint glass.

I had blown my chances of social contact outside of cycling, and after I sat my Higher examinations we had an 'end of college' gathering at the local pub, but I still was unable to put myself forward to arrange to see the people that I liked during the summer of 1988. Part of the problem was that I was still living with my parents, and I felt embarrassed to invite people back, and I knew that accepting friendship would eventually result in reciprocation, as well as the fact that deep down I still felt like a criminal.

I had a feeling that I had done well enough to get to University, and I had another season of racing to take part in. I reckoned that University life, with all of its student bodies and activities, as well as the intimacy of tutorials, would open up a whole new way of life for me.

If nothing else, Dorothy Patterson's class had given me a real appreciation of poetry as one of the most powerful forms of communication.

six: the chaotic years

The season of '88 was my best ever, with wins in Scottish TTs being quite emphatic from the start. The Scottish '25' championship was a sign of things to come, as I won it by three minutes, after taking a more serious training attitude. The Scottish '10' championship went much the same way, but I still had a parochial attitude to my racing ambitions by thinking purely at a Scottish level.

I still had touring in my blood, and had a short tour or two with Matthew and Gordon and a much longer tour through England to Holland, with Michael McTurk, camping most of the way, due to lack of funds. It was a good tour, but after a day or two in Holland, we reached The Hague, with our bodies and funds almost exhausted. We were soaked through with the constant rain, and we were swithering whether we should press on for our initial target of Amsterdam, another 50 or 60 miles away, or just turn back. As we stopped at a junction, a man with long hair pulled up on a recumbent bike, and asked if we would like to 'come back to my house'. Neither of us had seen a recumbent bike before, and this weird man brought out the stereotypical British fears about strange Dutch people that were latent in both of us. While Michael tried to refuse it, it only took a second or two for my intuition to overrule our fears and say, 'That would be fine, thank you very much.' When we reached his house in the outskirts, we soon realised that we had truly 'arrived'. He introduced us to his wife Michele and showed us round their three-storey house.

They explained that they were just back from a world tour, and after the hospitality shown to them around the world as real travellers, they decided that they would have a spare room, which would be for real bike tourists, whenever they chanced upon them. Nicer and more genuine people we could not have met, and I can still recall the early morning smell of pancakes and coffee as I write. We were their first guests, and they even stocked their fridge with Grolsch and other Dutch treats every day, and took us out to dinner. Thanks, Nop and Michele Velthausen.

After our three or four-day stay, we discarded the idea of Amsterdam and headed back home. On the journey back, I phoned home and found out that I had been accepted for a design-engineering course at Glasgow University. My future seemed set and I was delighted. It was not quite the end of the season, though, as I won Scotland's first mountain bike title.

My first days of university were exciting, and the ancient architecture of the main buildings made me feel like I had really arrived at a seat of learning. The course I was on was ambitious, more ambitious than I could have imagined with the entry qualifications I had – or more importantly, did not have. The course was run in conjunction with the School of Art in Glasgow, and it was basically the mechanical engineering curriculum, with design at the School of Art added on.

Because the university is only 25 miles from my parents' house, it was decided it would be best to travel up and down. The day would start with a 7.15 coach ride, arriving in the maths lecture at 9.05, and playing catch-up on the lecture, which had already started. That was five mornings a week, and by the Wednesday, I would be relying on either that night or the weekend to make good sense of it. Where the other students would have time between the other lectures and classes of the day, the design students would have to flit to the School of Art, either during or after the regular mechanical engineering day.

Sometimes in the day, when I got a chance, I would seek out the maths tutor, only to find a huge queue. I would rely partly on the marked papers, which were 'posted' at lectures, and received back, by post, at my home address. One problem was that, unlike at school, answers were either right or wrong, and no more.

The dropout rate of 50 per cent in the design-engineering course was pointed out to us from the start, so I was under no illusions of sailing through. The biggest obstacle to my success was my lack of computer studies. In the first two or three weeks, the task of writing a program came up, and that is when it became clear that there had been an oversight in my being accepted onto a course that required fifth- or sixth-year computer studies as a starting point. There was nothing for it but to institute a crash course.

The maths plus the travel time plus the computer programming plus other design work meant that it was normal to flick the switch at 2-3 a.m. and be up early for the bus back the next morning. All the while, I was still trying to keep fit, with the minimum of time consumption, so I restricted myself to short, hard efforts. All in all, the net result was a deeper and deeper stupor, which strangely enough, did not result in my becoming more sluggish, but more lively and childish outwardly, with a group of three or four other guys who made up our gang. Sometimes it seemed like a huge surreal party, laughing from one thing to another, while my student buddies thought I had gone slightly mad – especially when it somehow seemed such a great idea to fly paper aeroplanes from the top of lecture halls.

It was Anne, whom I had met again while helping Gordon build Christmas club bikes, who could see that I was not going to get on the level with my studies. During the Christmas recess I tried to get to terms with my comprehension deficit but could not bridge the gap and decided to throw in the towel. At this point, I was unemployed again, so until I found a replacement to university, I was determined to try and get something out of cycling. I knew I would have to think bigger.

Anne and I were seeing each other all the time, and by the end of spring, we had decided to get married. Anne is a staff nurse, and on the strength of her employment, we bought an ex-Council house in Irvine. In the meantime, I trained like mad, and the first big event that came up was the Champion of Champions 25-mile TT, which was held quite early in the season. The four 25-mile champions from Scotland, England, Ireland and Wales were riding. The result was a good one for me, as I beat the up-and-coming rider called Chris Boardman by a handful of seconds. It was held at Newtonards in Northern Ireland. We would cross swords again, but in the meantime, I had my eye on the British hour record. Since Francesco Moser broke the world record from Eddie Merckx in the early '80s, I had been captivated by the hour record, and now that I was going better than ever, the time would soon come to try it for myself. The record was held by Dave Lloyd, at 45.5km, but when I calculated it out, compared to speed on the road, I reckoned I had the measure of it.

I travelled across to Meadowbank Velodrome in Edinburgh a couple of times with Rolly McMillan from the club, and he helped me take lap times and get the feel of the pace beforehand. We went through for an attempt soon after, but it was rained off, and the next chance would be weeks away. Then a terrible thing happened that made everything suddenly seem unimportant. Matthew, who was so looking forward to being a brother-in-law to me, and vice versa, was killed in a motorcycle crash in Irvine. He was on a life-support machine for several days, but in the end, there was no hope.

It was a sad time all round, especially for Anne and her family. For me, it was so poignant because it brought back all my memories of the likeable lad who used to come into the shop and save me from depression and loneliness. He was my good friend who had come touring with my brother and me. He was a nice guy and a class cyclist who had so nearly taken victory from me in a mountain bike race, and the loss bore a heavy toll on all of us.

The next attempt on the hour record was only a couple of weeks away. I swithered whether I should postpone the ride, but Anne reckoned that Matthew would not have wanted that, so I persevered, with the attitude that I must do this thing in memory of Matthew's fighting spirit.

On the day of the event, the memory of him was still clear in our minds, but as long as I was successful, then I knew that was what Matthew would have wanted. It was the club who had managed to organise all the officials for me to go for the record officially. George Miller was a BCF commissionaire, but we needed one other, who was Jock Shaw. The schedule I had presented was deemed as over-ambitious by George Miller, who had the lapboard reduced to the number of laps needed to gain the Scottish record. In my mind, I knew there were six extra laps than the board stated, and my original schedule for the British record was the one I insisted be used by the trackside signaller. George was quite insistent that I should not get above myself, and that it was the Scottish record I was here for, after all. In my mind, though, it was nothing less that the British record I would be content with.

As the ride started, I was easily ahead of schedule, and by 10km, George was jumping up and down, saying that I had broken a British record. The next lap, he was waving his arms to signal me to slow down – in case I blew. I smiled to myself as I rode round, and I thought, 'George, you just don't have a clue.' The rest of the ride went bang-on to my schedule, and as I finished, I knew I had broken the record by a whole kilometre. Only to be told that false information had been passed up to me – to save me from overreaching myself. I was annoyed that they had played psychological games with me, but I was still delighted to have taken the record by a considerable margin.

After this success, I received publicity in cycling magazines on a British level, and I was asked by the track coach if I would ride for Scotland at the Cleveland GP. It was not long after my success at the hour record, but the meeting turned out to be a festival of poor results for me. Only doing TTs meant that I lacked the change of pace to deal with volatile track races, and trying to break clear was difficult. I had real trouble in the points race, trying to get points in the lap sprints, and I decided that I would have to break clear to have any chance.

The one good chance I had was ruined when Tony Doyle grabbed my jersey on the way past. Colin Sturgess was already clear, and I could not work out why he would want to protect a rider who was not his team-mate. Maybe the fact that I had taken spokes out of the front wheel of his team-mate Gary Coltman had riled him. It was not really my fault, as Gary Coltman had tried to lean on me on the line out, but instead of giving way, I decided to move a little closer to him, come what may. I used to work on the principle that if I held my own but caused a stack-up, then I would get more respect. When Tony Doyle later broke clear, my attempt to close the gap was chased down by Colin Sturgess, and again, I could not work out why he would help Tony, who was not his team-mate. In the end, I finished fifth or sixth, which was disappointing.

Soon after this, it was time to come up against Chris again, in the RTTC 'British' 25-mile TT championship in Beverley in Yorkshire. In my mind, it was going to be a two-horse race, and I knew that I would only beat him on my best form and with the best preparation and equipment choice. Anne and I, Jim Frew, and Jim Docherty, who had built my weird frame, all travelled down from Scotland the day before, so that I would be totally fresh and so that I could check out the course in advance. I was stuck with a fixed-wheel no matter what, and I think I was using 52 x 12 ratios at that time, which was bigger than I had used before. If I could use that gear and feel on top of it all the way round, then I would have a good chance of winning. I also knew that if I lost my flow and started dragging the gear round, then I would lose a disproportionate amount of time in the undulating sections.

I knew it was a risk, but with Chris riding so well, it was all or nothing, and on the morning, I reckon I was on top of the gear for most of the ride. Chris beat me by a minute or more, and even if the gear had been perfect all the way round, it would have been touch and go to have equalled his ride with the form I had at that moment. I went home with a desperate sense of failure, despite the fact that I was well clear of the third rider. Everyone tried to persuade me that I had done a pretty good ride, but as far as I was concerned, I was last in a two-man race.

The other major for me was my venture into the pursuit event on the track. It was the British Track Championships and the venue was Leicester Velodrome, which was a 333-metre open-air wooden track. My friend Tony Williamson drove down, and we stayed at the student halls in readiness for the competition the next day. After riding quite well in the qualifying, I was drawn to ride against Chris in the semi-final. The Scottish contingent (mainly the City of Edinburgh club) reckoned I would get beaten by Chris anyway, so I should ride within myself and stay fresh for the ride-off for the bronze medal the next morning. I understood their point, but I wanted to take him on. I was ahead for the best part of the ride, but I could not sustain my pace, and Chris beat me by two or three seconds at the end.

The ride-off for bronze was another lesson in tactics and psychology. I woke up with a persistent, deep but dry chesty cough, and I was informed that this is called a 'pursuiter's cough', and that I should just ignore it. This was my last ride, and there would be no holds barred. While I was warming up, I was told that Glenn Sword was putting a disc wheel in the front, and to put me on a level playing field, the City of Edinburgh club offered to furnish me with the same advantage. I was not sure as I had not ridden one before, but not to be outdone by my opponent, I gratefully accepted. On the starting line at the very last minute, Glenn Sword had his front wheel changed back, and as soon as the race started, I realised why. There was a slight crosswind, and with the disc, I was all over the track like a drunkard with two bags of shopping. I was well beaten, and afterwards, I realised that maybe I had been tricked, but from then on, I would concentrate on my own ride and not waste my energy or focus on my opponent.

Fourth place was not that bad, considering it was my first time at the event, and I had judged my pace badly and made mistakes. I did not leave with the same feeling of failure that I did at the '25', partly because I felt I had so much more to give to the event. There was one thing that had been regularly commented on, though, in regard to my image, and that was my hairy legs. It had been quite a long time since I had disregarded the rubbing of creams or irritants onto the skin before an event, in the belief that it would somehow increase velocity.

I was alone in this line of thinking within my cycling circle, and I was already seen as an eccentric maverick, with my straight forks, low-spoke wheels (fourteen and sixteen), twin double tube and cycling position, and my non-conformity was seen, I think, as an extension of my eccentricity. In fact, it was based on sound principles of physics and human anatomy, where the hairs help in a small way to allow the evaporation of sweat, which takes energy from the surrounding skin to do so. I was always hit by arguments like about how unhygienic it was and how much better a shaved leg would be. But I had read that shaved skin was more likely to suffer infection, which just left the questions about aerodynamics, aesthetics and conforming to my peer group.

In the end, I would buckle to the pressure of conformity and the need for an image makeover, but not before I got married to Anne on 1st September 1989. There was no way I was going to get married with shaved legs in a kilt. I would conform, but I would certainly not entertain creams or potions. It was also the end of the season, and as well as getting married, I started an economics degree at Paisley College.

The wedding itself was a traditional Scottish affair, with most men wearing kilts and hundreds of relatives and friends in attendance. My wedding day was a very special thing, and having all the people that were close to me in the same place at the same time was such a good feeling. One person who was not there, of course, was Matthew, but although we thought about him, we did not let his absence put a dampener on the day.

Soon after getting married it was time to start college, but this time I was on a course that I was qualified to cope with from the start. I was not very interested in economics, but it would lead to a lot of employment opportunities once I was qualified, and instead of travelling by bus from my parents' house, I would be cycling up and down to Paisley most days. Where I had had an image in my mind of social activities at Glasgow, I knew from the start at Paisley that my participation was purely for vocational reasons.

Depending on the weather, the journey would average about fifty minutes each way, but a lot of the time it would be well over an hour on the home run because of the prevailing west wind. I ended up being pretty fit that winter, with the daily hard rides, and because the road climbed to about 1,000 feet I would have a really good workout on the home run, climbing to the summit, straight out of the city.

On the strength of my rides that season, especially my fourth place at the British Pursuit Championship, the Scottish team manager Sandy Gilchrist asked me to ride for Scotland at the Commonwealth Games in Auckland. The games were taking place in January/February of 1990, which was right in the middle of college time. When I approached the college administration about having time out to compete for Scotland, I was told that if I went, then my place at the college would be terminated. It was a stark choice, but one that I would have to make quite quickly. My sense of responsibility prevailed, and I reluctantly turned down my chance to represent Scotland in New Zealand.

At the time of the games, I avoided looking at the results, because I felt so bad at having excluded myself. At the same time, we were struggling quite badly financially, because Anne was not able to work as much as she would have liked. She was suffering from stress and depression, as a result of Matthew's death combined with stress at work, and stress with her family at that time. The financial problem was compounded with the fact that I could not receive a proper student grant, on the grounds that I was still under the responsibility of my parents – unbelievable as it may seem. Being married and living independently in a different town did not cut any ice, and as far as the Scottish Office was concerned, I would have to go to my parents for money because I was under 25 years of age.

If my parents had written to the Scottish Office and stated that they had completely disowned me, and with not a penny they would part, there would have been a chance of a proper grant, but my parents were not happy about writing such a letter, and nor was I willing to go to my parents, cap in hand, to ask of them what the Scottish Office said I should. The total grant I received was in the order of £460, and under the financial constraints of the time, I quit the college at about the time the Commonwealth Games were being held, which was ironic to say the least.

For us, the 1990s started with financial stress and uncertainty about our future. I felt stupid, because if I had decided to go to the games, no matter what, then I would have been there, but as it was, I had the worst of both worlds by being out of college and the games, with nothing to show for it. The most ironic thing was that the form I had, with blasting up the Gleniffer Braes every day, was sound, and I could have done well at the games for sure. Leaving college was not a problem in terms of emotional attachment but I did have a touch of guilt and a slight feeling of failure at having dropped out for a second time.

It was not long before I found a job as a mechanic in Wheelers – a bike shop, which was situated at the far end of Ayr. It was almost the same distance to ride to as college, but it was dead flat all the way, and I could ride as hard or as easy as I wished to. The wage was not brilliant, but it kept us solvent in the meantime, which was the only reason I worked there, but when I left at the end of the day, I did not have to worry about bookkeeping or how well the business was running, as I would have if it was my own business.

That season of 1990 was not outstanding in terms of results, although I was able to better my own hour record at Meadowbank. It was only by a very small margin, because on the chosen day it was quite windy. I was in two minds whether to postpone and wait for another day, or just go for it regardless, seeing as the timekeepers and officials had freely given up their time to be there, as well as people from the club. It was probably a much better ride than the first record, but I was a bit disappointed to have scraped by, just to avoid embarrassment. I had hoped to push the boundaries out by another kilometre or so, but not long after the start, it became clear that it would be an all-out effort to avoid failure, and I only chipped on an extra hundred metres or so, after pushing myself to complete exhaustion.

I had also hoped to eclipse my Scottish 10-mile record that I had set the previous year at 19 minutes 49 – on a perfect morning – not long before I had broken the hour record. This I was unable to achieve, although I had been close on a couple of occasions, and I now had Scottish domination of TT events. At this time, I was still riding for Wallacehill CC, the club in Kilmarnock that I had first joined, which was sponsored by AOS/AEG. AOS (Ayrshire Office Services) was George Miller's own business, and AEG was a large German manufacturer whose products he supplied. I asked George if there were any way that sponsorship could be increased on a personal basis, as the club sponsorship only stretched to contributing towards travelling expenses. At that time, I needed sponsorship that would also cover material costs, because I had ambitions of competing at British level. It was not to be, and at the end of the season, I would have to look for a new club, with a view to receiving better support from sponsorship. In the meantime, though, I had ambitions of improving on my fourth place at the Pursuit Championship, which again was held at Leicester. Being an open track, it was at the mercy of the weather, and this year, the championship was plagued by showers. Each shower would delay the programme by half an hour or more, and my qualifying ride, which was scheduled for the afternoon, ended up taking place at midnight after a day of nibbling at food, warming up and warming down with each delay. When I did step up for my ride, I felt drained and unmotivated, and despite my hardest effort, I was only tenth fastest, and did not qualify.

To add insult to disappointment, I overheard a one-sided conversation, which the wife of one of the senior members of the City of Edinburgh club was holding. I was the subject matter, and her monologue contained expressions like 'disgrace' and 'fool of himself', which left me feeling betrayed and hurt, to accompany my disappointment of defeat. I left with the determination that I would not ride at Leicester again in the near future, after ending up so depressed at that place, and I held to it for three years.

I kept working at Wheelers, and things were pretty settled at home, as Anne started taking on more work, and we gradually improved our home from the condition we had bought it in. In the winter, I changed clubs to the Glasgow Wheelers, which did not have a sponsor on the jersey, but Billy Bilsland, who had sold me my first bike and who had been a first-class international rider himself, wanted to help in a bigger way than George Miller had been willing to before. I also made contact with Phil Griffiths, who supplied Zipp wheels and Assos clothing, so I would be provided with a disc wheel and carbon-fibre tri-spoke wheels and good training gear. There was a promise of financial help too for promoting the products – it was relatively small but enough to cover a lot of expenses that would accrue with travelling and tyres. Billy Bilsland, on the other hand, would see no direct benefit for himself or his shop, but he helped me financially, probably out of his own pocket. He had been a help to Robert Millar several years before, so it was not a new thing for Billy.

Before the season started in '91, the Wheelers shop closed down as a result of the demise of the then Henderson's group, which the shop was part of. It was the same downfall that caused the subsequent collapse of the speed skating club I had been involved in a few years earlier. Ironically, the shop itself was profitable, but as part of the group, it had to be sold as a going concern, or be closed down. When it became clear that closure was inevitable, I started looking about for alternative employment. I pretty quickly found a job at a mushroom farm, where I understood my role would be as a picker.

I quit the shop before the end and started at the mushroom farm.

On the first day, it was made clear to me that, due to the fickle nature of mushrooms, it would be necessary to work late quite often and at short notice. My actual work was shovelling and shifting debris and compost from the factory to a skip outside. The conditions inside were perfect for mushrooms – completely damp and humid. Normally I would be slopping about in inches of water, and it only took me a day or two to realise that this employment was almost intolerable. I had to work late every night, and managed to do no training at all in the first week. I would have to choose between this job and being able to race at all. I had a head-to-head coming up against Chris in Ireland, and I knew that I might as well cancel if I continued with the job, so I quit the job instead.

That was a big mistake financially, because when I applied for un-employment benefit, I was told that because I had quit a job, I would be barred for six months. The fact that Wheelers was closing down and I had done my best to find suitable employment made no impression on the appliance of strict rules. I went to the race in Ireland and got beaten by Chris, and when I returned, I started to think about what I should do in terms of employment. With no good options available, Anne and I decided that we should sell our house, which had gone up in value as a result of the work we had done to improve it internally. When we finally sold the house a couple of months later, we netted about £8,000, which, along with borrowings and credit accounts from suppliers, allowed us to start a small cycle shop.

It was in Prestwick, which adjoins Ayr, where Wheelers was, and our hope was that the closure of Wheelers would leave a gap in the market, which we could fill. It was a leap of faith for us, but my knowledge of the trade at Wheelers and my own bike shops previously, convinced me we would do all right.

In the meantime, we were renting a room at a farmhouse about five miles away, and since we did not own a car, we would cycle there and back, usually together, in whatever the weather could throw at us. During that summer, I also continued with some racing and probably my best ride was in the Scottish 25-mile championship. I had ridden a '25' two weeks before, and had done a 52-minute ride on the local course, which was the new Scottish record at that time.

I had decided, at the closing date for the British '25' championship weeks earlier, that I would not enter because of the hassle factor of travel, and the fact that the event is totally prizeless. I was also a bit disenchanted and depressed with everything at that time, and was even in two minds whether to bother entering the Scottish event, which had a much later closing date.

Luckily I did enter it, and my father volunteered to take me up. It was a cold and wet day, and still with an air of 'I can't really be bothered with it' in my mind, I decided that I would not bother with the usual warm-up. Instead, I decided that I would just wear my thermal longs and go for it, like a training ride. That is what I did, and at the start, I put it into the highest gear for the downhill section and tried to keep it turning as long as I could. Amazing as it was to me at the time, the moment when I would have to change down never came, and I rode the entire race in top gear. The longer I went in the race, the more seriously I took it, as I knew I was on a really good ride.

The result was that I smashed my own Scottish record by three minutes, and produced Scotland's first ever sub-50-minute ride, as well as winning the championship by almost six minutes. Most of the spectators and riders at the finish area were amazed and excited by the ride, as word had come back from the halfway turn that a 49-minute ride was possible.

My dad, who was usually pretty laid back about it all, had been caught up in the excitement, and when I zipped past the finish line in under 50 minutes, he was almost tearful with emotion, and that was something I had never seen in him before. I was then taken off for a Sports Council drug test, and after the presentation, we headed straight back to spread the good news.

I felt good about my ride, not because I had won the championship, which I would expect to win anyway, but because I knew I had pulled out a special ride on a bad morning. When I got back home, I heard that Chris had also done a sub-50-minute ride to win the British championship, but I was glad I chose the Scottish championship because I had received a good prize, good feeling from my ride, and I was home for lunchtime. Previous head-to-head encounters with Chris had involved me travelling south to the southern half of England, where I would be narrowly beaten by him, as he would receive time checks on me as last man off. I would then make the long journey back, sometimes travelling in the early hours of the Monday morning, feeling dejected, exhausted, under-nourished and demoralised. It did not bother me that Chris had won the British championship title, which is really the English and Welsh championship, organised by the Road Time Trial

Council, but is called the 'British' championship by most people south of the border.

As far as I was concerned, I had won my national title and Chris had won his, and if he was bothered about my scalp, then he could travel north and challenge me for it. Phil Griffiths was not long in conveying his disgust by phone, and called me a coward and a disgrace to the sport. I was not long in sending him back everything he had given me, as I slipped back into my despondency about the sport.

In the end, I became indifferent to the sport, to the point where I just stopped riding, and all I concentrated on at that time was the shop. Trade was building up, especially repairs, and it would soon be school-holiday time, which lifts trade even further. My future lay in building up a good business, rather than bursting a gut in the open road. I became so despondent and unmotivated about most things, especially cycling, that I had a clear intention never to race again. This was a new era and the past was gone. As far as I could see, I had nothing to show for my years of effort, but a reputation and large lungs, and now it was payback time for all the opportunities that cycling screwed up for me. At that time, I had an image of myself as a gross underachiever – a pathetic failure sitting in a corner, fixing punctures in a tiny bike shop, and cycle-riding was a good thing to blame for it.

Ironically, without my weekly infusion of success in bike racing, it would be difficult for my self-image to improve. Nonetheless, I was now a businessman, and my success would have to come from there.

seven: business as usual

It was a small shop we had rented, and there was barely enough room for my compact workshop, the new bikes in boxes and the repair bikes, which could lie about for weeks before collection. There was a tiny outhouse at the rear, which was already stuffed as full as it would go, so when the house, which was once part of the shop, came up for sale, we were very keen, especially when I knew that Christmas was getting closer every day. To be sure of getting it, we put in an offer that was quite generous, considering the house was in a poor state of repair.

By this time, it was getting on for the end of summer. Cycle racing was out of my life and I had not done any serious training for quite a while, when I received an interesting phone call. It was from Sarah Kozac, who explained that she was producing a TV series called 'Trailblazers', which would be in six parts, and would be filmed in Wales. All the parts would be filmed in one week, and it involved death slides and white water rafting and the likes.

The four home nations would have teams of three – two men and one woman – and I was to captain the Scots. It sounded like good fun, and there were good cash prizes, as well as the chance to get on TV for the sake of pure vanity.

Of course I accepted, but it meant that I was instantly catapulted back into training – not just cycling, but also all-round fitness, like running and pull-ups and the like. I only had six weeks to get into shape from a poor starting point, but it suddenly gave me an interest outside of the business, and could not have come at a better time as my morale was ebbing away.

The event came round soon enough, and it turned out to be the best week I have ever enjoyed. Every day involved doing an extreme version of an outward-bound course, which had been set up by the marines who had been employed for the job. Burma bridges, death slides, abseiling, rafting, going down rapids in car inner tubes, jumping into pools from great heights, and being flown a rough ride in a helicopter were the main highlights from a boyish-adventure perspective. We were all highly trained athletes, and everything could be taken to the limit.

The other side of it was that it was open bar every night, and all the athletes made full use of it, usually through the process of drinking games, which I was particularly poor at. It was a rare time in my life, when I was not drinking to feel better, but socially, in a group of fellow athletes whom I immediately got on well with. It was a laugh from start to finish, but halfway through the week three of us had to eat humble pie after almost setting the hotel on fire. In a state of partial inebriation, we thought that it would be a gas to throw everyone else's clean laundry out of reach, over the lampshades. We woke the next morning to find that the lights came on automatically on a timer, and that one piece of laundry had smouldered and set off the alarm. Worse still was the fact that it had been the prized platoon T-shirt of the best-built marine in the operations crew, and it was irreplaceable. He was a real nice guy, but he was justifiably angry, and it took a bottle of good whisky and sincere apologies to placate him.

By the end of the week we were aching all over, and apart from a food fight started by the Irish which spread to the top table where Suzanne Dando was seated, we had pretty much behaved ourselves. We all felt sorry for the Welsh team, who had abstained from most of the alcohol consumption and taken early beds, but had been last in so many events. We were quite happy to see the Welsh beat us into first place in the final event, which involved pulling a barrel up a gorge. That final evening was the pinnacle of alcohol consumption – so much so that Barbara Mills and I had to ask other passengers to make sure that Sean Langmuir was conscious at Edinburgh on the train the following day, after we got off.

Having such a good week with fellow athletes and being back in training made me think about racing again the following season. Anne and I decided that I would, but we would seek out proper sponsorship from established companies that were already investing heavily in publicity. We put together a portfolio of previous results and cuttings from major papers and magazines, as well as an outline of my intended objectives. We made up a hundred copies and a hundred colour prints to finish them off professionally, and we sent them to the promotion and publicity departments of the top companies most likely to respond.

There was no positive response whatsoever, and those companies that did expand on their reasons for rejection said that they could not support charity of this nature. As time went on we kept trying, but without any success, and as Christmas got close, we were more concerned with the sale, procurement and storage of bikes, as well as sorting out the house next door, which we had now taken entry to. Everything was 1940s – the windows, the wallpaper, coal fires in every room, and even the kitchen fittings, so there was an awful lot of work to be done to bring it up to a reasonable standard.

Anne had discovered that she was pregnant and would be expecting around April or May, so I was extra keen to make sure that most of the house was warm, draught-free and carpeted, sooner rather than later. We had been roughing it in the house, rather than keeping cycling up and down and paying rent, but now that I was an expectant father, it was important that the expectant mother had a reasonable bedroom and sitting room, if nothing else. There was not much we could do about the sitting room until after Christmas, because it had become a much-needed repository for bikes, along with one of the main bedrooms upstairs.

Trade that Christmas was very slow everywhere, and not just in the cycle business. There were regular reports in the news about how bad it was for retailers, and how it was the worst Christmas for a large number of years. It was comforting in a way to know that it was not just us that were affected, but in the end, a large pile of unsold bikes was the reality on Boxing Day. We would get by, but carrying the weight of extra stock, which we would have to offload at discount, was a financial drain we could do without, at a time of year when trade was at its very lowest.

While I was waiting for fatherhood and for trade to pick up, I was kept busy with the house, training, and a frame-design idea I had come up with. It was the first of its kind and everything about it evolved from the need for a mega-narrow bottom bracket. The chain-stays to the rear wheel were elevated to allow the cranks to almost touch the wheel, and there would be no top tube, so that the knees could almost touch together while using the narrow pedal width. It was early 1992 when I had it finished as a frame, and after a lot of cutting, shaping and filing, I had a conventional bracket and cranks that were as narrow as was possible. I built the bike up unpainted, and took it out for a road test, and found that the narrow bracket design felt good for me and my pedalling style. I had a design idea for a tailor-made even narrower bracket, but before I could realise it, opportunity would shine on us and I would have the chance to develop and commercialise my ideas with a business partner.

After all this time and effort of searching for sponsorship, the phone rang, and Eddie Tierncy asked to meet with us in regard to sponsoring me for the season, with an eye to the British championships and taking on Ekimov's world amateur hour record, which had been in the back of my mind for a couple of years. It would be necessary to go to an indoor velodrome, which only existed abroad at that time, but this would not be a problem as he explained that he had a good budget.

The new frame design was also part of the overall arrangement in which we would be partners, and my ideas, name and engineering input would be matched by a workshop and help from his engineers. This was the sort of break I was looking for in my idealistic notion of the Yellow Brick Road to ultimate glory, wealth and happiness. With hindsight, maybe I was naïve, but I shook on the deal and made steps towards our leap into our new lifestyle and venture.

There was no problem with the shop as Gordon, who had taken over my other shops, was interested in it. Eddie had suggested that when we offloaded the shop, we should relocate to Greenock a few miles up the coast), and stay at the hotel there, which he owned. This meant that we could start right away on development, and I would have a solid base to train from, which sounded like a great idea to me, in the world-conquering mood I was in at the time.

When we sold the shop to Gordon, we excluded all our Shimano equipment, all our tools and my oxyacetylene brazing equipment. Gordon bought everything else at trade, and once again, I was shop-free and heading in a new and exciting direction with huge opportunities to reach for. Anne was heavily pregnant and I had been working in the shop by myself, which was hard, because I would get tied up with cycling people talking to me for large parts of the day, which meant that any repairs would have to be done in the evening.

It was still pretty poignant to see the end of our little business. We were not looking back, though, and quite soon after that, we moved up to live in Eddie's hotel. Not long after we were there, little

Ewan was born and the emotions of fatherhood did not come immediately to me, but more slowly, during the following months.

In the meantime, I was training hard and looking forward to getting stuck in to the racing and the frame-building business. The first stage was to build a full working model of my bike, but with gears. This was not easy, because the narrow bracket puts everything out of line, but I managed to overcome this with a bit of alteration to the rear wheel.

At this time, there was a lot of talk about Chris Boardman, and how he had such a good chance of winning gold at the Olympics, and I would have a chance to race against him at the 'British' 25-mile championships at the Lake District.

I was riding the newly-built prototype, with handlebars made to allow my own riding style, and preparation was as good as it could be with local events and hard training. The bike was pretty much a copy of the one I had in the shop, and it was built with my own bottles and tubing, and because I knew it worked for fixed-wheel, I altered the chain-stay and seat-stay angles to allow gearing, and soldered on clamps for gear levers and cables.

With all the problems of selling up, fatherhood and not feeling like my own man, I do not think my form was at its best, but on the morning I went for it full-on. Chris Boardman was off last at 120, and I was 110. When I finished, I was first on the leader board, waiting for Chris's result. As we waited for the endless convoy of passing cars that edge past the last rider, we knew that he had time on me, and as memory serves me, I believe it was over a minute by the official result. I was neither pleased nor displeased with the result, as it sat well within the parameters of best-case and worse-case scenarios. Anne was there with Ewan, and I guess it was his first sight of a bike race.

Back at the hotel, I was still waiting for something to happen with regard to workshop space and materials to help tool up for production, but everything seemed so 'mañana, mañana!' I kept training, while we considered moving back to our house, which we had never sold, and sign on for unemployment. The mere suggestion of such a thing didn't go down well with Eddie, but the problem was that our initial sponsorship and business arrangement was now so ad hoc that we could not rely on having money from one week to the next.

One of my best rides of the season was not long after the '25' championship. My friend Tony was down from the RAF, and he took me to a 50-mile TT at Dundee, where we stayed over, had a curry and a couple of pints of beer. The following morning, I smashed the Scottish 50-mile record by a huge margin, by posting a time of 1-43-02, and at last, I had made good that season. I was also invited to the Isle of Man cycling week, where I would ride two or three events. The one that had most impact on the cycling world was the Mountain TT, which I won in a fast time. This was good for me, because a lot of riders thought that I was only really good on flat course.

Back at the hotel, things were not getting any better, and we were paying our mortgage out of savings, the time had come to tell Eddie that we had decided to relocate ourselves to our own house in Prestwick, because we had run out of money and that it was better for Anne and Ewan.

So, in the end, I did not get a chance at the Ekimov World Amateur Hour Record, and I did not get any of my tools, brazing bottles and equipment or my cycling components back. What we did get was a backlog of debt, six months of lost benefits and a lot of wasted opportunity. Not only that, we had given up our cycle shop business, small as it was, for an opportunity that did not materialise. At least we did still have our house, and we did have our beautiful little boy.

The house was in the barely habitable condition it had been in before we left it, and we would have to do a lot of work to bring it up to scratch, now that we had Ewan. My parents helped out with the overhaul of the heating system, and a new combi-boiler, which was ideal, as it was placed in the box room where Ewan would sleep, and the boiler meant that it was always warm there. Anne's parents also helped us out with things like carpets.

We were able to sign on, but because we had a mortgage on the house, we only received allowance to pay the interest part of the loan, and the rest we would have to pay out of our benefits directly. To compound matters, we had debts to pay on top of everything else. There was an advert in Yellow Pages, which cost in excess of £400, which I agreed to pay at £5 or £10 per week, and then there arrived a demand for £460 from the Scottish Office for the grant they had issued years before. Now they wanted it back, and again I had to agree to pay it off at £5 or £10 per week. They were not the only ones, as Council Tax also got in on the act, as well as a supplier of components, and all in all, the net result was that the amount of money we had left for living off was barely enough, even when shopping at the cheapest places.

About that time, we decided to get away from it all and head up to Anne's mother's caravan at Nairn in the north of Scotland, east of Inverness. Anne, Ewan and her mum Theresa drove up, while I decided I would cycle. It was the longest run I had ever done, and mountainous with it. It was 220 miles, which I covered in one day, although I carried a tent, just in case.

That was about September 1992, and that was the last serious cycling effort I did for the next three months or so. I became so disenchanted and depressed with everything, especially cycling, which I blamed for most of our predicament, and I was so convinced that I would never race again that I gave racing tyres and other personal equipment away. It seemed such a black time for us, just scraping by and paying debts, with almost no hope, and to make matters worse, we had to give up the phone, as it became a straight choice of eat or speak. If we needed to contact anyone, we would have to use the public phone at the end of the street.

At that time, everything seemed so pointless. Then I heard that Eddie had asked another rider to use my bike in a Christmas TT, just three or four miles from our home. At that moment, I just flipped out of pointlessness and into action. The event was only two weeks away, but I had not ridden in two months, so I went straight into action with the anger-driven thought that 'no bastard is going to win my local event on my effing bike! No way!' I had lost all my form, though, and trying to train half-hard was like self-torture, but as pride was at stake, I went out every day to get back as much as I could before laying off for the event.

The day of the event was fine and sunny, and when I arrived, Eddie and his entourage were there, so rather than take a corner, I got changed in the car park and left my gear in a friend's car. I spoke to the rider and pointed out that he was riding my bike. He looked humble and said that Eddie had been quite insistent, and I understood exactly what he meant. My own bike was one that I managed to cobble together from wheels and a frame from previous years. It was lucky that I had left a lot of standard design frames and some wheels at the house, but as it was, I still had to borrow a front wheel from a friend in order to ride at all.

On the start line, I was more determined than ever to do my best possible ride, and with the condition I had, it was a complete gasping effort from start to finish. Because I had almost no condition, it was a battle against pain and total all-body discomfort, which I ignored beyond the normal level of tolerance, simply because of the circumstances. In the end, it was worth it, as I beat Eddie's rider by a few seconds, and held on to my honour so close to my own house.

After the race, I spoke to Eddie. I was far from placated by winning a bike race, and I was still pretty angry the way things turned out, and started by asking when I would get my bike, my brazing bottles, my tool sets (including full Campagnolo, worth £1,000) and my other property. The response was not good, but not altogether bad, depending on how I responded to his questions. He wanted to know if I would come back to the fold and race for him next year. The answer was a definite no. The rest of the conversation revolved around attributing blame. He said I was turning down a great chance and that I would be nothing without him – nothing. To that, I said, 'Just watch me.' In the end, I was fed up arguing with him before he could finish telling me why he would not return my equipment, I suggested he could shove it where the sun don't shine. In the end, we agreed that neither of us would hassle the other, and that was that. New Year was just around the corner, an era was over and a new one about to begin – and how!

eight: onwards and upwards

The festive season of '92 was a time of reflection on a year that had been hopeful for business and sport, happy with the arrival of Ewan, and horrid with the meltdown of everything. The man who had been my rival had shown the world how good he was, in style, by winning gold at the Barcelona Olympics, and in doing so he showed me how good we both were. I had also enjoyed my success in my showdown at the Christmas TT, and in contrast to the long depression I was suddenly feeling that I could take on the world and win, that I was omnipotent and invincible.

It was just before New Year that I suggested to Anne that I would build the bike I had in mind and break the all-time record held by Francesco Moser. We were walking along the seafront at Troon at the time, and I was not quite sure if she would think I had gone off on another ill-conceived venture that would see us reflecting on a year of disappointment the following Christmas. To my relief, she totally backed me up on my unusually self-assured mission, with the proviso that it had to be 100 per cent full-on or not at all. I assured her that 100 per cent was my intention, and that I myself could not do it any other way.

In those few moments it was settled, and my wife had totally backed me in the decision I had already taken in my mind. To me it was not even a decision but more a statement of fact, as sure as the sun rising the next morning, yet to my cycling friends whom I dared to tell, I had really lost my sense of reality this time. In the end, I told very few people because I found it frustrating that they could not instantly see that this was a thing I would do, end of story. I also found the negativity and doubt very irritating, especially when people tried to convince me that my absolute belief in my future ability was irrational. As far as I was concerned, I had two arms and two legs, and that put me on a par with Moser, and any other shortfall would be made up by my ability to push myself harder than any other human being who had ever lived.

In the spring of '93, I was not good enough, nor had I ever been good enough to break the record, but all I had to do was make myself good enough. Sometimes I would find myself riding in gears that previously I would have though were pretty big for the terrain, but because I was Obree – 'the man who will break the record' – I could not accept mediocrity and change up into an even higher gear. The bleak retirement in the winter of '92 had taken its toll on my overall condition, though, and it took quite a while to get back on level terms, let alone break new personal barriers.

In the meantime, since the beginning of January '93, I was enrolled on a course of career training in secretarial and computer studies. It was not really my idea, but more a very strongly suggested course of action by the unemployment benefit office. It was called Employment Training (ET) but was referred to colloquially as the 'Extra Tenner' scheme, and to us, at that time, the extra tenner was pretty important in boosting our expendable income, which we could spend on things like nappies and food.

At this time, I was also beginning the process of working out the 'hows' of my dream bike. The question of how each piece of tubing or metal would fit together was resolved in my mind before any metal-bashing was started, and the acquisition of most of the component parts was done concurrently, so that nothing had to be redone or scrapped. The whole process of mental 3-D imaging took about three weeks and was well worthwhile, as the design changed several times before checking and rechecking could find no more faults or improvements. The main part of the frame is the centre beam going from head-tube to seat-tube, and no compromise can be made here, with regard to the mechanical characteristics of the tube. There was only one tube which I knew to be perfect for the job, and that was a Reynolds tandem oval base-tube, and nothing could begin without one of those. Ironically, I had several of these at Coastville, along with a lot of other tubing and my brazing equipment, but my latest attempt, by phone, to arrange retrieval was met with a rebuff by Ernie, and with violent overtones, so I decided to let sleeping dogs lie and just get Gordon to order another one through his shop in Irvine.

Gordon had relocated to about four doors down from the shop he had bought over from me in '88, to a purpose-built shop that was much bigger and had a roomier workshop. Gordon and his wife Isobel both thought that my plan for world domination was sound, and he had offered me the use of his workshop and brazing equipment to build my frame. I had discovered early on that remnants of tubing sets we had bought at Cosmos Cycles in 1984 were still surviving as a bundle beside the toilet pan. In purely metal terms, it was good tubing, and being designed for top-end BMX bikes, I knew that they would be a little heavier than I might get away with, but on the other hand, they could be manipulated to be even more aero-shaped than they originally were without fear of breakage.

Gordon said I could just have them, which was brilliant, because between that and some other Reynolds tubing that he donated to the cause, I had all the tubing I needed, except the main beam, which would arrive by post. The aero BMX tubing was made by a Japanese firm, but the lads in the shop called it 'pishrust tubing', which was a fair description of its condition after several years of over-spray. Being tied up in the 'Extra Tenner' scheme meant that my chance to get into production was limited.

The ET scheme was five days a week, 9 a.m. till 4 p.m., and mainly we practised office skills, like touch-typing, which I thought might be useful, filing and administration. My training had to fit in around these hours, and I would usually go out afterwards. I would do the static bike about twice a week and those efforts would be the key sessions. In between I would go out on the road where I had three or four circuits to choose from. I would never miss a day, even if my legs were stuffed from the previous day. If they were, I would do a recovery ride, where I would only go easy and turn my legs over quite fast so that my muscles would loosen up for the next day's session. Sometimes I would head out feeling tired, but after a bit of riding, I would feel good and really go for it, and sometimes my legs would be tired enough that an aerobic TT-type effort would be counter-productive, but I would still be able to do strength work, where I would climb hills slowly on a very big gear.

Between training and the ET scheme, my time on my dream bike would have to be planned. Saturday was an obvious time, but as this was the busiest day in the shop sometimes it was not possible. Luckily for me, it was the quietest time of year for bike shops, and if I came early, I could do quite a bit of work. The ET scheme was a dead-end route as far as I was concerned, but I treated the computer training and the touch-typing as useful for me privately, and all of my thoughts were consumed by my dream bike and my training. From first thing in the morning I would think about my session that evening, and how hard I was going to go. I would be obsessed with twitching my leg muscles, and trying to analyse or convince myself about how strong I felt.

With my impatience, it was not long before my dream bike was taking its basic shape. Everything was in my head, and there was not as much as a scribble on the back of an envelope for guidance. Instead, I put marker points onto Gordon's concrete floor, which owed more to Greek mathematics than modern frame-building techniques, and pieces of string were even used. Of course, I knew from years of adjustment, what my exact hand and seat positions should be, and by using those as starting points, the rest of the marks came easily. To anyone watching, though, it looked more like surrealist metallic art than made-to-measure frame-building, and I think the lads in the shop thought it was more 'hash and bash' than anything.

Nothing could have been further from the truth with the frame, but with the forks there was an element of innovation, which had been started at Coastville and the ruin of at least three sets of fork blades. I had almost perfected the technique of turning the oval form of the fork blade into a wing-like, very narrow, very aero tube. It took the ruination of two more blades to perfect the technique without collapsing the tube or causing it to crack at the edges, but the end result was worth it and the knowledge allowed me to produce a seat pin that was also blade-like.

Pretty soon, the frame and fork were ready, including internal strengthening parts to reduce flex that were hidden from view. By March, I was still to fit a bottom bracket to the frame because the bracket of my imagination could not be bought, and I would have to produce or adapt this myself. I reckoned I would work backwards by innovating any way that I could to get the narrowest bracket width and then making the clamping bracket that I would braze onto the frame. There was a quite new but dysfunctional washing machine at our back door, and the turning parts might be adaptable in some way, I reckoned. As it turned out there were good bearings and the housing to hold them, but the dimensions were all wrong. After a days' worth of metal-bashing though, I had something that conformed to my vision and by the end of March, I had a bare-metal bike that I could try out.

Stepping astride my dream machine for the first time was a moment of excitement and apprehension, but my fears died and my excitement mounted with every pedal stroke, as I got the huge gear winding up on the dual carriageway. I had my light training gear on because I had cycled to Irvine from Prestwick and intended to give it stick on the way back. I was only intending to give it a quick spin round, to check it out before setting about the paint job, but I knew my baby had soul, and I could not help myself from going to the measured 10-miles TT course and ripping round, full-on.

It was a perfect day for it, with almost no wind and a mild temperature, but I still could not believe my watch at the finish point – 19-49 – I had equalled my own Scottish record from 1989. I knew then that my baby and I were going places. By the time I got back home, the ride seemed a little more ordinary as I calculated that I would have to go a lot faster than that to consider myself good enough for the record, but nonetheless it was uplifting to be on target. When I got back, I told Anne about it, and she was really made up. I also told Anne's parents, who were behind me from the start, especially Anne's mother, Theresa, who had as much belief in me as I had in myself at that time. I did not tell anyone else, because I knew I could not afford any negativity or rationalising of my plan. I suppose I could have told my brother-in-law, Martin Coll, who was a Scottish International rider, but I hardly ever saw him at that time, and he was also one of the quiet sceptics.

The third of April was Good Friday, and if I had started the whole thing earlier and not had my retirement, I could have made for the Herne Hill track meeting, which was the biggest in the country, other than the British Championships, which would not be until August. It was a great pity that I was not ready, because if I could have attacked and broken my own British record, then I would have been on the serious sponsorship trail to go to a covered track abroad. As fate would have it, though, the meeting was rained off and rescheduled for the end of May, and if I was as good as I knew I was going to make myself, then I would smash my own record that day.

I had seven weeks to play with, and the first thing I wanted to do, other than train even harder, was to spray my dream bike. I wanted it to look as good as possible, because sponsors do not like to be associated with a bad image, and the first thing I had to do was fill up the joins so that no-one could see the construction detail. At this time, I had become a member of the Leo Road Club, which is based in London, and it was through Vic Haines whom I had become acquainted with through mountain biking, that I had my main contact. We still did not have a phone, because of our worsening financial squeeze, and I would walk along to the phone box at the end of the street to get in touch with Vic.

The club did not have a structure, such as clubrooms, committees, AGMs or the like. It was basically an elitist grouping of riders under the same colours, where riders would hardly ever see each other, except at races – in other words, it was a club of convenience. It was sponsored by Alan Rochford, who had a cycle shop in his own name, and he would help riders out with travel expenses and some equipment, but the centre of the club and the driving force was Vic. Most riders were in it because they were fed up with committees and the like, but I was there because Vic seemed to have his finger on the pulse, he was in London and he believed in what I was aiming for. Not only that, but Vic could talk, he was a salesman for his own business, and he could certainly promote me if I let him.

Nothing could happen if I was not able to improve myself even further, and training became even more obsessive than before. Because I was using the same circuits for training, I knew what gear I was getting round at which bits, and I would chip away at riding harder each time I went for it. Sometimes the pace was almost intolerable, but I had a vision in my mind of my ideal velocity, and I would simply make myself do it.

Home life was stable at this time, and everything had a routine for me, which was mainly dictated by the ET schemes. Ewan was getting bigger and I was really taken on by fatherhood, but when I looked at myself as a father, I only saw someone who was a failure. However I knew that when I did what I truly believed I would, I knew that my son would be proud of me later on, when he was older. My mum and dad knew we were at the borderline of financial survival, and sometimes they would come round with what they called a 'Red Cross parcel', which was a big box of vital foodstuffs. I used to have a mixed bag of emotions about this. Primarily, I would feel even more of a failure than I already did, because it only served to highlight my inability as a grown man to provide properly for my family. On the other hand, I felt gratitude for my parents' thoughtfulness, knowing full well that the donations would make a useful difference to our larder, but at the same time, I would feel the need to politely decline their generosity for the sake of my pride. Anne felt this too, but I would never say anything for fear of hurting my parents' feelings. I knew that I had to break the record, no matter what the physical cost, otherwise I would never be able to live with my shameful failure and self-hatred.

Sometimes, despite the fact that I had been gifted with an almost arrogant belief that I can do anything I set out to do, I would feel like I was a cornered animal that had to fight tooth and claw to survive. There was no Corinthian ideal for me, and I knew it. It was a case of success and survival or failure and emotional death and self-destruction. So, for me, with a mindset like this, my interest in the weather conditions was purely a matter of knowing what clothing to wear. I had stumbled upon the most powerful of training aids – the intertwined emotions of total belief and total fear.

Despite having done my fast '10' a few weeks earlier, there was a time when my morale and confidence could have plummeted to the point of no return. I had set out on my training TT bike to ride a 25-mile TT privately, and at the end of my all-out effort, I only managed it in 56 minutes, which was so far off the pace that I could hardly take it in. Then, a few days later, I was just finishing an hour-long effort on my static bike at the back door, when my father arrived.

At this point, I was in the condition that I had set out to be in by the end – on the verge of death by exhaustion. I was hyperventilating as a matter of necessity, my heart rate was nearing 200, and I was literally dripping and shining in sweat all over. When I finished, warmed down and dismounted, I could barely focus or walk, let alone speak clearly.

My dad had brought a 'Red Cross parcel', and shared with me his thoughts that I should forget all this nonsense and just find a job – any job. Parental support and enthusiasm would possibly have turned around the effect of having ridden so slowly in my private TT, but hearing my dad's view of reality did not help me at all. This was on top of being summoned to the Tax Office to explain our position on tax for the shop, as well as having run out of money. Round about this time, I remember our lowest point where I found myself searching down the back of cushions on the suite and into the back of drawers, in order to find 19p, which was the exact price of a cheap loaf of bread at the local supermarket. I remember clearly that it was two days before Giro day, and this loaf could last us until then. I believe a 'Red Cross parcel' arrived at the appropriate moment, but the fact that we could do with it only served to make me feel even more useless as a father and a husband.

I kept training nonetheless, but shortly after the Giro arrived, I did succumb to cheap beer in a depressive dip. Luckily, it was a one-off, but the alcohol did not help my feelings of panic, failure and sadness at our situation at the time. Somehow, though, I was soon in a mood of invincibility and confidence once again, with total vision and energy to battle on regardless, to make myself better as a cyclist once again. The time had also come to show myself and my baby to the world, and 27th May 1993 would be the day, if I could arrange to ride at the postponed Good Friday meeting in London.

I had discussed my plan with Vic, and he had contacted the organiser to see if it was favourable for me to ride. I also contacted the organiser directly myself, as Vic had suggested I should do, and he said that he would pay my expenses for travel and overnight stay. All I had to do was stay focused and train harder than ever before, while the days to the moment of truth passed by and it would be time to taper down for total freshness on the day. I had also built a special pair of wheels with only half the number of spokes and the extra holes filled in. I had been using these types of homemade specials for about seven or eight years, and I knew exactly what I was doing in terms of rim and spoke combinations. I had special tyres for them that Alan Rochford had given to me, and along with Vic's Aerovic helmet, I felt that I had left no stone unturned in my quest for maximum velocity.

My dad offered to drive me down to London the day before, and my mum wanted to come too, since she had not been to London since she was a little girl. The journey took over twelve hours, due to traffic and getting lost in the city. Thankfully, it was dry the next day, so I cycled down to the track where I would meet Vic and Alan, while my parents took in an open-topped bus tour. I tend to get disorientated wherever I go, so after a few rides up and down Brixton Road, I finally found it in plenty of time for my full mental and physical preparation before the start.

There was not much mental preparation needed on the day, as I had spent the last five months thinking about how fast I could go for an hour. All that I had to worry about was the uncertainties, like the wind speed and how my maximum output through the pedals would equate into speed in the real world. These were factors that I could not change by worrying about them, and if mechanical failure is going to happen, then it will happen. I was in both a good and bad situation at the same time, in regard to the fact that I was a dead cert to smash my own British record. On one hand, there was no pressure from the public to do any more than break my own record, but in my own mind, I had to produce a ride that would be seen as world-class, and having a soft option to ease back on might not help me during the ride. I was so determined to go to the absolute limit of my ability, like I had done on my static trainer several times, that I was sure this would not be a problem.

After a good warm-up, the time had arrived for me to go to the start line, in front of the assembled crowd. Vic and Alan would be handing over my schedule that I had given them earlier. I was thinking big, with a schedule for 50km, which was over 3km further than my own record. Initially, Vic reacted by saying, '50?! Are you sure?' but once I had assured him that that was what I wanted, then he accepted it and said that would be fine. I was so glad I had not been faced by doubters at the start of this ride, like I had been at the last one, with George Miller.

As I pulled away from the start line, I knew from experience that I would have to settle into a pace of my own before trying to hold to a schedule, but within a few laps I realised that it might be possible to hold to the 50km mark. I rode to that pace for quite a while before I realised that I would have to let it go and ease it back a touch, or I would blow completely before the end. I was still going flat out, but in a more controlled way that would allow me to sustain it for most of the hour. By the halfway point, I was down on my 50km schedule, but I was ahead of Eddy Merckx's record of 49.435km set at altitude in Mexico City in 1972. I knew this because the announcer, Roger Shays, was in full vocal swing, and was informing the growing crowd that an historic ride was being made here as they watched. The crowd was getting excited at what was unfolding in front of them, with every lap being reported as a step nearer to the classic Merckx record, and the crowd started hanging the hoardings at the side of the track to encourage me on.

I was just on the pace for it, and with my schedule, I could see how close it was to his record, but the breeze across the track was rising slightly, which was enough to take the edge off my pace. With 15 minutes to go, it was touch and go for a Merckx ride, and with the last quarter of an hour record ride, I was trying desperately to cling onto the pace that I needed. The crowd was going wild now, and I gave it everything I had to hold on, but despite this, I could not help but slip ever so slightly off the magic pace, to take a huge psychological edge. With five minutes to go, I was just 100m down on Merckx's record ride, and a really strong finish might have pegged it back, but despite the thunderous noise from the crowd and Mr Shays, I had nothing left but to make it to the end of the ride.

I had achieved my goal of total annihilation, and although I had just missed the Merckx figures, I was well pleased with my day's work. I had smashed my old record by 3km, and had shown myself to be at world-class level with my ride. If there had been a sea-level outdoors world record, then I would be the holder, or if the amateur record of 48.5km by Ekimov had not been scrapped, then I would have been the world-record holder there and then.

Most observers were blown away by the ride that I had done on a less-than-ideal track, with less than perfect weather conditions, and by the reaction of the public and the reporters, I knew I could now talk openly about Moser's all-time record set at altitude and be taken seri-ously. One freelance writer who had come especially for this ride was Adam Glasser, who was more than confident that I could break it, after what he had witnessed.

My mum and dad were surprised by the size of the crowd at the track, but I am not so sure if they understood the significance of the ride as an excellent first step towards my ultimate goal. I myself felt a slight touch of anticlimax because nothing happened, like celebration or anything like that – I would just have to wait and see what turned up. I had shaken the tree, so to speak, and now I could only hope that something would fall out, but to increase my chances, I made sure that it was made clear in all the press reports that I was hell-bent on getting my hands on Moser's hour record, and that I needed a sponsor for the foreign endeavour. With the demonstration ride I had just performed, I hoped I would have a reasonable chance; without it, I would have had none.

The Moser record was considered to be almost unbeatable because he had taken the record to 51.15km from Eddy Merckx's record, which I had almost equalled at sea level. Top professionals had looked at breaking the record, but changed their minds after private tests, so for an amateur Scots rider to have the audacity to come out and challenge it was incredible, but conceivable after my Herne Hill performance. What I needed now was a company director or a marketing man with vision and an interest in the sport to come out of the woodwork to sponsor the whole thing. I had a feeling that I would get a response from England rather than Scotland, because Scots companies – and Scots in general – tend to be negative about

[handwritten in margins: 'real-world thinking' vs ingrained image of self as useless]

other Scots' ability to achieve. What I hoped more than anything was that it would be soon.

Before I left the track to head north again, I heard the news that Chris Boardman had smashed the British 25-mile record to just under 46 minutes, which is a fantastic ride by any standard. The front cover of Cycling Weekly had an equal split with me and Chris depicted head-to-head, and that was exactly right, as we were due to face each other at the British 25-miles championship in Cornwall that coming weekend.

Vic and Alan had arranged the transport and accommodation for the weekend, and all I had to do was get to London. We arrived at the hotel in good time to check out the course by car and by bike. It turned out to be a pretty rolling if not undulating course in most parts, but I had my regular TT bike with gears and Obree special wheels, and I had my baby, which was fixed-wheel. It was a bit of a decision as to which bike to use for the terrain, but in the end, my heart was drawn towards my fixed-wheel bike, on the basis that I was strong enough to punt the big gear up the hilly bits, but flexible enough to keep it turning fast on the downhills.

On the morning of the TT, it was sunny and quite warm, and considering the remoteness of the event and the time of day, there were a fair number of people dispersed about the course to see Chris and me do battle once again. I was off before Chris, and I knew that I would have to try and get into a pace early on, so as to get a rhythm going for my fixed-wheel, but after a couple of miles, when I was struggling up the first hill, I knew I was just not going well. I thought it must be like that bad training ride I had when I just had a bad day, with no real explanation. As I got further and further into the race, I started to realise that this could be my biggest ever humiliation, and that Chris was bound to be minutes up on me when he came through – I wouldn't even be in the medals! I battled on in a sense of panic, and then I did something that I still see as a most shameful act. I slammed my brakes on to a complete stop, dismounted and proceeded to loosen the quick-release of my front wheel, with the intention of having a phantom puncture, rather than try to shoulder the terrible weight of failure on my own on the long journey back to Ayrshire.

Within seconds, I came back to sanity, and realised I had let my ingrained image of myself as useless affect my real-world thinking. I got back on my bike in double-quick time and got stuck into it with renewed vigour and confidence. I caught my five-minute man just before the line, and then I knew I had been on a brilliant ride from the start, and when I looked at my watch and saw that I had gone under 49 minutes, I knew I had been so stupid with what I had done.

I had a bit of a wait to find out if I would get away with my cowardly act, but in the meantime, I heard that I had been 24 seconds up on Chris after about ten miles. I also heard that I had been in arrears by about the same amount at a point just after my battle with my own insecurity, but when I heard I had been beaten by just ten seconds, I felt angry and ashamed with myself. I felt such hatred for myself when I spoke to Vic and Alan, because the sport means everything to them, and they were so disappointed that I had been beaten by such a small margin.

Alan was the most visibly shaken, especially when I made the excuse that I had to stop because my wheel had pulled over and the tyre was rubbing. He and Vic had been so meticulous in my preparation, from driving round the course to getting the right food to making sure that my bike was perfect. How could I tell them the awful truth, when I did not really understand it myself, and if I did, I would have to explain my whole life. The worst thing was lying to Alan about the bike, when he was so perfectionist about every tiny detail, but the truth about my aberration would be more awful than anything.

The guilt was mine to live with, but the result was still good enough to put me side-by-side with Chris as a potential world record breaker, and for me personally, the '25' championship meant almost nothing in my scheme of things. Despite my self-sabotage, the end result showed that Chris and I were both world-class, and the fact that we were four or five minutes clear of the bronze medallist only made the fact stand out more clearly.

It was clear to everyone that there was only one man to challenge the Olympic champion, and it was me, and the fact that Chris had done the business at the Olympics was good for me, because I was suddenly being compared at the highest world level. Chris had also declared that he wanted me to go for the hour record and there was a bit of a quiet friction between us as sportsmen, because it would have been ideal protocol to follow the British queuing ideal, where whoever announced their intention first should be given free rein by the other rider until afterwards. This would be good sportsmanship under normal circumstances, and I would consider Chris and myself both to be 'good sports'. The run of circumstances since December of '92 meant, unfortunately, that the luxury of good sporting behaviour could not be afforded by either of us. Chris did not hear of my hour record plan until at least May, when it was in the public domain, and I honestly believe that he saw it as a direct attempt to get one over on him, since his plan was public news much earlier. For myself, I had lived and breathed for the hour record since December, and it is unfortunate that I kept silent until May, for fear of negativity and ridicule. There was no going back for either of us, because we each had agendas that could not be easily compromised – Chris had to go on the day that the Tour de France came to Bordeaux to break into the pro ranks, and I had to go some time soon, as a matter of emotional and financial survival. There was no backup plan for my season, my cycling career or my life; Moser's record was all there was.

Not long after the '25' championship, the cornerstone of my plan fell into place with the news from Vic that I had a sponsor for my attempt abroad. Vic had done most of the talking with Kelvin Trott of Choice Accounting, regarding what sort of backing would be needed for a full-on professional assault on the record. I did not know much about the sponsorship details, but all I needed to know was that it was now a reality, and that the first steps of organising it were taking place.

The first problem Vic had to overcome was the location. With all the covered velodromes in Europe, it would seem like an easy task to find just one with a couple of free days, but that was not the case. Vic tried Bordeaux, but it would have been really unsporting to go there when Chris was based there for his preparation, so in the end, the options were singled down to just the one – Hamar in Norway. The velodrome was freestanding on what would be an ice rink, inside a newly built sports stadium, which was called the Viking Skipet because it was shaped like an upturned Viking boat.

The first step, once we knew the venue, was to get a chance at a tryout for the record in advance of the real attempt. In the second half of June, I travelled to Hamar with Vic and a reporter from *Cycling Weekly* so that I could have a dry run. Hamar is about one and a half hours' drive from Oslo. The ride went well, with a finishing distance of about 51.5km, which was unofficially a new world record, but during the ride I experienced some steering problems, and a couple of times I ran off the track for a moment. This was at its worst when I got really tired towards the second half of the ride, and during the actual attempt, this would be unacceptable, because the sponges would be out all around the track. Part of the problem was not being used to the tight angles of the 250m track, which was almost half the size of Herne Hill, where I had broken my own British record. All that mattered to me was that I had proved to myself and to *Cycling Weekly* that I could take the record and, as far as bike-handling was concerned, I knew I would be all right on the day.

I was really on a roll, and the next major event on my calendar was the British 50-mile TT Championship in Kent, but Vic's knowledge of the English TT scene came into play as he suggested I ride a 10-mile TT the day before, because it was held on a stretch of road that could allow me to break the British record.

I came down to London and stayed at Vic's house some time before that to see about having a replica bike made that would serve as a backup for any eventuality. Our destination was the business premises of Mike Burrows, who had been the driving force behind the Lotus bike on which Chris had been 'catapulted' to success.

I had been a little taken aback by Mike's comment the year before, about Chris's gold-medal-winning ride. He had been quoted in some press interviews as stating that Chris would not have made even the bronze without his bike. I was sure from my knowledge that his figures of between thirteen and seventeen seconds advantage over just 4 km could not be correct, on sound scientific calculation, but I had never met the man, and I wanted to greet him with an open mind. Vic and I came in and introduced ourselves, and Mike took a quick look at my frame, which I was proudly grasping, and stated that, 'You'll never break the record on that thing, son.'

I had realised early on in cycling that almost all of the physical aspects of the sport are governed by Isaac Newton's three fundamental laws of physics. Everything about my creation had been a result of my inter-pretation of these laws, and my confidence in scientific principles allowed me to ignore his remark, although I respected him as an engineer. He convinced me to use a mono blade (a single-sided blade to the front wheel, rather than forks), which I personally agreed with in engineering terms, although the advantage over my blade forks, which had taken so much time and labour would be slim, if any.

We spoke about a replica bike, and Mike offered to help us out, but as frame-building was not his department, he said that if we could get someone to 'join some steel sticks together', he would be happy to make it aero with a layer of protected carbon fibre. I mentioned that the frontal width of my own creation was only 19mm, but standard round tubing plus layering of carbon would make the replica bike at least 30mm. Mike assured me it would not matter, so long as the aero tapering was on a 4:1 ratio. At the time, I thought that, by Mike's reckoning, a jumbo jet would have the same aerodynamic drag as a single-seater, but I was not bothered if he was right or wrong, because the advantage that can be derived from a frame is very small anyway.

What mattered to me was that the whole reason for my bike was not compromised – the bracket width had to be as narrow as possible, – 65mm on my own bike – which I could only achieve by mounting the bearings directly onto the crank areas. This was new and radical thinking in cycling, as well as being difficult to carry out, because not a single component could be standard to cycling, not even the shell, which is a standard for all frames. Unless someone was willing to hack up a washing machine, there were only two options – try to defy the laws of physics with standard parts, or undertake a serious amount of engineering work to replicate what I had done with a lot of thinking and toil.

The only way that compromise would be avoided was good liaison between the frame-builder and the person working on the bracket. I decided that I would leave the entire project to the engineers, who were freely giving up their time and materials, and concentrate solely on my racing. It would be Alan Rochford's frame builder who would be joining the steel sticks together, and Royce who would produce as narrow a bracket as they could to fit into a standard frame bracket. I went away happy in the knowledge that the rule of the UCI (Union Cycliste Internationale, the world governing body) requiring two identical bikes for the record attempt would be satisfied.

In the meantime, I would be riding the '10' on the Saturday afternoon, and the '50' Championship early on Sunday morning. Vic was right about the 10-mile course being ideal for record-breaking, but when I was preparing to ride, I had the next morning's '50' in the back of my mind. When he told me that Kelvin, my sponsor, had put up a special prize of £1,000 for anyone who broke the British record of 18-34 in the event, then I totally focused on the ride at hand. It was a downhill start, and even in my huge gear I struggled to keep up with the pedals, and on one of the roundabouts, I was so determined to get that £1,000 that I stuck my hand out to the traffic coming round and just sailed on through. On the return leg, I knew I was on it, and I never tried so hard in my life as I did on the last three miles into the headwind. I finished with 18-27, and I was the record holder and £1,000 less poor. Money could never be a real motivator for me, because I am really not a materialistic person, but the lack of money certainly was, and to have helped provide for my family really was a psychological booster for me.

The next morning was the '50', and when I was warming up, my legs really felt quite stiff. I decided I would set out at a moderate pace and gradually pick it up, rather than set out fast and diminish as the ride went on. I knew that water was the most important thing on a ride of that length, and I drank a litre of straight water just before taking the line. I knew from training that it would slosh about my stomach a bit at the start, but that my body would not be long in starting to use it up. The net result of my tactics was that I felt good through most of the ride, and I broke the British record again, with 1-39-01. Unfortunately, there was no £1,000 special prize this time, but at least I had won the championship by about nine minutes, and had achieved back-to-back records in the process.

While I was at the championship, I met Richard Hemington from Specialized, who was providing me with carbon tri-spoke wheels to use in time trials and the hour record. His initial contribution was in hardware, but Vic and I had negotiated a good bonus should I break the world record on Specialized wheels and provide him with the worldwide publicity that comes with it.

That was my last public preparation for the record, and the anticipation of the cycling public could not have been greater after the rides that I had done. All I had to do now was hold it together mentally and physically and not catch a cold. In the period of waiting, I did some good training, while being careful not to overcook it.

Anne and I were both paranoid about being with anyone who as much as coughed, and I became more nervous as my one moment of ultimate truth and destiny grew nearer. The days passed by just the same, and soon enough, it was time to depart for the race with no second place. Every shred of my being would be questioned, and I would have to provide the answers or face a lifetime of failure!

nine: the big test

It was the middle of July 1993, when Anne, her mum Theresa and I set off on what would certainly be the most important journey I had ever taken. We met the rest of the party at London, to fly onwards to Oslo, where we would pick up a people-carrier that Vic had pre-arranged, and a taxi to take us all to Hamar.

We made ourselves at home in the hotel, and headed down to the Viking Skipet that evening, which was ghostly empty. It was built for the forthcoming winter Olympics, but I would have the honour of being the first athlete to compete there. It was a metal outer structure with ridges, which were similar to the Sydney Opera House, and when it was empty, its huge void and eerie echo certainly did not make it feel either warm or friendly.

Atmosphere was way down on my list of concerns that evening, as Vic and Alan unpacked the replica, which was sparkling, immaculate and beautiful. Its flawless dental-white flowing lines made the Washing Machine Bike look drab in comparison. The immediate desire was to initiate it to the virginal boards of Hamar Velodrome. Vic and Alan had the replica put together in the time it took me to check out my own bike's flight damage, if any. On the walk to the trackside with the replica, I noticed it was a little overweight, but on pedalling off, I could feel how stiff and inflexible it was. The extra 2kg or so would not really matter on the flat curves of the black line.

I rode at 48-plus kph, for 20 minutes or so, which was good enough to get the feel of the new bike, and far enough off the pace not to be a workout. No two bikes could ever be exactly the same, but I soon got used to the handling characteristics of the replica and, although the bottom bracket was a good bit wider than my own bike, it was as narrow as it could be within the constraints of convention. Overall, the bike felt a bit different from my own, but once I got used to it, it seemed quite all right and did not half look the part!

Getting a ride in and knowing the backup bike was fine, put my mind at rest in terms of mechanical failure, and sailing round the bankings also helped to dispel that subconscious fear that most athletes must have, that suddenly their best form will desert them. All there was to do now was to get as good a night's sleep as possible, as my nerves and restlessness grew with the relentless approach of my finest hour. Seeing the sizable group of team and supporters at the velodrome, and riding around on my own, brought it home to me that they were here for me – just me. It was my moment to shine in front of the whole world – suddenly it seemed like the greatest party trick I would ever perform.

There was a question about which bike I should ride, now that there were two to choose from. I always had it in my mind that I would use my own bike to break the record, but now that the Washing Machine Bike had a beautiful little sister, it was inevitable that there would be sibling rivalry. Vic and Alan were both a little besotted by the sexy curves of the little sister. Her beauty may have been skin-deep, but I was convinced by it myself, after a little persuasion about how good it would look.

I was not completely convinced, though, as I remembered the knife sticking out of Chris's back after using the Lotus bike. My wife and her mum had 'female vibes' that I should use my own bike – it had served me well – and I remembered Jimmy Train always saying, 'Never change anything before a race'. Nonetheless, aesthetics won out in the end, and it was decided that I would use the little sister, for the sake of image to the press, and for reliability.

That night, we had a good meal together as a group, including the UCI commissionaires, and timekeepers, who had been flown in first-class to officiate the attempt. There was a good rapport, and the atmosphere at the hotel was buzzing with anticipation. Anne and I retired early for a good night's sleep, but unfortunately there was a loud function on downstairs from our room, which did not cease until about 3 a.m. Normally I could sleep through this sort of disturbance, but on top of nerves and excitement, it was enough to keep me awake.

I finally got to sleep at around 3.30 a.m., which would not be a problem, as the attempt was scheduled for the afternoon, and a long lie would see me right. Wrong. I was awakened by knocking at the door at 7 a.m., and a loud Cockney accent. It took me a minute or two to come round from my deep sleep and work out that it was Vic, with a message that the press were here, and that I should get up. Not being assertive or forthright in nature, I did what I was asked and, partly out of respect for Vic's wisdom in managing events and partly out of curiosity about what was so important that I should be wakened at such an early hour, I donned my clothes and went downstairs.

It turned out that that was the start of my day, as I proceeded to interviews from the press people that were there. The press people that I spoke to apologised that I had been woken, as they had not come to speak to me directly, but just to find out what was happening. They were from *L'Equipe* – the most important sports paper in France. I decided to speak to them anyway, seeing as I was up already, and now wide-awake. They had not heard of me in France, because time trials are not common there – road races are what get reported more than anything else. They had heard about a bike built from an old washing machine, and they wanted to know all about it.

I proceeded to explain everything about it, from how it was built to why I had to build it myself, and how the narrow bracket dictated every-thing about the design. They had also never seen my crouch position, and I explained that I had been doing it since 1986, and that I simply did not change over to tri-bars when they arrived. They understood all that, but they wanted to know what to call this bike – it had to have a name. Right then, I instantly said that she was my Old Faithful, without as much as a moment's hesitation, and in that spontaneous moment, my baby had been named – but not yet baptised.

All this was before breakfast, and just when I thought I was off the hook, I had a TV camera filming me eating my toast and jam. I did not really like it, and it would be accurate to say that I felt really uptight and anxious by this stage, but Vic reckoned I had to please the press to get maximum publicity. By this stage it was only 9 a.m., and I felt like a performing monkey, and there was no end in sight, as other people's wants and demands just kept on coming and coming. Everybody wanted the best for me, but all the reminders of how momentous a task this was did not give me any chance to relax, during what turned out to be a six-hour build-up. Being quite an introverted person, I found it hard not to be drained by it all.

The build-up continued, and we were taken to the velodrome a long time before the starting time, and I spent most of that either talking or being talked to. Vic and Alan both spent a bit of time trying to psych me up, which was very nice. I did not have the heart to tell them that I would rather slash my wrists than fail. How could they understand? Could they understand in a thousand years? Their psych-up talks were very quaint – excellent by sporting standards – and they were nothing but well intended. If I told them the truth that the hour-record was not about glory, achievement, money, being the greatest, or even sport itself, but justifying my next breath, then I would have confused them, to say the least.

The moment of truth surely came, and after a few laps of the track, I pulled up to a stop as the feeling of abject fear twisted my stomach, tightened my breath through my dry mouth, as the stench of adrenaline eased through my nostrils. I wiped my shaking sweaty palms on the side of my skin suit, as the official starter said, 'Take a deep breath – remember this is Moser's hour record.' Then, as he asked, 'Are you ready?' I felt like I was shaking all over as I tentatively said yes.

I drifted away from the line, and wound up the big gear to cruising speed and tried to settle into a pace before checking out the schedule. I was riding a slightly bigger gear than I usually use in time trials, because if I got on to my scheduled pace, then my pedal rev-rate would be fine. I was using 54 x 12 ratios, but Vic reckoned that my usual 52 x 12 would be much better. There would be no way of knowing for certain without much more track time to check out the differences. Either way, it was too late now, and as I came round, I saw that I was down on my 52km schedule. I tried to lift it slightly, but I was just not getting the best of myself, and I was still slightly down on schedule.

Now I was starting to panic as I gave it everything, and I was trying to use every muscle in my lower body to pump the pedals round just a little faster. Now Vic showed me that I was on Moser's schedule, so now I would be up or down on the record itself, which was 51.151 km. I was behind on this schedule too, but not by very much. I kept on pressing and pressing to get on level terms, but I just could not get comfortable and into a flow. I felt like I was moving about the bike, trying to find my rhythm, and I was just pedalling as hard as I humanly could to catch up on the schedule.

By the time halfway came, I was still in a position that if I could just get everything out, I might get back on top. At the same time, my lungs were heaving, and the onset of all-over exhaustion was setting in, as I would have expected, but in past efforts, I have had the luxury of being up on the record, so that maintaining the pace is all that is necessary.

Now I would have to find extra pace, no matter what, but nothing I could do would raise the pace enough to get back, but I kept going, because somehow I had to achieve it.

My attempts to attack the deficit could not be sustained, and in the last ten minutes, I knew I could do no more, unless a sudden burst of energy came from nowhere. It was so frustrating; I was only a lap or so down, but it might as well have been 100, and I felt the humiliating weight of failure, as I tried my best to the line. It had been a totally lonely and isolated experience. It was my own personal battle with the black line, and the schedule and everyone else was just a blur, as the black line was my total universe. At that time, no past or future existed. All that existed was the need for survival and pace.

When it was over, I was defeated and exhausted, and it was only then that I noticed the audience that had come to see me in action. I was immediately brought in front of the cameras of France 2, where I was asked what I thought about my ride. Throughout every part of my being, I felt like a failure, and I gave the same opinion of my ride. It was pointed out to me that I had broken what would be the sea-level record, also held by Moser, and the French crew tried to give me flowers to celebrate the ride. I instantly could not accept them, as I honestly felt at that moment that I should be flogged at the minimum, and I abjectly hated myself for the disgraceful failure.

At that moment, I saw Old Faithful sitting sidelined and lonely at the side of the track, and something just snapped inside me. I stated that I was going again – on Old Faithful. Everyone round about was incredulous as I went on to say that I would go again that afternoon if necessary. Normally a ride of that intensity would require at least 4 days' recovery, but at that moment, I felt like a drowning man clutching at straws. Then I was a different man – where I had been a cowering cornered animal, now I was fighting my corner for survival.

It was arranged that I could go the next morning, provided I set off at 9 a.m. on the dot, because the officials had flights to catch. Anne and her mum slipped in at this point, and my wife – who is normally quite reserved – suddenly took control and laid down the rules that we would go back to the hotel and keep ourselves to ourselves, and no-one would bother me in any way. She finished with the statement that 'Graeme needs to do things his own way, and you lot are bossing him about'!

At this point, still dripping in sweat, I stepped back into the discussion myself, with a request that the people-carrier pick up Anne, her mum, me and Old Faithful at the hotel at 8.50. There was a bit of mutter about warming up, and the like, but now I felt really truculent, and insisted that ten minutes to nine would be the perfect time. I already knew exactly what I was going to do, and the three of us executed our plan with a good meal and an early night, which was devoid of psychological talks or anything of the kind. The three of us had total belief that I could take the record, and 'talking up' would only have shown an element of doubt.

There was just one thing that could cast doubt on my ability to break the record the next morning, and that was the slight problem of physical exhaustion and muscle fatigue. I knew without doubt that my tiredness from that afternoon would affect me the next morning to some degree, but when the chips are down, they are down, and I was in no mood for trivialities getting in the way of me getting a hold of my record.

I had this angle covered anyhow from previous experience of recovery. I knew that I could not sleep long before my muscles really stiffened up, but I did not want to set an alarm, because it wakes you from a deep sleep with such a start that the overall effect would be exhaustion by the morning. Instead, I used the 'bladder alarm', which is a technique of drinking loads of water before going to bed. It would only be an hour or two before I would waken in need of the toilet, but before going back to bed, I would do five or ten minutes of deep stretching, have a small bowl of cornflakes for carbohydrate, and another load of water. And so the cycle went, five or six times during the night.

In the morning, I conveniently woke at 8 a.m. from my last bladder cycle. I had my last bowl of cornflakes, shaved and got my skin suit on. I did some stretching exercises in the room, and Anne, her mum, Old Faithful and I caught the 8.50 ride to the velodrome. We arrived just five minutes before the starting time, and I went straight into my new mode of 'blitzkrieg'. I put on my tracksuits and my shoes at a distance, and I remember striding over to the waiting crowd like Butch Cassidy, before putting on my helmet and going straight up onto the track. I was careful to say almost nothing and to not catch anyone's eye, as a matter of keeping my momentum. It was now almost 9 a.m., and I was right on time. I did three laps of the track and pulled up to the starter, who grabbed the back of my saddle to steady me at the time. At this moment, I had no sweaty hands, no tightness of breathing and no sense of fear or anxiety. Instead I had a 'blitzkrieg', arrogant impatience to 'bring it on', and I knew that I would succeed with this mood. What I did not want was the starter to utter the same words that he had done the afternoon before. I was afraid, deep down, about thinking about the greatness of the record or how taking a deep breath to humble myself to it would break through my thin veneer of arrogant aggression and reduce me to a cowering, tired and beaten athlete before the start.

I was having none of it, and just as he was about to speak, I got there first with a loud and clear, 'Are you ready?' Now, that is normally the question that the starter asks, and to hear it from the athlete must have taken him aback, but in any case, he instantly replied 'yes'. Such was my fighting spirit that I attacked from the line there and then, and such was the unexpected nature of my start that I could see the timekeepers fiddling with watches from the first banking, while out of the saddle.

I gave myself four laps to settle into the time-trial-type rhythm with Old Faithful that I could not find the afternoon before. Andy – the schedules guy – had suggested the evening before at dinner that I use a schedule for Moser's record itself, and I agreed, as it seemed to make good sense. On that schedule, I was up from the start, and I was into a flow that I was gradually building a margin over the record, and the more ground I gained over the record, the more gung-ho I became.

The ride was no easier than before, and it was a full-on effort to maintain my pace and my rhythm. Where it had been a battle against the black line, it was now a battle against myself to not lose my rhythm, as the effort needed to sustain my ride got greater and greater. The vocal support from the team and supporters was greater than it had been the previous day, and a lot of people spread out along the inside of the track so that I could pick out individual voices, hearing their message as I sped around. Anne and her mum stood on the apex of a banking so I could glance at them as well as hear them every time I came round.

By halfway, it felt like hell, as my effort from the previous day started to tell on me. Minutes seemed like hours, and lap after lap, it got harder, like going up a steeper and steeper incline. Many times, I thought about how nice it would be to stop and end the agony. I was up on the record, though, and I would go on and on, no matter what – even if I had to ride to death by exhaustion like a horse – and every lap I thought about the failure. For a little while, I imagined I was that horse, galloping on and on and on to its oblivion.

I was in agony by the last quarter of the ride, my feet, ankles, geni-tals, hands, face and scalp had all gone completely numb. Every muscle in my legs was on fire, and I had to think about how each muscle moved individually to keep them pedalling in some sort of rhythm. My eyes were a flickering blur now, though I could still see my line, and my lungs were rasping air in and out like bellows. Still, it was a beautiful feeling to be breaking the record, and when I got the 'ten minutes to go' shout, I knew I could hold on, no matter what – I would ride through any misery now to grasp my prize.

Misery it was, but just before my time was up, I heard what was – and always will be – the most beautiful sound in the world. A pistol shot rang out to mark the point where I had completed Moser's distance, and there and then I was the record-holder. I had an extra half minute or so to add distance to the old record, but in my head I was celebrating already, and I had an official finishing distance of 51.596km.

There was happiness and reconciliation all round, and after a short celebration and a few interviews with those members of the press who had had enough insight to stay, we had to start back for Oslo. My own feelings after the hour record were strangely subdued in relation to how desperate I was to not return home without it, and those that I did feel were ones of relief. I felt like I had survived a near catastrophic event, rather than performed one of the greatest turnarounds in sporting history.

We spent that evening in Oslo with Kelvin and his wife, just relaxing and talking about the day that had been. We thanked him for his vision in stepping up to sponsor me when he did, but we still did not know how much the whole shooting match had cost him. All that mattered to us was that the attempt took place, and that, in the end, I was walking with a slice of cycling history in my back pocket.

Part of the effect on me of breaking the record was that I was able to see clearly beyond 17th July, and suddenly there was an alarming lack of sporting targets lined up. Now I was thinking about what I should do next, and part of me was hoping that Chris would break the record on the 23rd, so that there was always a target to fall back on. Ironically, I hoped he would succeed, because he had banked on the hour record almost as much as I had, and I knew now from personal experience, how painful and emotionally debilitating it would be to step up and fail. The thing is, you see, from a European perspective, the most important thing is not holding the record, but having broken it. By cycling philosophy, I already had my prize in its entirety, and nothing now could take me out of the record books – and nothing could stop me from being referred to as a 'record man' for evermore. Some people round about me were expressing wishes of failure on Chris, but I never felt that. How could I, after what I had felt after my first ride?

Chris's ride, six days later, was a welcome distraction to the void I was seeking to fill in my cycling career. My forward planning had been absolutely nil, which was typical of the stark difference between Chris and me. This definitely was highlighted by the type of questions that I struggled to answer on my return to Scotland under a deluge of press interest, most of which came from mainland Europe.

The way of life we had before we left for Norway was over and our new life began well and truly at the deep end, and Anne and I were out of our depth and struggling to know exactly how to handle the situation. I knew already that the hour record was a really big deal in most places except Britain, but what happened in the aftermath was almost overwhelming. Our phone never stopped ringing, and we were doing constant rounds of interviews for television, newspapers and magazines. At one point, we had three camera crews at once, which had suddenly appeared at our house. Although they had arrived without appointment, we were keen to oblige them, since they had travelled from abroad to do a piece, and it just was not in our nature to be inhospitable to people who had travelled such a long way just to see us.

If I had been a little less naïve, then I would have declined the photographs and TV pieces that were keen to depict a stereotypical image of a cycling Scot, with images of kilts and tartan, and bottles of whisky and ruined castles as backdrops. It was fun at the time, and it did do my general public recognition a lot of good, but at the same time, it also undermined my credibility as a serious athlete to some degree. Although we were now temporarily solvent, we reckoned that getting as much publicity as possible could only be good in the longer term if I were to be able to convert performance into cash, through sponsorship or whatever. It was the 'whatever' that we were not sure of, and we were waiting for opportunities to show themselves, and it was the feeling that publicity would open doors for us that drove us on to accepting most publicity opportunities that came our way. Our publicity campaign must have worked, since I became a known name in cycling with just one ride – not that we had to seek out publicity, it just kept finding us.

Such was the demand on us that, one afternoon when we decided that we would go out to the town and get away from the constant phone-ringing (a recent development since Kelvin's £1,000 bonus), we returned to find 64 messages on our answering machine. One of the messages was an invitation to compete and do demonstration rides in Denmark. It was my first paid appearance since my hour record – or, to be more specific, my first paid appearance ever. It involved a series of pursuit rides on Old Faithful, and since I had decided to go for pursuit again as a career move to keep me going in the competitive arena, I thought that the rides in Denmark would get me into the way of it. In the meantime, Chris had broken my record on the 23rd, with a ride of 52.27km, and beating the hour record helped him break into the professional side, which was his plan and his destiny.

Martin, my brother-in-law, had been seeing more of me since I broke the record, and he volunteered to accompany me as a helper, since the organiser Ib Van Hansen was paying the expenses. I had entered the British Championship pursuit before I set off, and I viewed the trip as an opportunity to get up to speed physically, because of the sheer intensity of the effort, and also to get a fix on pacing myself with a schedule, as well as tuning in mentally to the demands of the ride. When we got there the change in status that the hour record had suddenly brought me was made obvious by the way I was received and treated, both by cycling people and the general public.

Martin and I were both touched and taken aback when I was greeted at the track by a fully kilt-clad pipe band playing 'Scotland The Brave'. I cannot remember exactly what the rides entailed, but I can remember doing 4-43 outdoors to beat my opposition by a small margin. I did two or three lung-bursting efforts that day, before being displayed on a float that was being pulled round the grounds of Odense FC, whilst being serenaded once again by the sound of 'Scotland The Brave'.

I rode at another track with a pursuit match against a team, which was a close-run thing, but the actual result I cannot remember. Then we moved on to Copenhagen, where I did a couple of hard pursuit rides as well as leading out the Keirin riders. The public response there was good, but the ambience of the place is what sticks out in my memory. The track dated back to the dawn of cycling, and had largely escaped renovation since then, and everything was as it would have been during the early twentieth century. The track mechanic invited us to see his workshop/cabin, and it was like going back in time with signed pictures of track stars who have long since passed away. There were even pieces of ancient equipment dating back to the turn of the century. The whole room was like a living museum, and I got that same feeling that I had when I went up into Alistair Gow's attic when I was fifteen. When he asked me to sign a photograph for his wall, I realised then that I really was part of cycling history for evermore.

I came back from Denmark with a good feeling about pursuiting that I had lost in 1990, when I had ridden badly and been ridiculed at Leicester. Now I was in the way of thinking big, and I asked Doug Dailey what I would have to do to be selected to ride for Britain at the World Championships to be held at Hamar. His answer was instant and direct: if I won the British Championship at pursuit, I would go – simple as that. I liked his performance-based policy, since I was cynical about committee selections or 'face fits' selections that are justified by hunches.

With Doug, my selection would be in my own hands, which was good for motivation, but now my focus would have to be squarely on those British Championship rides. I had a little while at home before I would have to taper down to be fresh for the Championship. I reckoned that after my time in Denmark, I had done some really good pursuit efforts, but my longer, more aerobic efforts had been neglected out of necessity, and if I only had enough recovery time for four or five really good efforts, then I would have to choose them carefully.

I worked out that I could get a good pursuit effort in, even if my legs were a little tired, but I would have to be fresh for a proper aerobic session, and a huge gear strength effort could be done any time. With this logic, I worked out that I could do a time trial effort, recover a bit, then do a pursuit effort, recover a bit, and then finish off with my strength session, before recovering fully from all of it. I was lucky to be living in a part of the world where quiet and hilly roads could be found, and one of the hills on my training circuit takes about four minutes to climb. This is where a lot of my efforts took place, and I think of it as 'pursuit hill'.

With my own knowledge of training and recovery, I had prepared as best I could for my latest challenge. This result would be vital to my cycling career, and there would be so much interest in me now that I simply could not afford a pursuiting mishap like the past. No matter what, I would be the 'record man', but if I were to make some sort of career in cycling, I would have to be able to compete at world level.

In the meantime, life went on in the new way, with press and public interest still strong, and with Anne dealing with most of it. Things would never be the same for her either. We had started the year and lived most of it with little more than hope, but now things had totally changed. Just when we were almost coming to terms with our new order, I was off again on another campaign, where I could not afford to do badly. For us, the past was safely banked away, but our future was exciting yet uncertain, as I was about to embark on a quest that could lead to huge failure or to huge rewards. I was searching for pursuit glory, and there would be no second chance this time.

ten: making it a double

I went to the British Championship in Leicester with a bad feeling, after what had happened three years earlier, when I finished tenth at midnight and also got slated verbally, into the bargain. This time I had a few people who were out to help me as much as possible, especially Alan and Vic. I was riding the same equipment and gear as in Denmark, and I knew the maximum pace I could expect from an outdoor track. I would not know for sure how Leicester would compare to the Danish tracks, but I knew that it definitely would not ride any slower. The big question was how my form had held up or improved.

I had learned the necessity for a long but gentle warm-up for pursuit efforts, and before the first ride I was most nervous, so I started even earlier. Thankfully there was no rain and after the first ride I felt much more confident as fastest qualifier. I had ridden faster than I had done in Denmark, and felt in control of pace judgement. The second ride – the quarter final – went the same way as I caught my opponent before the end.

The real test was to come with the semi-final and final, with rides against the best riders. The semi-final went well with an easy win over my opponent. Then a problem blew up out of nowhere, as one of the riders complained that my Aerovic helmet was not up to regulation standards, and on inspection, Willie Tarran, the chief commissionaire said that the helmet could not be used in the final. Vic took offence at this and whilst in a temper he used several expletives towards Willie Tarran, which I later apologised for. In the meantime, Richard from Specialized brought out a suitable helmet, which I was pleased to wear, and I carried on regardless in my preparation for the final.

The rider in the final was Bryan Steel who was favourite for the title, and I knew I could afford no mistakes with him, as he was an international rider of high reputation. We took our places in the starting gates, and my heart rate soared as the five bleeps counted down to the release point. This is where I strained every muscle in my body on the out of saddle effort to push and pull the pedals with as much strength as I could muster to get the bike rolling as quickly as possible on the high gear and from the static start of the starting gate.

My entire selection for the world championships rested on this one ride. Just out of the starting gate it all went wrong as on one of the super hard up strokes to get rolling, my foot came flying out of my right hand pedal. I just panicked and panicked trying to click it back in, but luckily it did go back in eventually. The whole time span seemed like an eternity and amidst the shouts of 'Fall Over' I had no thoughts at all other than setting in about the ride and trying to catch up.

By the time I had started to get rolling, Bryan had almost made up his half lap and was breathing down my neck. It was one of those situations again where the chips were down and I had no choice but to fight my way back. Once I was up to speed I was clear of Bryan, but I had only 4km to claw back the deficit and beat him to the line. At half way I was still in arrears, but the flow was running my way and at this point the message of survival desperation reached my legs as I upped the ante, to drag Bryan back on terms and by the finish I had him well beaten.

I did not realise it until afterward that when the spectators shouted 'Fall Over' they meant that if I fell over on to the track within 20m, I could claim a restart, but on reflection, I am glad it worked out as it did, because it made my rite of passage into the Worlds' team more emphatic, and it also highlighted a problem that I would not get away with at world level. In the course of the championships, I also broke a championship record of some kind, but I was too excited by my Worlds selection to make a mental note of what it was.

I spoke briefly to Doug Dailey, who was quick to welcome me to the team, and was equally quick to point out my weakness in the pedal department. It was a problem other riders had had in big events, even with the best of equipment, and I already had a solution in mind, although I said nothing about my plan at the time. I had a burning question at the time for Doug about whether he would have considered me if I was clearly the faster rider, but had not quite gotten on terms with Bryan before the line to win the championship. Like a good poker player, Doug refused to reveal a bluff, but he did say that he had stipulated the British Championships by way of forcing me under pursuiting pressure before riding the Worlds. It was a wily tactic, as without it my pedal weakness would have remained hidden until too late.

Mike Burrows also met me at the championships with the message that he did not build bikes to sit around as back-up, and that unless I intended to use his machine as my main one, then he would like it back. I duly obliged, as I knew now that I would always ride Old Faithful. That was the end of my contact with Mr Burrows.

Also meeting me again at the championships was Adam Classer, with whom I had become very friendly. He had gone out of his way to see me at Herne Hill, where it all started, because of a feeling that I would do something special, and he had come here full of positivity and 'good wishes'. He wanted to take a photo of me with my British Champion jersey just outside the velodrome. When he was ready to shoot after focusing his camera, a rainbow had appeared right over my head. He took that shot and started dancing up and down, and saying, 'It's an omen, man! It's an omen!' – the rainbow being the World Champion colours.

I would see more of Adam in the coming months, as he had persuaded Channel 4 to produce a documentary on the rivalry between Chris and me. It had taken most of the season for him to finally get the go-ahead, but now that the film crew were finally organised, he and the crew would be filming Chris and me in Bangor, Northern Ireland, in our next encounter. It was another rerun of the Champion of Champions 25-miles TT, except it was held later in the year in the hope of attracting all the 25-miles champions from the home nations, as well as Ireland.

It was held a week or so before Chris and I would ride the Worlds, and I suppose we both must have been thinking that it would be an ideal TT workout before we funnelled our final preparation down to pursuit distance and intensity. For me, it had been a difficult time between the British Championship and the TT because I had to undergo an acrimonious and imposed change of management help, through outside pressure. It was my brother-in-law Martin who had stirred up the problem by implying to my wife and her family that Vic was egotistical and 'inappropriate' financially and managerially. In the end, I had to bend to the pressure and tell Vic, who had not made a penny from his efforts, that he was off the case. It was difficult for me to do, when I knew he was so passionate about the sport and that he had believed in me all along.

At the TT in Ireland, I was not left alone and unaided, as the humorous and happy-go-lucky Martin had volunteered to take over from the man he had helped to depose. I did not really know Martin that well, because he did not come round much before June, and I had not encouraged him because of his negativity and fun-talking about my hour-record intentions. I liked Martin fine, though, and he would be the person who would be in a following car, which Chris and I both had.

On the morning, a lot of spectators turned out to see the crunch match between Chris and me. The race was tied up between the two of us, and on paper it could have gone either way. To add to the tension, there was the TV crew out filming for the start of the documentary, which Adam had been pressing for all season. For me, it was a bad start to my place in the documentary and a possible morale-blow to my Worlds preparation. Five or six miles into the ride, I sustained a puncture in the rear wheel, which is a real problem if riding a track machine, because it is bolted in.

I changed over to my training road bike for a good distance, until Martin had changed the rear wheel on Old Faithful, but my training bike with no tri-bars and heavy wheels felt so sluggish in comparison. I rode that for seven or eight miles before dismounting again to finish in 53 minutes, which was still good enough for second place, but Chris pulled out a sensational ride in under 50 minutes – a new all-time Irish record.

Chris and I both said our piece to the camera, but with just one week to go before going in front of the world's media, luck did not seem to be on my side. Still undismayed by my build-up, I proceeded with my cunning plan to eradicate any chance of my pedal problem happening again. I had already been thinking of my idea before the problem surfaced, but now it was a necessity. I had little time to play with, however, so on the Monday morning after my return, I turned up at Irvine Cycles with a pair of pedals and a pair of shoes.

My original idea was to mount the shoes directly onto the pedals, so that my feet could be closer to the axle point and I could drop the saddle height. One of the benefits of the narrow bracket was the fact that it brought the pedals closer in, so the height of the bracket could be lowered with the same track-clearance, and mounted shoes could lower the body even further. To take the pedal axle as close as possible to the sole of the feet, I melted a groove into the sole of the shoes for the curve of the pedal to nestle into. I bolted the shoes to the pedals and smoothed everything off with filler. I went a quick blast up and down a back street to test them before packing my bags for the Worlds.

When Martin and I got to the airport in Oslo, it was Doug Dailey himself who picked us up and took us to Hamar. We had come just two days before the championships started, and Sandy Gilchrist (the mechanic) and Gordon Johnson (the masseur) were familiar faces to us both. The first thing I showed Doug was my latest secret weapon, and we reckoned that when Sandy arrived, we could well wind him up.

His first question as mechanic, of course, was 'Did you bolt them on?' to which I replied, 'I just glued them, but I banged them against the front step and they were fine.' After Doug and Gordon added their piece, poor Sandy spent the next five minutes on the laws of physics and common sense, before being welcomed to the truth. For Sandy, my innovations gave him a nervous disposition, because he knew that if anything went wrong with my 'strange bits', he would be helpless to rectify it before the start. That is a position that Sandy is just not used to, as he comes with the tools, parts and experience to deal with any eventuality, but with Old Faithful, he was almost afraid to touch any home-made bits, just in case. Sandy, though, is as thorough and partic-ular about my bike as I would be, and with Sandy I knew that when I sat on my bike, on the line, it would be meticulously prepared and having that confidence meant I would only need to think about me and my mental and physical preparation. There are few people in the world I would trust my bike to, without even a second's thought about whether it would let me down in the ride, but Sandy is one of them.

That evening, we settled in at the guesthouse, which was quite small, and the British team had more or less taken it over. The building was stereotypically Norwegian, with its wooden structure. More importantly, it was quiet in its location, and on this occasion, Doug had chosen wisely. The next day, we headed down to the track to get a ride round during open session, but it was so busy that it was hard to get a good gauge of the bike on the track and a feel of the bankings at race speed. I managed to get her up to top speed, though, by weaving in and out of the other riders. Forty minutes or so was enough, and after a reason-able night's sleep, it was race day – and the moment of truth.

Surprisingly I was nowhere near as nervous about the opening ride of the pursuit as I was about the hour record. I had no pre-planned expectations of how well I would do and neither did anyone else, except

Adam, with his rainbow photograph from the British Championships. I warmed up and prepared in my own way to be at my very best for the qualifying ride, which would be make or break right away, as only the fastest four riders progressed directly to a semi-final. Such was my lack of experience about how fast I could go, that Doug and I had to guess what sort of schedule to use.

We had decided on 4-30, and if I could raise on that, then I would have a good chance of going through to the semis. At the start of the ride, the French riders in the audience were sniggering and joking about my huge gear (now common, if not standard) and the riding position, but pretty quickly it became obvious that I was going well ahead of my schedule, and the sniggering died away – or so I was told by the British riders sitting behind them. Towards the end of the ride, Doug indicated that I was close to world-record pace, but I chose to ease back slightly and save a little for my next ride, as I knew I was sure to qualify at that pace.

It was the standard format, where the fastest and slowest riders would ride against each other, whilst the second and third fastest also ride against each other for a place in the final. I could not believe it when it turned out that Chris and I were facing each other that evening as second and third fastest qualifiers respectively. Where I did not feel apprehensive or nervous before, I did now, as I realised instantly that this could be my most important ride of the season, and thoughts of a place in the final and maybe even winning were still non-existent at this time, as the immediate fear of defeat and the terrible feeling of abject failure that comes with it took precedence. I cycled back to the guest house and arrived an hour late after getting lost, which is a habit of mine if I do not make a mental note of landmarks.

There was a hushed quiet in the British camp, as the 'grudge match' of the year was set to take place that evening. It was a beautiful sunny day, and it was only early afternoon when we were all sitting in the sun in anticipation of the result to come later on. Chris and I were both interviewed as part of the Independent Image documentary instigated by Adam. The documentary team could not have been at a better place at a better time than this, as the 'Battle Of The Bikes', as the production would be called, was set to film its two protagonists in direct combat on the world stage. It was at this point that Adam decided to give me the rainbow photo, and he pinned it beside my bed, where I had gone to contemplate in quiet solitude, and reassured me that this was destiny.

The day passed quickly enough and the tension in me only got greater as the time got nearer. The team would watch from the stands whilst the team officials had to decide who would look after each rider for the ride-off. Sandy had checked out both bikes in the afternoon, so he would help Chris with his preparation and take his bike to the line, while Doug would deal with me. It was certainly a weird feeling being at a World Championship and facing my own team-mate, but we both treated each other respectfully and mainly kept to our own space. In the warm-up, no-one tried to psych me up, especially Doug or Martin, knowing full well that nothing could add to my desperation to not be defeated and my strong desire to succeed. Where I had Martin, Chris had Peter Keen with him, and there was Gordon Johnson and another official who could help in our divided camp.

It was a truly British affair, in that there was no favouritism from anybody at any time, and I think everybody was eager to see what would transpire as there had been fractions of a second between us in qualifying, although no-one knew I had eased off a fraction in that ride. The whole affair was conducted with complete dignity, which is what one would expect in such a situation, but I had heard that in a lot of teams the winner might be chosen beforehand so that the best rider can have an easy passage to the final.

As it came up to the ride itself, my body was bursting with emotions, but the same old patterns emerged as fear of failure was much more powerful than the allure of victory. As I sat on the line and looked over to Chris, I knew that this was everything – not for a place in the final the next evening, but for this ride itself. I had to concentrate on my own ride or I would devote valuable mental energy on Chris that I would need for myself, and I had decided that I would not even think about pushing myself mentally until after 1km, and to that point I would just ride it like I had done in qualifying. I reckoned the last 2km would be decisive and it was that last half where I rode like my life depended on it, and with Doug 'walking the line' – a system where the coach walks forwards or backwards in relation to the rider's lead – I should have known that I was up on Chris in the last part of the race.

In the heat of the race and lack of clear-thinking due to hyperventilation, I could not work out if I was up or down on Chris, and somehow with two or three laps to go, I thought I was down, and put in a death-or-glory effort to the line. The result after three last laps from hell was victory and a world record. I came round to Martin and Sandy, and I had to ask them if I won, but by their jubilation, I should have known. To them, I seemed unmoved by what had taken place, and they were right, as what I really felt was relieved, and a big bit chuffed, but as soon as I knew I had won, my mind clicked straight onto the following evening's final where I must not fail – even more so.

Chris was a sportsman in defeat, and offered me his helmet for the next ride, which he reckoned was a fraction quicker than the one I had used, and facing a Worlds final, I was not going to turn down fractions from anybody, especially as it might be the fraction that I lose by, and then live to regret. The tension in the team was also gone now that it was just me stepping up for the chance of gold, and everyone was behind me for the ride.

When we got back to the guest house that night, my mind had already pitched forward completely to my next task, although I had a warm glow from having gotten back on terms with Chris and having broken the world record. It was Adam's photo that seemed to captivate me more than what was now history, and the thought of gold was a driving force. The thought of facing myself and the world with silver was the image that tormented me to the point where I knew I would rather die of heart failure in the ride for gold than live with silver. For gold itself, I could only try my hardest.

I hardly slept that night, as I visualised myself from a riding angle, and the exact pace and rate of pedalling I would have to do to be sure of avoiding silver. I rode the race over and over in my mind from the starting effort, right through to near the finish, and I imagined with it the pain, the hyperventilation and the signals from my body, telling me I could not push any further and how I would over-ride them and continue on my planed groove to oblivion. I never quite reached the end during my visualisations, because at that point, what I visualised was riding on through the harm or death zone, and the real ending could only come from real life. Where I decided not to think about the first part of my ride against Chris, I wanted to be on my groove from the first pedal stroke against Philippe Ermanault, my French rival.

On the morning of the evening to come, Martin and I went out for an hour or so on our bikes so that I could loosen off my muscles from the other two rides, and then I returned to spend most of the day thinking about Adam's rainbow and deepening the groove in my mind that I was going to follow. When I got to the velodrome that evening I could sense the anticipation in the air, and where the ride with Chris and me had been quite a British thing, this was the final and it was a world thing, and the stakes could not be higher. The interest from the world media was huge, and where my old bric-a-brac bike did not create much attention before, she was now a star in her own right. A lot of press people and photographers wanted to see her in the British enclosure, but Sandy had put a blanket over her to keep people guessing. Chris's and Shaun Wallace's bike (the new Lotus) were parked either side, but most of the press wanted to see that one-off bike that everyone had heard so much about.

On the start line, I could taste and smell the fear and adrenaline, and like a hunted fox, there only seemed to be two outcomes in front of me – death by groove or success. I had been here many times before in my mind, and as the five beeps started for the gate release, I was sucked totally into my imagined effort, pedal stroke to pedal stroke exactly following my mental groove. The pain, hyperventilation and the 'don't push me any further' signals from my body all happened as I had visualised over and over, and I rode right through it all as part of my programmed ride. I was riding to annihilation like a metronomic robot, still totally in my groove with over 1km still to go, and at this point, I had ignored more safety alarms from my body than I had ever done before, but now, I started catching glimpses of Philippe on the corners, so I was up on him, and with 1km to go, I was able to switch to 'hard as I can' mode and out of my groove, which would have caused physical damage if I had to see it through.

I won. I broke the world record again in the process, but as soon as I sat up after passing the line, the painkilling effect of the adrenaline, fear and ambition immediately wore off and the need to lie down and gasp was overwhelming. First of all, I had to ride a lap or two just to regain some control of my body, and then I put one arm in the air as a traditional celebration of victory – and nearly fell off! I had forgotten that my bolt-on shoes would stick out a fraction further than the pedals I had calculated for in building, and I clipped the banking at low speed, resulting in good TV, but an embarrassing dive-bomb wobble off the track.

When I finally got out of my shoes and hobbled to a chair, I was still gasping for breath, and could not speak, while my body felt beaten up and my lungs were on fire. When I finally got my breath back, I could taste the blood from my lungs in my mouth and could not stop coughing as they were irritated with every intake of air. As I sat trying to compose myself and not heave up my lungs, I saw Philippe Ermanault crying from his very inner being, and that really touched me deeply, and made think about how the fountain of sport can taste so sweet or so bitter to all of us who drink from it. Much as I felt sad for a moment in empathy with his feelings, which I could totally understand, as well as a fleeting tinge of guilt that my existence had brought about his downfall so close to the altar of glory, I was glad I was World Champion.

Before I knew it, and before I even had a chance to absorb the intensity of what I had achieved, the world about me went haywire with photographers and media people all around, competing with each other for a piece of the World Champion. Old Faithful helped distract some of the throng for a little while, and the more I got myself together and my body recovered, I was sucked into a whirlwind of tasks. I had been so fatigued until that point that I had not even noticed the standing ovation from the crowd, including the French team, despite the fact that their rider had been beaten. I only knew from Martin afterwards what had happened, but there was no time to dwell on the ride now, as I had a sample to give at Dope Control, and a ceremony to attend.

At the medal ceremony I did not look very moved, especially at the playing of the national anthem, and to be honest I was not. For me, being World Champion was not something I had dreamt about, and I had not even thought about it seriously until I had beaten Chris, so the idea of it from inception to fruition had been less than 24 hours. More than anything else, it took all of my concentration and self-control simply to not bend over double, coughing up the taste of blood so that I could stand tall on the podium.

Right after the ceremony, I was tied up with organisers of events trying to sign me up to compete at their events. I signed most of them after hiking up the price to breaking point, and after dealing with some of the press as well as the documentary team, I headed straight to Dope Control before the time cut-off. Once we were in Dope Control, I had time to sit down and take the few deep breaths that I could without coughing and let my body relax. It was a sanctuary from the ever-present press, and while I waited in the quiet of the white-tiled room, I was in no real hurry for nature to take its course as I gradually unwound. It was not until then, when I had time to reflect, that I finally thought, 'Wow, I'm World Champion!'

After Dope Control, Martin and I had to run to the other end of the building for a press conference that I was running late for. Then there were individual interviews, and after we had finished with them, we headed to the press box to test the power of the rainbow, by asking for a phone call or two back home. Obviously I phoned Anne and my family, but one call I wanted to make was to old Jimmy Train, who was not keeping very well. I was proud as punch that the boy who had walked into the club with Doc Marten boots and a Parka jacket twelve years earlier had finally made World Champion.

By the time this was all over, I was almost fainting with hunger because, for me, I found it best to reach the start line slightly hungry, and that was two or three hours earlier. We headed back to the guest house and had something to eat and waited to see if it was covered on Norwegian TV. When I saw myself on the screen, I could not believe how it looked, and the whole team were rolling about laughing when they saw it. My head and shoulders were bobbing up and down as I spoke, and it looked as though I had an extreme nervous disorder. I had been filmed on a static bike as I pedalled, but on the TV, all that could be seen were my head and shoulders, and to round it off, they decided to show me almost falling off without style.

On that note, there was a general consensus among the riders that a celebration was in order, and that there would be one. Doug knew nothing about it, and most of the riders put pillows under their quilts in case he looked in on them, but he always goes to bed early, so there was not much danger. I do not know if Martin had planned his mission or if we simply headed to the largest venue in town, which would not be very hard to find, as the town of Hamar is actually quite small. Either way, I cannot remember, as I just tagged along with the crowd as was my schoolboy conditioning. While we were walking, Sandy revealed that he had to change my rear tyre after each ride because the starting effort twisted the frame and chain-set just enough to rub the sidewall on the second pedal stroke. Normally it would not be a problem, but these tyres were £100 each and ran at 240psi, with super-thin sidewalls. Sandy explained that the problem was kept from me so that I would not be distracted from my best starting effort in the final.

When we got there, we discovered that the tales of mega-priced Scandinavian drinks were true, so Martin – in his very own exuberant style – dragged me to the bar, resplendent in my World Champion rainbow jersey and my medal, and started to talk to the barman. A few minutes later, he announced that I had a beer tap to myself, and I could imbibe as frequently as I wished – at no charge. The power of the rainbow had worked again, and in no time, we were smuggling pints around liberally. In no time, I was in more of a party mood, and despite my continual cough, I went up on the dance floor and 'gave it large'. For a laugh, and as a result of free beverage, I started dancing in the crouch position – with medal-swinging for added effect – and moments later, the whole dance floor started doing the 'Obree Dance' which continued sporadically all night, and every time I went on the floor.

The next day, it was history, but I still had my cough, my medal, my jersey and my memories. On the flight home, I had almost reached emotional overload and I had aching limbs, a hangover and my ever-persistent cough to go with it. Just when I thought it was safe, an announcement came over the speakers that we had a world champion on board, and that helped bring it home to me that things would not be quite the same again, especially in Britain, where World Champion really says something, even if the public do not really understand the event. Being the hour-record breaker, on the other hand, means a lot in mainland Europe, but the general public in Britain do not under-stand its true significance in the sport of cycling.

When we got out of the airport, I was greeted by Fullarton Wheelers, with a huge banner, an assortment of press and TV people, as well as family members. Anne and I headed home in the full expectation of multiple phone calls and press people wanting interviews, but we were prepared for that – because now that was my business. We were doing OK as it was, as the Specialized Wheels were on a big bonus deal, as were some smaller items, like glasses and shoes, and when the contracts I already had for appearances were added in, we were sitting pretty, with more opportunities surely to follow. My time of winning the Worlds was over, and now was the time to make the most of being World Champion. The real journey was just beginning.

eleven: the power of the rainbow

Coming home with a gold medal was a special feeling. I felt like a prince who had slain a dragon and come back triumphant, which was brought on by my gradual emotional acceptance of my achievement and by the response of others. When I thought back three or four years, to when I had spotted Colin Sturgess in his champions jersey cycling the other way at Leicester, and how I had politely waved at him with a sense of reverence, I realised how people must think of me now. Wearing my rainbow jersey certainly gave me a feeling of warmth because it was like King Arthur and the sword in the stone, as only I in the whole world had the right to wear it. Anticipation was another feeling that added to the emotional minestrone that was cooking at the time. After all, I was World Champion and hour-record breaker, and I had just arrived home, less than 24 hours since I had stood tall for the British anthem, and it was inevitable that things were going to happen in any of many different ways, and I could not wait to grasp my opportunities.

As I expected, the phone rang an awful lot during those first days of my reign as World Champion, and a lot of those calls were congratulations, press or invitations to events abroad. Martin was dealing with foreign organisers, but neither he nor I knew very much about what the going rate for a professional cyclist like me should be, with my latest pulling power. He would always come back to me to find out what I thought about the deal, and it did not take long to find out what the parameters of a reasonable deal were. We knew already what was on the table for my track meetings in Italy, and that gave us a template to work from, but the truth of the matter was that organisers did not have an exact idea of my professional worth either, as I was regarded as a one-off in most respects, although a world champion would have a certain market value that could be a starting point.

Life was hectic at this time, but mainly in a good way, with TV and newspaper interviews and sponsorship opportunities. I wanted to be wanted, and now I was, but the most hectic time as World Champion had not yet begun. I had dealt with all the press demands and a lot of phone calls, as well as having been received by the Council in Ayr. I walked into a surprise party organised by Martin and his wife, Miriam, and I was also trying to keep myself in shape as best I could. Training had become difficult, because my cough had not improved at all in the three weeks since the Worlds, except that the taste of blood had disappeared, so Martin suggested that I see a doctor friend of his who specialised in this field. He reckoned my lungs had gotten strained or damaged 'somehow', and become infected, so antibiotics might help.

A week after starting the antibiotics, my cough was finally subdued, and I would have a chance to recover from my feeling of exhaustion from continual bad sleep. I also had the Grand Prix des Nations TT coming up in the following week, which I wanted to ride and I was happy not to have to break a professional contract. I managed to get together a TT bike with gears for the event, which had my position exactly right, and I would ride in a standard skin suit. This would be the biggest TT event in the world, as all the big hitters that matter would be riding and only those who had satisfied certain criteria had been invited. For me, I was only allowed an invitation on the strength of being World Champion at pursuit.

Martin came with me to northern France to help me with the event, and on the evening of our arrival, we struck lucky as Dominic, who had very good relations with the promotions department of BiC, noticed that I was planning to ride in a plain skin suit. It was not a plain skin suit to him, but an empty billboard, and we shook on a deal that night for a nice, bright orange skin suit the next day. Now I was a true pro, with a contract to be there and a contract from a sponsor, which is as well because I found the place completely depressing – almost before I even got there.

On the morning of the event it was sunny but still assuredly depressing as an environment, or so it seemed. I spent quite a while warming up for the 50-mile event over undulating roads, before taking to the start line and all the press and live TV action that comes with it. As soon as I wound up the gear to get into my flow, resplendent in my orange skin suit, I could not quite reach my potential. Something just was not right, so I looked down to check both my front and rear brake callipers to see if they were rubbing and slowing me down, but they were not, so I checked round everything else as I rode along, but everything was just fine. That just left the engine, and then I thought about the cough and the antibiotics I had just finished, and halfway up the first hill, I really knew I was going to have a really, really bad day.

I felt terrible the whole time, but the thoughts of stopping I had well before halfway were overruled by a voice in my head, saying, 'Don't stop,' and I knew that although I would only manage a poor ride by my standards, I would have to push myself to the very limits to avoid embarrassment. In the end, I was so destroyed I thought I would never reach the line, and most of the ride had been spent forcing myself on and trying to will forward the passage of time. Despite my efforts, I pulled out a terrible ride and finished seventeenth out of twenty pros, and when I saw it on TV, it looked so bad that I had to cringe. The only thing that kept me going was the knowledge that I would still be World Champion tomorrow. Martin and I went away with our money and my BiC track bike, which somehow got into the deal, and went about the business of squaring away my ride as history, and looking forward to the next ride, which was the Eddy Merckx Grand Prix. I deposited my newly acquired bog-standard track bike, which I would need soon enough for some track appearances, into the garage as soon as I got home and closed the door behind me on the whole episode. I had heard the old saying that 'you are only as good as your last ride' so many times that I had worked out the flip-side of the equation to be 'you are as good as your NEXT ride', and on that principle, I was only looking forward to the forthcoming Eddy Merckx Grand Prix.

The event was held around Brussels, starting and finishing near Atomium – a famous landmark of the city – and was organised by the great Belgian rider of the past, Eddy Merckx. I had heard that the course rolled a little, but was not hilly like the GP des Nations had been, and I decided to take a chance and ride Old Faithful for the event, but when I saw the course the day before, I realised that, because of the corners and the short hilly sections where I would lose time, it would be safer and more sensible to ride my geared bike. It was a pity because it would have been nice to have had Old Faithful on display for the sake of the public and also, if I got into a flow on the fixed-wheel bike, then I knew I was onto a good ride.

When Martin and I got to the event the day before, and rode round the course, I was not sure how good I felt. One thing was for sure, and that was that I felt better than I had done at the Nations GP, although

I knew my form was less than it had been at the hour record. I was not unduly concerned about that, because I had always ridden races on the premise that this could be a day where I might excel myself, despite my underlying form. And I had anecdotal evidence from the past to back up my philosophy.

On the morning of the TT, the entire starting circuit round Atomium was packed with people and it was difficult to get out of the changing area without getting tied down with reporters and the public – all meaning well, but all wanting a little slice of my precious time. As I approached the start line, I remember feeling overwhelmed by the whole atmosphere and the press and TV interest. The start was on a wooden-bandstand-type construction in the middle of a long, straight road leading to Atomium, and there was stimulation to every sense as I lined up to face the stopwatch.

I could feel the cold, damp, northern European autumnal air chill my arms and legs, while the colours, the noise and the pervading smell of hamburgers and chips distracted me from my goose bumps. More than anything, I could taste the fear and adrenaline in my breath, and I remembered my recent bad ride as I was taken to the bandstand to be asked a few questions over the huge public address system.

As I started, my legs felt like jelly from the cold wait, but after a little while, I started to get into it as I rode my way into the race. The TT was two laps of the same circuit, which twisted and turned quite a bit, and on every turn there was a large crowd assembled to cheer on their stars. I was not on a great ride, but I knew it was not so bad as it seemed because I had held back so that my second lap could be the strongest.

Just as things were starting to look reasonable as opposed to bad, luck took a turn for the worse. I approached what looked like a left-hand 90° corner in the outskirts, but the large building and the people standing there obscured the true extent of the corner, which was nearer 110°. There was no getting round it after I had skipped sideways to miss a hidden drain lid, and with the crowd standing out on the road, they were right in my line. If the public had been standing on the pavement, then I might have just made it round, but what took place was an impact with a gentleman taking a photograph, who at least had the decency to give me a soft landing!

Martin was in the following car, so when I went to remount and discovered a badly buckled front wheel, I was able to swap over to Old

Faithful for the rest of the ride. Thankfully there was only part of a lap remaining and, despite the lost time, the end result – although poor – was not so bad as the Nations GP, and I ended up with tenth place, or thereabouts. Chris had won it, and there had never been such a margin between us, but somehow I just did not seem to care about it, as it seemed so unimportant in the scheme of things, as race after race seemed to come and go in a war-weary daze.

The race was not the only thing that we had gone to Brussels to deal with. In the aftermath of the World Championships, I had been approached about cutting a record, of all things, and since I did not foresee my musical career budding in other directions, I agreed to do it. The song was actually quite apt in its title of 'Who Am I?' and the lyrics went on to question who and what I am as a mysterious, enigmatic non-conformer. We went to the recording studio the day before the race and tried out the song, but it turned out exactly like I had warned them – I could clear a pub in half a minute, and my singing voice was no better in the studio. Not much was said about it, but I reckon they knew that no amount of dubbing would make it sound even reasonable, so it was not surprising that we did not hear much from them after my return home.

In the immediate aftermath of the race, I was whisked off to Belgian TV, where I was a guest in a live sports show. I was in a panel of three and feeling quite up for it. I 'happened' to mention my sponsor in the course of conversation, which to all intents and purposes was Specialized, but being public TV, this was not allowed. In my 'don't care less – life is such a laugh' attitude of the moment, I also made special mention of the man with the camera, and thanked him for his soft landing. After some irreverent comments about football, it was all over and time to go home, to pass time wisely until the next event.

In between races, we were thinking about moving house, as the one we were in was in Ayr, but Anne really wanted to be in Irvine, and the only reason we lived in this house at all was because it used to be needed for the bike shop, which was no longer there. We were looking for a slightly bigger house in Irvine, where Anne would be nearer to her family when I was away racing so often. The date was closing in when I had to leave for my next race.

The Firenze–Pistoia (Florence to Pisa) TT would be my last time trial of the year, but this time I was looking forward to the event, as I knew I had a better chance of a good finishing position or even winning.

The course was almost flat, and that was more akin to a British time trial than any I had ridden. More importantly, it was ideal for Old Faithful and a fixed-wheel. When Martin and I arrived before the race, we were picked up at the airport and made most welcome by Mr and Mrs Petrucci, who were both in their 60s.

That night we went out for a meal together and we talked for ages, and it was only after a while that we realised that Loretto (Mr Petrucci) had been a big star in the '50s in Italian cycling, and he could have made it bigger if post-war rationing and prejudice had not worked against him. He had been second in the Tour of Italy in the early '50s, and he won Milan-San Remo in both 1952 and 1953, and most people seemed to treat him with respect. That evening while we talked, he discovered that we did not have a jersey sponsor, and he said that he knew someone who might be interested in a deal. Within seconds, he was on his mobile, and within an hour or so, the man from Selle Italia was joining us for a suit deal. We had struck lucky again, but this time I wanted to give my sponsor a good result.

On the morning of the event, the man from Selle Italia came round with some saddles and some clothing. There was no point in being sponsored by Selle Italia and having a rival's saddle on my bike. It was a beautiful sunny morning, and Martin and I were waiting patiently in the yard for our car to take us to the start at Florence. We were almost thinking that we had been overlooked when our car arrived half an hour late, and at that point, we thought we were still all right for the official start time. The next thing we knew was the driver pulling over and asking us where we were going – the obvious answer was Florence. We did not know anything about directions, so he pulled over and asked a local. After a short conversation, we were finally on our way, but our schedule was now dramatically tight.

I had a set start time, and as we approached the area of the race start, there were cars, police with whistles and people walking everywhere. The whole thing seemed chaotic, and as minutes passed by, I changed in the car and put my cycling shoes on, so that I could go straight to the line if I made it on time at all. Just as I was resigning myself to a restart, with the possibility of a time penalty, the Italians broke the laws of physics and created instant order out of utter disorder and chaos. We were waved and whistled by the police, straight through to the start area.

At this point, I suddenly had enough time to answer a call of nature, while Martin put the wheels in the bike. I went straight to the start in time for the countdown and I was off. I had no time to compose myself or get nervous about the ride, and because I had more or less just jumped out of a car, I did not really feel like I was in a big event to begin with, which was all right because I wanted to set out slightly under race pace to make up for my lack of warm-up.

The ride itself is simply a matter of going flat out for the whole distance to Pisa, and this time my ride was an improvement again, with fourth place, but I was disappointed to have missed a place on the podium. It was not a great ride, but it was not an embarrassment, which I was relieved about.

The next day Martin and I would be flying out of Bologna Airport, and Loretto offered to give us a lift in his van. It was a long, winding climb over the mountains, and on the descent, Loretto started telling us how he had won a stage of the Tour of Italy down this very road in 1952, and the more he relived his victory, the faster went his van. After screeching round every corner and almost scraping every barrier, Loretto and I both laughed as Martin – normally the prankster – was silent, white-knuckled and even whiter faced.

We thanked Loretto for his lift and headed into the airport to find that the flight home would be delayed by ten hours, so we decided to head into town, check out some action, and come back in good time for boarding. In a way, the delay was ideal since it was a fine day and we were in no real rush to return to our Scottish autumn. More than anything, I wanted to bag the Asinelli Tower, and when we reached the top after an endless spiral of wooden trestles and stairways, we were rewarded with the most magnificent view of Bologna. The child within me demanded that I fly a paper aeroplane and the 'floater' I built just drifted on and on into the distance, until it could barely be seen as a speck of white against the red tiled background. As we just made it out drifting into someone's back yard, accompanied by a puff of confused birds, I wished I had left a message on it.

After our childish entertainment, we were back home to reality that night, and for me, I was glad that was the last time trial of the year, although I knew I had a whole load of track meetings to take part in. At this stage of the season, it all seemed so long and endless that I could hardly remember a time before I was riding race after race. At last, though, here was a chance for a week or two to unwind just a little before hitting the track circuit, so I and Martin and my other brothers-in-law, Damien and Aaron, went out to town. The net result was that

I returned mega-intoxicated after a constant flow of self-demanded 'just one mores', as Anne had seen on previous occasions. She had seen the pattern before, of me being violently ill and at the same time going on about how useless I am and the like.

Apparently I would always say something like, 'I hate myself, I'm so useless, I can't understand why you stay with me, I am a total waste of space, I'm a failure. It's true what they told me – I'm a failure.' In the morning, I would rarely be able to remember uttering such deep and ingrained thoughts that have been with me since childhood. As usual, I would refuse to accept that I had a problem – either psychologically, with my barely repressed feelings of failure and self-hatred, or with alcohol, which allows them to re-surface. I would always make light of it and say I had a bad packet of crisps or a strange mushroom on my pizza topping, but the whole syndrome had not been altered or soft-ened by my absolute success at that moment. Nothing, it seemed, could improve my hidden inner image. It could only be appeased by yet more success on top of my success.

Sobriety put my demons back in their box and allowed me to think about doing some pursuit efforts to keep myself sharp for the next engagement, which was one that I signed up for in the immediate after-math of my victory in Hamar. It was good having some time at home despite my moment of drunkenness and I was glad I had looked after my form once I was at Crema, the first stop on a tour of European tracks.

I had done a deal on the spot with sweat-dripping skin suit, that Martin and Miriam could both come as a weekend break, expenses paid, and I would be happy to sign the contract. That was at the Worlds and now it was time to step up and perform at my best in whatever event or events that the organiser thought best. We had gone to the track in the morning to check things out, and everything seemed quite low-key. I got a look at the large outdoor track while the local school was using it as part of the sports curriculum, and it looked in good enough shape. I hoped, for everyone else's sake, that it did not rain as we headed back to our plush, marble-floored four-star hotel, where we had been given the two largest rooms.

After a siesta and lowering the gear on Old Faithful by just under 2 per cent to account for the sluggish outdoor conditions, it was time to ponder on what the evening would bring. We had discovered already that trips like these tended to come as 'magical mystery tours', because from the moment we stepped out of the airport, we would be met by someone new to us, who would take us to an unknown hotel or destination. In this case, there was the added complication of the language barrier, and because of that, it was hard to find out what races I would have to ride on the track; I would have to be prepared for anything.

As it turned out, I would only be riding Old Faithful in an attempt on the track record, which was something like 4-49. As we approached the track that evening by car, we thought that there must be a big football match on because of the droves of people marching down the streets. When we got to the gates of the stadium, all became clear, as huge posters of me were plastered on the gates and walls. We made our way to our pen in the track centre, and made ourselves at home with nibbles and water.

The crowd just kept coming and coming, and those who somehow made it to the track centre formed a blockade about twelve-deep right round the perimeter of our enclosure. All that most of them wanted was a glimpse, a photograph or a signature. Trying to be obliging, I started doing some signatures, but the demand was endless. A lot of people, especially girls, seemed to want signatures directly onto their skin, and some of them in quite strange places. The whole atmosphere was charged, as thousands of people milled around with us as their focus of attention, and Miriam found it a bit unnerving, because she had never experienced a situation like this before.

There were two TV channels there, wanting interviews in English, and the only way to get there was by following close behind Martin as he carved his way through the crowd. Once I had done those interviews, I dealt with some other reporters before heading back with Martin to the enclosure, where I could warm up for my ride, which would not be easy by any means. It had been set by a good rider, and the track here was open-air with quite a slow surface, so I had not adopted any inkling of complacency about breaking the record, and if all these people had come out to see me, I must give it my very best in my ride.

As I took the line, there was an uncanny silence in the huge crowd, but they made up for it when I started pedalling, and at the end of my unscheduled all-out ride, I had broken the record by five or six seconds. I was stood on top of a podium and received flowers and a huge cup, and I was feted like a champion after that one ride. Of course, it did not end there, as there was fresh demand from the media and the public, which I was happy to accommodate in any way I could, now that the pressure of producing a class ride was out of the way.

I had barely gotten my breath back when Francesco Moser, the man I had looked up to for all my cycling years, and Ercole Baldini, who had held the hour record in the past, were accompanied by a host of media people and the two TV channels to meet me. We were in a sea of people, and the atmosphere and excitement at this place and time was almost overwhelming, but with these great riders in front of me, it was un-believable. My Italian was poor then, and Francesco's English was little better, so to break the ice, I said – as a joke – that he could try my bike, while gesticulating that we were the same height.

Well, breaking the ice even further, Francesco called my bluff and rolled up his trousers. A minute later, my absolute hero was riding round in a full-tuck position on Old Faithful in front of thousands of cheering Italians, and I did not know whether to laugh or cry with emotion at this incredible moment. The entire evening was that moment, and the media knew that too. From that moment, everything seemed to turn into a stupefying frenzy and the only solution was to organise an impromptu press conference.

Martin managed to get hold of his cousin, who lived nearby, and she kindly agreed to interpret for us, which made life an awful lot easier. Francesco and Ercole were at the meeting and Francesco said that he was very interested in the Old Faithful concept and the riding position for future reference. When the press conference was over, the track meeting itself was over, and most of the public were leaving. Some people stayed behind for autographs, but quite soon we were on our way back to our hotel.

When we got back to the hotel, we were all buzzing and shaking in the aftermath of that incredible and most unusual evening of bicycle racing. I found it almost impossible to sleep that night, and the next morning, the three of us decided to walk along to town and check out the shops. My feeling that people were looking at us was confirmed pretty quickly as a shopkeeper dashed out to the street in front us, saying, 'Obree! Obree!' He beckoned us into his shop, where he gave me a nice gift and back out again, where he gesticulated to see if it would be all right to take a photograph. He got one of his assistants to take a shot with him and me together, before he announced proudly to the people in the street about who I am, although the only bit I made out was, 'record man del ora'.

The rest of our visit to town took a similar pattern and in the end, I had a good armful of gifts to remind me of the time we went to Crema. That was not the end to my riding commitment in Italy, as we would be moving on to Forli, which is a good five-hour drive from Crema, but the organiser from Crema was also helping at Forli, and he arranged a driver to take us across there and back. The atmosphere at Forli was good, but it was not such a good night of the week for a track meeting, and the exceptional response at Crema did not quite happen there, although I can remember spending ages just doing signature after signature.

The ride at Forli was cleverly thought about by the organisers, as they had me ride against the junior team pursuit squad, who were capable of about the same as I was as senior individual champion. Everything was totally straight up as far as I knew, and I do not know of any whispers in the ear to make it look good, as far as the juniors were concerned, although it is possible that they knew instinctively not to humiliate me if they were riding up my tail. That never happened as it turned out, and the race was touch and go all the way as to who would win, as I went flat out all the way. In the end, it was so close, and I was so tired on passing the line that I did not know if I had won or lost, and because of the language barrier, I had to wait to see where I was directed on the podium to find out. But not so, as these particular Italians refused to see a champion stand in silver position, so the five of us shared the top tier together, and I found out from one of the juniors with my pidgin Italian that they had just got it on the line.

Who won or lost was not really that important to most people, as the spectacle of the contest was all that mattered. On the long drive back to Crema, I spent a bit of time thinking about what it was that made these people's sport so vibrant and alive. Before, where I had thought that a lot of people were just fanatical about the sport, now I could see that they were passionate about it, and I realised that it was the passion that had touched me so much in Crema that other evening, as opposed to fanaticism. I also realised that I could totally empathise with that philosophy, as I would find it difficult to be fanatical about anything because I was too much of a realist, but being passionate about cycling was a sentiment I could totally relate to in the present tense.

Our few days at Crema were over soon enough, but the time I had spent there seemed like so much longer as I boarded the plane with my huge cup and the memories that I will cherish. I thought it was such a great pity that Anne had not been there to enjoy the experience, but at least I could show her the largest cup I had ever 'won'. It was called the Baffi Memorial Trophy, and because it was soldered shut, it had tiny beads of solder inside, so when I showed it to Anne, I told her it was some of Baffi's ashes inside. The cup was relegated to the garage until I told her the truth.

It was not long after our Italian trip that Martin and I set off on what would be a four-week continuous tour of European track venues. I believe the first of them was Grenoble, where we had been booked into a really nice hotel. We decided that we would forego the hotel menu and seek out a good curry, so after a long search and asking a lot of locals, we ended up in this tiny place in the back streets. It was nothing like Glasgow in either quality or quantity, not to mention price. We headed back to the hotel a bit disgruntled, only to find a police cordon at the front of the building.

Showing our key and giving a name against a list, we were let in, and in the foyer there seemed to be a bit of excitement. A man with strange bright clothes stepped into the lift, accompanied by two policemen, so Martin and I took the same lift. Halfway up, Martin nudged me and said, 'Do you know who that is? It's the Dalai Lama!' – and it was. At least I got to share a lift with the Dalai Lama, because I have scant memories of the racing there, except that I was riding a pursuit event of some kind.

The next stop on our tour was Zurich, where the temporary track was revealed for its once-a-year usage for the six-day race. It was one of the oldest indoor tracks in the world, and I had heard reports from Danny Clark, the Australian rider, that it ran fast because the wood is so well matured, like an old Stradivarius violin. The ride there was a pursuit against a four-man team pulled from the six-day race, who were riding standard bikes. I remember being delayed in some way just before the start, and running up the tunnel just in time to be introduced to the crowd, before mounting Old Faithful with no other warm-up.

Either I was on good form or Danny was right about the wood, but pretty quickly into the ride, I was way up on the six-day quartet, and I had to swing up to the very perimeter of the track on the banking to avoid a rider dropping back. I eased up from pushing it to the max, and humiliating the four-man team, and still finished with 4-25, which was just five seconds short of my own world record.

I spoke to the other riders after all the racing was finished, which was about 2 a.m., and they explained that they were pretty stuffed from the racing to be doing good times in team pursuit. It was after Grenoble and here that I started to pick up the vibes of resentment as riders saw me stepping up for five minutes and getting paid more for it than a lot of them were netting for six days. I had a feeling I was viewed like a humming bird that sucks the nectar and flits on to the next flower. It is fair to say that at the same time, I was treated with utmost respect by most riders.

That was that, and next on our schedule was Geneva, where Gerald Oberson and Daniel Perroud were organising a one-night track meeting, where a revenge match between Chris and me was the central theme of the evening. We were there a couple of days beforehand, and it was Gerald who took most to do with us by showing us round Geneva and escorting us back and forth from our five-star Hotel du Rhône, where Martin and I certainly must have looked out of place amidst the suit-clad guests.

I had been riding on the track since I arrived, and I quite enjoyed being on it, because it was so different from the tracks I had ridden previously, in that it was a diminutive 166.6m, as opposed to the 250m that I was used to. I liked swooping round on the top of the track on Old Faithful, down to the bottom line for extra velocity and 'pulling Gs' on the 52° bankings. It was not an easy track to ride for pursuiting, because the extra gravity on the bankings could almost double your weight, so keeping a good line at the bottom without drifting up the track took a lot of skill whilst giving a full-on effort in your ride. I probably had an advantage over the state-of-the-art pursuit rider, because the large gear I favoured meant that I could lean on the pedals a bit, which helped soak up some of the downward force from the tight bankings and my crouch position was inherently more stable in these conditions.

Chris had arrived the day before to check out the track, and he explained to me that after the end of season time trials, he had gone into winter mode to rest a bit before the long campaign to follow in his season to come, and for that reason, he just did not know what to expect from his form. We both knew that because it was a small track, there would only ever be 85m between one of us catching the other, and that it would only take a small difference in our form for one of us to be humiliated. When we spoke, we sort of edged round that fact without actually saying anything, but in the end I knew that when it came down to it, I would stick the knife in but I would not twist it. I understood it as a mutual, yet unspoken, professional understanding.

On the night of the event, the hall was filled to capacity, and the track centre was mobbed. We were introduced like combatants in a wrestling match, with spotlights, razzamatazz and rousing music. In the ride itself, Chris did not know if he was up or down on me at all, as it was impossible to see across the track past the track-centre diners and the wall of bodies in the way. The arena was partially darkened for effect, but Martin managed to stand on a chair at the trackside, and pass simple finger signals to me about my position against Chris – in seconds, up or down, with one hand for the number of seconds and the other to say if I was ahead or behind.

Well, before halfway, my lead had grown alarmingly to about three seconds, and if I kept going at this rate, I would be on top of him before long, and I would be in the same straight. At this point, I felt fine and decided to ease off the gas a bit, because with the form that I had obviously acquired from my previous track appearances, I knew I was in total control, and winning without insulting Chris by passing him mid-race became my objective. At the end, there was four seconds between us, and I finished with 4-28, a very quick time for a tight track, and even Chris's time of 4-32 showed world-class form. We spent another day in Geneva with Gerald and his family, which strengthened further my instant friendship with him.

After the Geneva meeting, Martin and I headed back to Scotland under pressure to attend a sports award hosted by the *Sunday Mail*, and when Anne and I were there at the plush dinner, the reason they were keen to have me became apparent, as I had won the top sportsman award for the year. It was a dinner-dance, and it was my first chance to chill out in ages, and as such it seemed obligatory to partake of the red wine in moderation. It was a good function, but unfortunately I still had not learnt the lesson from the past that there is no such thing as moderation for me, and in keeping with the trend that had been set by that first pint when I was fifteen, I was intoxicated by the end of the night.

Anne was pretty annoyed by it, to say the least, especially after another of my drunken diatribes about how I hate myself and how she should leave me 'because they are all right about me – I am useless and not worthy', which I again had no recollection of in the morning, and this account comes only from what Anne and others have recounted to me. What I did remember early in the morning was my flight to Dortmund to race against the ex-world champion, Jens Lehman, that evening.

I was still half intoxicated and half hung over as I checked in for my flight, and by the time I reached Dortmund via London, I was sober but completely drained – physically and mentally. I only had a short time at the hotel to ditch my bags and get ready for the track, and all the while my body felt beat-up, but I had to make do with strong coffee and plenty of water. When I got to the track, I knew I had done a stupid thing and I was not sure how much slower I would go, but the way I felt was pretty sure a well-deserved humiliation was on the cards. In an attempt to minimise my humiliation at the hands of Jens Lehman, I offered him the 'double indemnity' in plain English, where if I am clearly going to win, I would hold back from catching him, and vice versa. Unfortunately he turned me down flat and said that we just race direct, come what may.

From the starting blocks, I just rode as best I could and hoped that I could keep it going and try to avoid being lapped by the German. Jens always starts hard, but after a kilometre we were even, and from then on in, my alcoholic paralysis – less than 24 hours ago – seemed to mean nothing as I scorched round the boards to catch Jens in 3 kilometres. I had no professional qualms about rubbishing him in front of his home crowd, as he had refused to take out his verbal insurance policy, and I carried on for the full distance on my own to set a new track record of 4-28. Jens was all right about what might normally be a little unprofessional in front of an opponent's home crowd because he knew he had given me permission. Luckily there was no problem between us as professionals and it turned out that he was a really nice guy in real life, and he and his wife even gave me a lift back to the hotel.

After I arrived back home, victorious and with a very thick wad of Deutsche marks in my back pocket, Anne was even more forgiving than she already had been, but she knew my behaviour was not normal and that my inferiority complex, self-hatred and lack of confidence were deeply ingrained, but not so deeply buried, and that they stemmed from my childhood.

Soon after this, I had to head out to Bordeaux, where I would be riding against Chris in a three-race series of pursuits during the six days – one on the Monday, one on the Wednesday and one on the Thursday. To add to my schedule, I would be flying to Brussels Airport on the

Tuesday morning to race at Ghent against Philippe Ermanault before flying back on Wednesday to meet Chris again that night.

I travelled alone as my friend Gerald was coming to Bordeaux and he would give me any help that I needed. When I got there, I met Gerald and settled in at the hotel, we met Chris and his manager and we talked about how if it happened to be close in the races that it would be more entertaining for the public – especially if it was one each, going into the third and final race. As it happened, Chris happened to win the first of the three races by a narrow margin, before I headed to Ghent for a man-to-man confrontation with Philippe.

When I arrived, I met Philippe, and it was he who offered the double indemnity policy of no humiliation. We both had too much respect for each other to want to trash the other in the off-season, but each of us knew it would be a hard race, as I had heard that he had reasonable form. It was not a straight ride against Philippe, as both of us had to defeat a Belgian rider to progress to the final. Philippe dealt with his opponent easily, but my ride was a different story, as a rider, whose name escapes me, started so fast on the small track that he closed on me fast in an unsustainable burst of speed from the gun. My own arrogance and complacency played a part, as I started slower for him than I would have for Philippe, because I knew he was a slower rider, but I soon knew about it, as he covered the 85 metres between us and was sheltering on my back wheel to get his breath back before coming past me for victory. Everyone in the crowded stadium were on their feet, including Eddy Merckx, as they could not believe the spectacle before them.

At this point, there was still 3km to go, and all he had to do was draw his front wheel level with mine and he was the victor, and all I could do to prevent him was to hit top pace so that, even on my wheel, he would be struggling. The inevitable happened and he sprinted off my wheel to take the race, but the combination of full air resistance away from my slipstream and the spurt in effort I put in when I sensed him attacking, prevented him from quite getting his nose ahead. The Belgians were going wild as he got within inches of the biggest upset of the season, but it was not to be, as he tried the same tactic two or three more times and failed by the smallest of margins. Not that it mattered because all he had to do was hold my wheel until the end, which was not very far now.

At this point, I knew I had to attack with everything I had to try and dislodge my opponent. On the second such attack, a small gap opened and I kept going with everything I had to get free and gain back my time. It was all out to the line, and it was a close result, which, as luck would have it, went my way. The ride against Philippe was textbook stuff in comparison, and although I finished with a two or three seconds' margin over him, there was never any question of being able to catch him, even in this small track.

I stayed at my friend Rudy Seger's house, whom I had met at the Isle of Man Cycle Week, before heading back to face Chris again at Bordeaux. The ride against Chris was the same 4km pursuit as on the Monday, but this time I was more sure of victory and I knew that if I happened to win it, then it would be one race each going into the final, where the rider with the form would undoubtedly win the series, and it would be an entertaining final – as we had all agreed. It was a close race most of the way, and on the last half-lap, I looked across to check that I had a reasonable lead over Chris as I sped up to the line for victory. Unknown to me, as I made towards the line, Chris had put a race-winning half-lap in, to clinch a very close 2-0 lead over me.

I was not pleased at the situation, and Gerald certainly was not, and our anger grew, the more we thought about it. The last race was over 10km and was worth double points, and I was so riled that I decided that my full form would shine, come what may. Out of the starting gate that night, I had no concern for professional etiquette – or anything else, for that matter – and I could and did pass Chris in just 4km, and Gerald told me that Chris was on world-record pace for 10km when I caught him. This time I was riding round with the flowers, while Chris was left to ponder on his unprofessional humiliation. Things were not very good between Chris and me after that, and they certainly were not very good between Peter Keen and me, and my Swiss friend Gerald did not bite his tongue when it came to squaring the debate. Still, it had been a good week of racing and I had enjoyed really good support from the public, although some of the astute among them were wondering how my form could happen to be reasonable on Monday and Wednesday, and exceptional on Tuesday and Thursday.

About this time, I was invited to the Scottish Sportscene Sports Personality of the Year Awards. 'Sportscene' is a sports programme on BBC Scotland, and the awards were based on voting from the public. The programme was broadcast live from the studio. I was amazed to have won ahead of all the footballers and sports stars, like Stephen

Hendry and Colin Montgomerie. I was invited to the British awards, but Stephen Hendry's scepticism about them was confirmed when we both received two seconds of airtime for our trouble.

Then I was back on the fast lane again with a visit to Paris for a race against Philippe again – this time on home soil and on a slightly larger track, which would give Philippe a marginally better chance than our last encounter. I rode as hard as I could and the lead see-sawed back and forth in a man-to-man battle where no quarter was given and none was asked. With a lap or so to go, I could see with a bleary glance that we were about even, and whoever could find the most within himself on this last lap would win. Philippe must have been more desperate for the win in front of his family, as he pinched it from me on the line. I had tried my best, but as I saw him going round and the delight of his family, I remembered how he had wept in defeat at the Worlds, and I was glad in a way that he had won, to become a hero for a day in his own back yard.

While Martin and I were in Paris, we had to see Gaumont about a proposal to make a film, and we also went to *L'Equipe* to do an interview that would be more in-depth about me as a person, at which point, Martin decided that it would be a laugh to make me look bad in front of the press, by way of a practical joke. The joke worked in a lot of respects by giving me a sort of comical image, which was exactly what I had hoped to dispel, after the washing machine heritage in Old Faithful had caused me to be wrongly portrayed as a less than serious engineer, designer and person. I was pretty fed up after that, and I thought about how other people seem to control me all the time. I thought about Vic and how much better he would have been at that meeting. He would have talked over me to take control, like Martin did, but at least he would not have rubbished me in the process.

Martin and I had a few more venues to go to across Europe before finally getting back home, and it was not too soon for me. I was starting to get pretty jaded with it all, and sometimes I would wake in a darkened hotel room in a panic, trying to remember where I was. I would jolt my memory to remember what country, what city I was in or what airport I left last. As I would fumble for a light switch, I would be totally confused about everything, especially about what I was doing there in a foreign place I had absolutely no recollection of getting to, and certainly no recollection of my purpose there.

My last venue of the year was Vienna, which was a two-ride affair as part of the six-day race, and Anne was coming with me to make a bit of a holiday of it. I cannot remember much about who I was riding against in the two rides, but I went pretty quick in both of them. When the organiser asked me if I would try to attack for my world record for 4km, I agreed but I told him honestly that I could very likely get close to it, but I would be less likely to go under it.

On the day of the ride, we decided to go into the city on the train, and on the way out, I bumped my mouth and the cap came off my front tooth. Instantly, the freezing air stung into the exposed stump. To make matters worse, we lost our way back to the right tram line, and we went round in circles before we could find it, and we stumbled into the track centre with just enough time to warm up for the attempt. I was taking it seriously, with my fastest helmet and skin suit, and I was keen to do well because the hospitality we had enjoyed was outstanding, and a fast ride that could create some excitement was what I was hoping for. Alas, it was not to be, as I only went as quickly as my other rides.

Not long after that, it was Christmas, and that marked a year exactly since it all began with my uncanny self-belief about breaking the hour record. All the appearances were over, and I could look forward to a rest, at least until our second child arrived in March – or so I thought!

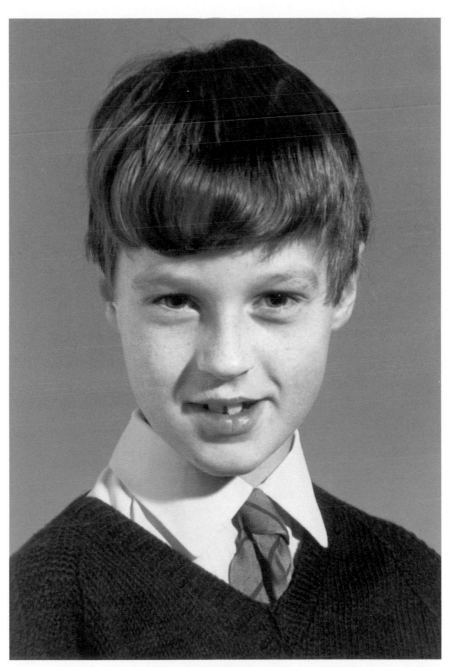

Me aged nine.

Wallacehill club 1981. The two men who influenced me most: Billy 'show the b*****ds' McFarlane on the right with bike and Jimmy 'get the miles in' Train – second row from front, right.

Loudon Road Club group photograph 1983. Trophies all round.

The Scottish 25 miles national championship, 1987. I risked riding a single gear but, on the day, it blew a gale. Dave Hannah won in 56 minutes 11 seconds and I was second 41 seconds behind.

Attacking the hour record at Meadowbank in 1989. Spot the spectators.

Jimmy Train enjoys a celebratory cuppa after I break the British Hour record at Meadowbank in 1989.

Our wedding day, 1 September 1989.

Spring 1993 at Irvine Cycles – my workshop would never be this tidy. The goggles offered protection from the brightness of the jacket.

May 1993–the chips are down and it's time to get even.

Ewan teaching me to play guitar.

Big brother Gordon, Ewan and me. I'm the one with the feather in his cap. I build frames better than I hang pictures.

Richard from Specialized – one of the few who never lost faith.

Me and the Junior squad at Forti in 1993. 'I bought you a beautiful plate, darling'.

August 1993: Chris and I receive awards for our hour record successes, four weeks before our big head-to-head at the world championships.

L'INCROYABLE MISTER OBREE

Phénoménal Graeme Obree ! En réalisant 51,596 km dans l'heure samedi près d'Oslo, l'amateur écossais a démythifié le record détenu depuis 1984 par Moser (51,151 km). Seul journal présent, L'Équipe vous raconte tous les détails de cet exploit. (Pages 2 et 3)

LE QUOTIDIEN DU SPORT ET DE L'AUTOMOBILE

L'ÉQUIPE

LUNDI 19 JUILLET 1993   ★   48ᵉ ANNÉE — N° 14 680 — 6 F

FRÉJUS. — Paes (ci-dessus) avait donné le ton en battant Boetsch. Krishnan s'est mis au diapason.   (Photo Jean-Marc POCHAT)

Les arènes de la peur

Insoutenable suspense à Fréjus : le match décisif entre Gilbert et Krishnan a été interrompu par la nuit à 4-4 au cinquième set. Il reprendra aujourd'hui à midi. (Page 12)

PERPIGNAN. — Un quart de roue sur Perini (à dr.) qui fait le bonheur de Lino.   (Photo Denys CLÉMENT)

Lino sauve l'honneur

Le Breton a remporté hier à Perpignan la première victoire d'étape française du Tour 93. Aujourd'hui, place aux Pyrénées, où seul Rominger paraît capable de menacer Indurain.
(Pages 4 à 8)

ÇA MARCHE, TINTIN, ÇA MARCHE !

The French sports paper L'Equipe thought my achievement was incredible and they gave me their front page, and their second page, and their third page! (See Appendix, page 240)

On the other hand the British tabloid press would not take me seriously. This piece, from the *News of the World*, was entitled 'I'm on Wash Cycle' and ended by saying he was certain to reclaim his world hour record '. . . on Hotpoints'.

Celebrating the hour record at Bordeaux in 1994. But I am caught in a dilemma: mum and wife are both present but only one bunch of flowers.

Here I am, World Pursuit Champion in 1995, in space age kit and demonstrating my 'Superman' position.

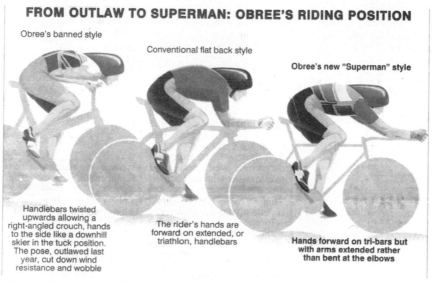

FROM OUTLAW TO SUPERMAN: OBREE'S RIDING POSITION

Obree's banned style

Conventional flat back style

Obree's new "Superman" style

Handlebars twisted upwards allowing a right-angled crouch, hands to the side like a downhill skier in the tuck position. The pose, outlawed last year, cut down wind resistance and wobble

The rider's hands are forward on extended, or triathlon, handlebars

Hands forward on tri-bars but with arms extended rather than bent at the elbows

A graphic from *The Times* in April 1995 illustrates the different riding positions. The governing body said if I used clip-on bar extensions they would be happy. Not!

(From left to right) Sandy Gilchrist, me, Doug Dailey and Yvonne McGregor in Columbia.

Ewan and Jamie providing the extra pedal power, in summer 1996.

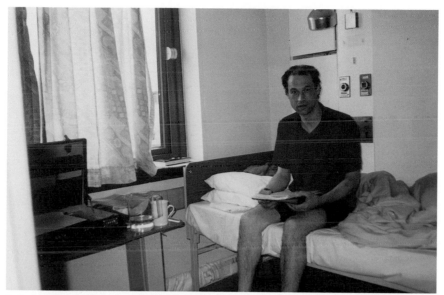

What does an author have to do to get peace and quiet? I worked on my manuscript whilst recuperating in hospital.

The Obree family, summer 2003.

twelve: it's take-back time

It was the start of 1994, and after a year of intense and continuous training and racing, I was just as much mentally fatigued as physically, to the point where I could only ride at one pace – as hard as I could. At this point, I do not think I could have raised it beyond the red zone, even to win a major championship. Such was my fatigue-induced inability to psyche up latterly I was riding races like a wind-up toy, where I would just count down the bleeps and go.

Needless to say, I was glad when I got off the cycling merry-go-round and was able to get into the way of the normal off-season by way of recharging my batteries, with longer gentle rides and time spent at home – even if it was three months overdue. I was not too concerned about raising it that side of March, since the World Championships were late in the year, and I qualified by right as the defending champion. I was just getting into the way of my recuperation programme, when I received a phone call from Gerald who, having his ear close to the ground, had found out that the UCI were going to make rules to outlaw the tuck position on the 7th May.

I had already seen what Francesco Moser had done with the riding style, and so had the UCI, and they did not like the way it was going. Francesco is an innovator – that is partly why I had admired him over the years – and if anyone was going to take the position further, it was him. He had invited me to train with him in Milan when we were both at the cycling exhibition and I had seen his forward saddle and chest support at the time. What an experience it was to ride with the man who had been inanimate on a poster for all these years – the man who had ridden the ultimate time trial, the Hour Record. What's more, it was something else to give him a hard time on my wheel with the form that I had at that time. There is another talent that Francesco has that I can reveal in this book – he can half an apple with his bare hands whilst driving a car, which I discovered to my amazement on the way to the track. After I had seen this, I whiled away many an hour trying to emulate the same feat in the comfort of my own home, but with little success.

Francesco was set to use the position during his tenth anniversary ride in celebration of his famous ride in 1984, and what Gerald said in his phone call was that I would have to use my position too before the cut-off date. He was proposing that he and Daniel could organise an hour record attempt – with sponsorship and everything taken care of – at the end of April, so I would have ten weeks or so to train. Because it was Gerald, I knew that everything would be sound, and there and then my winter recuperation came to an abrupt end as a result of circumstances. I got straight into training again, which was not as straightforward as it might have been, because most of the track appearances I had ridden in were 4km pursuit efforts, and most of the time that was as much training as I got before shuffling through airports to the next venue. The net result was travel and emotional fatigue, as most races came with a whole lot of talking and social interaction but very little longer-distance aerobic time-trial type efforts. Sometimes a ride could be as late as 2 a.m. amidst the smoke and beer aroma of the six-day arena.

At that time, the lack of control over my direct affairs, as well as Martin's inappropriate remarks to the press – which had seriously damaged my image – meant that Anne and I had to terminate as gently as possible what had originally been put forward as a very short-term arrangement. Martin had been thinking about the USA before he got engaged to Miriam, who has dual nationality, and now that we had settled financially, he and Miriam had enough money together to emigrate, and everything ended amicably.

That was the end of another era in my short career, but also the start of a new one, as I was setting forth on a quest to regain my hour record and to defend my title. I had heard from great champions of the past that doing it the second time round can seem harder in terms of sheer drive and total motivation. For me, there was no problem with motivation, as I knew that I could have gone a lot further than I did at Hamar if things had gone perfectly from the start – not to mention the largest part of my drive, which was to not fail at all costs.

Soon after I resumed my proper training, I went out to Geneva to see Gerald and Daniel about the hour record, which they would organise completely from start to finish, including sponsorship and travel. I signed an exceptionally good deal, where DPO (Daniel Perroud Organisation) would pay half the fee for a good attempt and the other half for breaking the record, and I need have no hassle with anything else except training. The exceptions to the sponsorship sign-over were the Specialized wheels, the bike frame and the shoes, because I had my own deals already that were based on bonuses for achievement. Gerald was a partner in DPO and it would be his job to run around to find sponsors and do deals with the media for direct coverage, but he was in a good position because he was centrally placed between Italy, Germany and France and could get by in four languages including English. His enthusiasm and belief were his greatest assets, and since he and Daniel had organised large events like the Davis Cup, then I felt safe to leave it in their hands while I concentrated on the sweat side of things.

There was also the ongoing project to build a genuine second bike that was as good as or better than Old Faithful. All the while that I had been doing the rounds in Europe, I would open my bike bag with apprehension at what could be my worst nightmare at that moment – Old Faithful suffering untold injuries at the hands of a baggage handler. All the while I promised myself that as soon as I got out of the circuit at the other side of Christmas, I would set about building mark II, which would also save Sandy and Doug from the risk of apoplexy at major championships.

Doug had helped me get in touch with Chris Field at Hotta Design, who had agreed to wrap the frame in carbon once I had built it to my own specification in steel. The main problem I had with Old Faithful was the bottom bracket, but this time I was able to finance the machining of a special shell that could be brazed onto the frame directly and this would accommodate the crank-mounted bearings directly. The design was altered slightly because of the carbon wrapping to follow, but it was effective as a frame already so I would not be relying on the carbon to give it its essential strength. In other words, the carbon was to give it a smooth aero shape but as it turned out, the frame ended up with a much stiffer rear end once the carbon had been applied.

Now that I had two bikes I felt much better about my hour record campaign and when I tested the complete bike, I was very pleased to find that it performed at least as well as Old Faithful. I had my two bikes and my training was progressing well, but the thing on my mind at that time was the imminent birth of our second child in mid March.

I had an arrangement for just after the due date to ride in South Africa for just over a week, and I thought this would be good for form. As the time got closer and closer, there was no sign, and eventually the time to depart came up, with still no sign of labour pains from Anne. All of the family were on hand and we decided that we should just go because it seemed like I could be back before anything might happen, and besides, there was only six weeks until I would be on the start line to face the ultimate truth again.

South Africa seemed like a good place to go for some good training because it was consistently warm, and although the flight was long, it did not involve much shift in time zone so I would not be suffering jet-lag at either end of the journey. I would be riding on the track at Cape Town, Durban and Johannesburg, as well as riding a road race in the Cape Peninsula that had 19,000 riders. Riders were set off in groups of 500 to avoid congestion, and groups would be setting out before the first light of dawn. It was a good training ride for me because I kept attacking, but in the end, the midday heat just killed me off with a few miles to go. On the track, I was riding pursuits, but I had plenty of opportunity to train on the road, and when I was at Johannesburg I took advantage of the 6,000 foot altitude to get a couple of good aerobic sessions in. While I was there I heard the news that Anne had gone into labour and given birth quite quickly, and that we had had a little boy who we named Jamie. That was the 22nd of March and I was back home a few days later but the emotion of it seemed to bypass me in the same way that it had done with Ewan.

Now we had two beautiful little boys and a bit of money behind us, we would be moving back to Irvine, where Anne and her family come from. Long before I had gone to South Africa we had agreed a moving-in date for a four-bedroomed house in Irvine, and our plan was to rent out our own house rather than sell it. Anne was more keen than me but I agreed with her logic that we needed more space with the children, and if I broke the record again there could be lots of media people wanting to do interviews with me, and it would be preferable to entertain them in our new, more spacious house.

The move was no hassle to my training, and in mid April the moment of truth had arrived for me as I set off for Geneva with two bikes and Gordon Stead from the bike shop. The idea was that I would train for a couple of days in Geneva's velodrome and then I would attack the world records for 10km and 20km, which were broken by

Chris on his way through to the hour record. When Gordon and I stepped out of the airport, we spotted the posters that said in French that I would be attacking these two records, but in even larger letters, it was rounded off by the notice of an hour record attempt. I had understood that the main attempt would be made at Bordeaux nine or ten days later, and Gerald, who had picked us up at the airport, assured me that it was Daniel's idea and that Bordeaux was the big hit as far as he was concerned.

The whole Geneva part of the campaign was created to provide a bandwagon of publicity for the proper attempt at Bordeaux and to satisfy sponsors who were Swiss-based. Gerald was an ex-pro himself and he understood that doing an hour at full tilt on a 166-metre track is just not sustainable because of the tight bankings. He reckoned that if I could manage 10 or 20km in record time, it would look good for the ride itself on the bigger, faster track. The first thing on my agenda was a trial run for the media, and that turned out to be a disaster as I was off the pace from the start, and only proceeded to lose more time as the ride went on. The press were not impressed by my initial trial but the big test for them would be my serious run the following night, under the pressure of real conditions. Daniel was not very impressed either as he had hoped to generate a lot of momentum within the press, which did not materialise.

The next night I was a nervous wreck, after being unable to get into the pace that I would need, but under proper event conditions and after a couple of equipment adjustments, I was hopeful that I could scrape a result from the edge of my pain threshold – as I had done many times before. One of the changes I made was to my helmet, which was a blobby type that I would have to wear because it was part of the sponsorship package. Gordon suggested that I could stretch the helmet cover over my own aero helmet so that I could get the benefit of slick aerodynamics yet still sport the advertising of the helmet sponsor. It was a tight stretch but it worked, which meant that I took to the start line with a psychological lift from the previous afternoon's bad ride.

The evening was organised to the high standard that Daniel and Gerald had set for the ride with Chris and me during the winter. Half of the show was taken up by the spectacle of kick-boxing with top names from the sport taking part and the other half of the show was me taking on three world records, including the one hour record itself. The build-up and whole atmosphere was first class, with dancing girls, spotlights, music and all the razzmatazz that a top event could have. The kick-boxers were on first and I would have to be ready to take the line at a set time – and ready I was.

I cannot remember which bike I stepped up with, but on the first and most forceful pedal stroke, the bottom bracket axle sheared in the middle with the immense twisting force that the left leg generates from a standing start. At that moment it was a case of absolute panic as Gordon, good to his trade, quickly changed over the rear wheel and shoes to my other bike while music blasted out in the arena to appease the waiting public. The record attempt quickly got under way and it was in my mind to do the 10 and 20km records but no more, because I knew that I could not even think about trying the hour record on this track where I would be hitting a banking every five seconds.

Gerald was giving me up a perfect schedule to be right on target to break the 10 and 20km records, and luckily I was able to get onto the pace and raise on it slightly in the early stages.

I knew that I should have had the basic pace to start with at least, because I had done a couple of really good pursuit rides in South Africa a month prior to this and had even broken the South African record, with 4-35, on an outdoor concrete track. After 5 or 6km I thought that, in terms of physical output alone, I might just be able to go to the 20km distance, but the constant centrifugal force on my body started to weigh on me very quickly, and well before 10km I was in agony, as my whole upper body started to seize up. It felt like I was riding with a large ruck-sack on my back, with an extra brick being thrown in as I rounded each 52° banking. I had already mastered the art of switching pedalling style between straight and banking – on the banking I would really kick in with my calf muscles, which helps offset the downward force on my legs and lift the pressure on my body as a whole. This had been instrumental in beating Chris in the pursuit here, and Philippe Ermanault at Ghent on the same size of track.

To maintain a pedal action like this for a longer ride is well nigh impossible, and even if it were possible, it can only reduce the near-double body weight to a manageable level. The short of it was that I could have thrown in the towel at 8km from sheer pain, but I counted down the seconds until the moment that I could escape the unseen fire burning through my body. At 10km, I sat up the moment that I knew I had a world record under my belt. Gerald and Gordon both understood that I had the fundamental pace, but that it was impossible to attack distance records on what seems like the wall of death after a short while. Daniel, on the other hand, was not quite so forgiving. Before the show was over, and while Gordon was dealing with the bikes, he asked me to come into the office for a talk. Gerald came in too, and as soon as we got seated, he let rip with his thoughts about how I was so unprofessional with my bike problems, and then not even doing 20km. He accused me of just being here for the beer and that all I was after was the half of the fee for attempting the record and that I had not trained or taken it seriously at all. Gerald stepped in pretty quickly to my defence, despite the fact that Daniel was his partner, and told him in direct language that he was wrong. At this stage everything was in French, but I had a good enough grasp of French and unambiguous body language to know exactly what the topic of conversation was. I had put my jacket on over my skin suit before going into the office, and I noticed that a Dictaphone that I was using to take down ideas for my book (yes it took me this long!) was in my pocket. Realising a classic moment could be passing me by, I switched it on for later interpretation. I am glad I did, as the discussion only got more and more heated between Daniel and Gerald, to the point where both men were thumping the table in defence of their viewpoint. At this point, Daniel made it clear to me that it was all off and the Bordeaux ride was cancelled because I could not break the record. My friend Gerald raced to my defence before I could, with the absolute confidence that I had not witnessed since Anne and her mum had broken their silence on the eve of my ride at Hamar. He stated in clear English, 'I know that Obree can break the record, I am sure, sure, sure!' as he thumped the table in front of Daniel for added emphasis. I was touched by this display of loyalty and belief that I had not experienced from anyone except my wife and her mum Theresa. At the same time, I was riled and concerned by the scene in front of me. To counter Daniel's claim that I was only there for the half fee for attempting the record, I stated that I would willingly go to Bordeaux on the premise that if I failed I would get nothing. After a continuation of the debate, it was agreed that it could happen like that, provided I rode 2/3 of the distance ahead of record schedule three days before the actual attempt. Angered and more determined than ever I stated that that would be just fine, but to try and lighten what was now a bad atmosphere with near-total fall out between these two former friends, I said that it would be on condition that Daniel shaved his hair when I did get the record.

I never needed a friend like Gerald more than I needed him now, and the first thing he helped me with was to repair the bracket spindle that had sheared. Gerald had been a professional for a short while and a merchant banker for much longer, but more than anything he was a hands-on man of boats, which meant he had the means and know-how to repair the bracket in his own small workshop. The other thing Gerald was helping me with was my training, and because I had so little time before going to Bordeaux, I had to make the couple of serious rides I could fit in really count, and that is where Gerald came in.

Overlooking Geneva is a mountain called Selev, which is not huge by Swiss standards but it is possible to do 3,000 feet of climbing. Since a main part of my self-made programme was strength training in a large gear, getting out there and going for it on my road bike would be ideal training. Gerald revved up his Honda Goldwing with Gordon on the pillion, and paced me out to the start of the climb, where every one of Daniel's fist pounds was fresh in my mind with every heave of the pedals on the relentless slope. What had happened had given me real drive to succeed, and Gerald's confidence only made me more fired up to step up there at Bordeaux and justify his trust in me. Ironically, the whole affair only served to heighten my fear of failure and my sense of how terrible that would be.

We did another aerobic session behind the motorbike before it was time to set off for Bordeaux. The atmosphere was heavy with enmity, as Gerald and Daniel just avoided each other at the departure lounge, and while we were in Bordeaux things did not really improve. I had a few days at Bordeaux before Daniel's big test, and it was strange setting out for the best part of the hour record in an empty stadium, but what had to be done, had to be done. With Gerald giving up the schedule from his laptop computer for Gordon to communicate to me via a black-board, I knew right away that I was hitting the pace with a smooth rhythm that I knew I could sustain. The smooth, solid boards of the velodrome were a delight to ride on after the small track at Geneva, and the sweeping curves and short straights were even better than the geometry of Hamar.

In the end I did over 53kph for 40 minutes, and everything looked fine for three days' time provided I could recover sufficiently from this effort before the big day itself.

There was nothing to be done now but wait and hope that nothing went wrong in the meantime. There was nothing I could do to improve my chances now, but there were plenty of things that I could do that would jeopardise my ride, such as having poor sleep or having something bad to eat that would upset my system. The food that Gordon and I were eating was becoming monotonous as we rejected about three-quarters of the hotel menu, which restricted us to boiled chicken with either rice or pasta. A couple of days before 'R Day' we asked the fluffy-white-hat-bedecked chef if he could make chicken curry but the reply was an indignant, 'Oui', as he explained he is a top French chef and can make anything. We came back that evening, and as we took our restaurant seats, the chef proudly came over with his chicken curry, which consisted of exactly what we had had every other night – boiled chicken and rice. The only exception was a light dusting of dry curry powder over the top. It was a treat to have a change from our mundane diet!

As time drew nearer, my nerves became more taut and the atmosphere grew more intense as press and media people began to arrive. Anne and her mum arrived along with my own parents and my brother Gordon, whom I would have asked to accompany me from the start if he had not been so tied up with work. I did not see much of my parents, as they took off on a trip through the Pyrenees and into northern Spain, but they would be back in time for the ride itself. The atmosphere between Gerald and Daniel did not improve either, but I hardly saw Daniel in the build-up period except for the eve of the record attempt when I was conscripted into kicking off a football match between Bordeaux and another French side who were vying for a place in the European Cup. Not only was I nervous about the forthcoming ride, but to kick off the match was more nerve-racking than anything, because I had absolutely no idea what was expected of me. I had never seen or taken notice of a football match being kicked off before. In truth, I had hardly ever seen a football match at all – either on TV or live. My mother could not stand sport of any kind on the TV at home, and my knowledge of it was scant to say the least, and my over-riding fear as I strode out to the centre of the pitch was exposing my total ignorance in front of a capacity crowd. I tried in a vain panic to ask in French what to do, but it was to no avail. As everybody was standing around waiting for me to do something, with the ball at my foot, I kicked it to the nearest available player and headed swiftly off the pitch. I forced myself not to run, as I could feel every judging eye burning into me, like I had done that day at primary school as I sat lonely as an exhibit to ineptitude.

That night we played Monopoly until quite late, and at a certain point, Gordon and Gerald mysteriously decided in unison that they had had enough and were going to bed. It was not until the next morning that I realised that my friends had really been looking out for me by giving me no option but to do the same. The morning of 'R Day' was like the calm before the storm, as the weather was dead calm and subdued and everything seemed so quiet and mundane just hours before cycling's greatest record could be broken.

That feeling of calm was deflated pretty quickly when we got to the track. The family members walked the 1km to the velodrome, and my mum, who had not been to a world-level event, could not believe that the overflowing car park and vehicles parked up and down every street were the result of this one record attempt, but closer inspection proved it to be true. I did not see them until I was almost ready to go out into the track centre, but my brother came round to the changing room to tell me to just go for it, come what may. My mum and dad were in the track centre along with Anne, who had Jamie, and her mum, with her.

There was a huge crowd assembled and there was a lot of media interest, including Eurosport, who were covering the event live. When I finally got to the line, the atmosphere was intense, and I realised at this point just how much everything centred around me and me alone. At Hamar I did not get that feeling because the crowd was tiny, but now with this huge crowd and with the absolute faith that Gerald, Anne and her mum had shown in me, the fear of failure and the determination to succeed were both more intense in me than ever.

The most important thing for me to do was to get level with the schedule and into a rhythm. Thankfully, as things turned out, I was racing constantly on record pace from the start, and at the half-way point, I had a bit of a cushion to fall back on if need be. At that point, I was averaging my previous 53kph, but from there things just got so hard as that usual feeling of hanging on and hanging on to the pace while my body went through hell started to take over. My average speed started to drop down and down, and I could see my cushion being eaten into, and in the last 15 minutes it was absolute hell just keeping my cushion up. The last five minutes seemed longer than the first half hour, but I had been here before, and nothing on earth was going to prevent Daniel from shaking my hand at the end of this ride. I had the usual syndrome of numbness in my extremities, especially my scalp, and overall physical and emotional exhaustion, but it felt so good to be out of the emotional vice I had been squeezed in for the previous two weeks. Things ended amicably between Gerald and Daniel once it was all over, and Daniel knew I had been genuine all along – but he never shaved his head!

After the ride I was surrounded by a scrum of people, and in the centre were the media people who all wanted interviews and photographs, which took quite a while to break free from, which was a pity because I wanted to go to the crowd who had come to support me. All the family were there with me in my moment of glory, except my brother, who adopted the role of a shadowy figure in the background, because he had always hated cameras and publicity. At the champagne reception afterwards, he came up and gave me a brotherly hug, but little did I know that that would be the last time I would see him alive.

At that reception, there was a drunken gatecrasher who was more fanatical than anyone else in the room. He made a bee-line for my mother, whom he proceeded to kiss on both cheeks, and when she directed him to 'Papa' he was treated to the same greeting as her – the response from the British male was the funniest sight of the day. It was a happy, smiley time all round, and we took photographs in the sun, before heading back to our respective countries to quietly return to our pre-record lives. Post-record, the lives of Anne and me would be full of press interest and hype to deal with on our return, as well as our hoped-for sponsorship dealings.

No matter what transpired in the wake of my ride, I would be justified in carving out a clear run for the World Championships since I had gone a long way to achieving my season's target before the end of April. One thing was for sure and that was that I would be in danger of being too fit, too early. Since I had effectively missed my off-season, I was in real danger of suffering fatigue and burn-out unless I satisfied myself with lighter training and domestic racing for a while. Those were my intentions on my return, as well as spending some time with my family in our new house. Life was certainly less stressful, and in my spare time I would be looking for a wise investment for my hard-earned cash.

thirteen: losing my grip

After the hour record, nothing much really happened. I half expected phone calls and invitations to track meetings, but all that it stimulated was interest from sponsors for the season, and the World Championships that would take place at the end of the season. I hardly raced at all for a couple of months after the Hour, and I also missed the British 25-mile Championship for a reason that I have now forgotten, but I think that the lack of Chris Boardman made it seem like a non-event to me.

Two weeks after my non-participation in the English event, I took part in Jimmy Train's memorial race, which was also a 25-mile TT. Jimmy had died not long after I had become World Champion in 1993, and it had been one of the most fulfilling moments of my life to visit him in hospital with my rainbow jersey and medal. The club had decided that a one-off event should mark his passing, and that the event should be meaningful in stature. Jimmy's long-time friend George Miller was organising the event and he had managed to persuade the winner of the British 25-mile Championship to come up to Ayrshire along with a lot of top time-trialists to compete, along with myself.

I was in good form that day, and I knew the course well as it was the one I had ridden my first '25' on as a schoolboy and umpteen others since. The net result was that I had caught the champion, who had been set off two minutes ahead of me, and passed him before the finish. I had started fast, and after just five miles, George shouted up a signal to me that I was 15 seconds down on him, but I immediately knew that it had been two-minute gaps between the top riders at the end of the field, and worked out that I was in fact 45 seconds up! It was a fantastic result for me, and because the champion had been sporting enough to come up to Scotland to take me on, it meant that my non-participation in the championship two weeks earlier had been swept aside.

After that, there were a couple of track meetings that I rode and also a return to Denmark, where I was to ride the world's longest one-day classic road race, the Fin Rundt, which is a lap of the Island of Fin, where Copenhagen is situated. I was apprehensive before that start because I had never done well in races of this length, and with the diet of training I was on at that time, I was more geared towards short, fast races, like pursuits and time trials, but I reckoned if I boxed clever and did not over-expend myself, then I might just get through it. My plan worked for most of the race, but as the field split up and I found myself in a small group working hard near the head of the race, my fuse suddenly blew and I went straight from putting in a good effort to going straight back through the field. Pretty soon I was right out the back and in a state of complete exhaustion, and as I looked round at the voices from behind me, I knew I was the last rider still on the road.

The vehicle behind me was a single-decker bus, which the cycling club owned. And two of the riders were hanging out of the side doors and shouting to me to come in. I was lucky, as there was only one seat left in the bus, and this is where the best part of the field had disappeared to. I had already spent five hours racing, and had done 220km, but with quite a long way to go. I felt bad that I had not gone the distance for the sake of being professional about my sport, but the Danish riders in the bus assured me it was fine, as I had gone most of it pretty much in the action.

As quickly as the circus came to town, it had gone, and I was left alone to stay over at a motel, where I would be picked up early in the morning and driven to the ferry to take me to the airport, where I would fly directly to Belfast. I would be riding in Belfast in a criterium (circuit race) at Newtonards. In a state of exhaustion, I would have no trouble sleeping, but before I did, I would have to set an alarm. To my horror, I found that I had neglected to pack one. I sought out somebody from the motel, but it was locked up and abandoned, like a ghost town, so I had no choice but to go to plan B. I had met a man called Jack Black a few months earlier, who makes a good living out of motivational talks and coaching the public on how to make the most of their untapped mental strengths. I had my mental strengths well honed by that stage, but he was talking locally and convinced me to come along and see what I thought about his presentation. Out of politeness and curiosity, I went along, and one of the things that he talked about was the ability to dispense with alarm clocks and tune the mind to waking at a certain time.

I went through the process that he had talked about, but I was surprised to find that not only had I slept through my silent alarm, but I had also failed to respond to the knocking on the door from my lift to the ferry. At this point, there was no point in panicking, as I had slept about three hours longer than I should have, and nothing would get me to the airport on time. I asked the caretaker who had shown up if there was anything I could do, and he suggested I go to the local airport to try my luck, but normally the flight was full. As luck would have it, one man on the fully booked flight did not show up, and I made my connecting flight to Belfast at little extra cost. Maybe Jack's subconscious system had meaning after all!

I was not long in Newtonards before it was time to race again. The race was round the town centre, and with the field being mainly Irish riders, it was hard. Sometimes in British races, the main group goes fast, in a steady way with occasional attacks, but in Ireland they take the bull by the horns right away, with attack after attack after attack, from the start. The problem for me was that I was the rider that everyone was marking closely, and any attempt to break clear myself was followed by four or five riders, and that was the way of it here. A small group of us finished together as the others would never let me get clear of them for victory. The finish was a short sprint after a tight right-hand corner, and the rider with the most bottle would win it, and as such, I finished third or fourth.

My trip to Newtonards was not over yet, as I had the Champion of Champions '25' to ride the next morning, and the criterium was just a warm-up. It was the same organisers as always – Bobby McGreeghan and Billy Kirk – and it took the same format, but there was not that traditional sense of challenge and excitement that there had been when Chris was my No 1 opponent. It was lucky he was not there, as my saddle clamp broke when my rear wheel smashed into a pothole, and I had to ride the last few miles with my saddle balanced on the bare pin. Luckily I had enough advantage over the next rider to get away with it, as well as the deep fatigue that had set in after three days of hard riding.

My season was now getting busier as the time for the World Championships drew nearer, and one of my next outings was to Sicily, where the championships were to be held. It was Richard Hemmington from Specialized who organised the trip through the company contacts in Milan, whom I met before taking the onward flight to Palermo in

Sicily. The whole idea of the trip was to get a feel for the track and to see round the time trial course at Catania. The track itself was pretty standard, and was a large outdoor concrete type that needs no special practice to ride on. The people there were unbelievably friendly and helpful in any way that they could be, and sidestepping rules, regulations, schedules and the like for the sake of common sense was refreshing to experience, especially for a status quo, jobsworth national like myself.

The ride round the TT course to be used in a few weeks' time for the World Championships was an experience that blew my mind at the time. Richard and I were invited to the mayor's office before being escorted by Sicilian police and motorbike outriders around the entire circuit of the course. It was midweek, midday traffic in the city of Palermo when the two leading outriders led the charge through the town with sirens and flashing lights full on, as their unambiguous hand signals forced oncoming traffic to pull over. One-way streets and red lights were no problem either, as we sailed through with a Judge Dredd-style flat-palm signal to other traffic to halt.

At one point I was riding along a dual carriageway and all traffic was prevented from passing by the police car and two outriders at the rear. The long tailback made me feel guilty, and I rode as hard as I could in the searing heat of this cactus-strewn island as the drivers behind waited patiently with little or no horn-blaring – as would be the norm in Italy. A couple of miles down the road, I realised there was a little more respect for authority than I would witness at home, as a man on a moped decided to quietly pass. He was clad in a suit and tie, with his briefcase sitting on a rack behind him. He almost made it, when the outriders realised that this was the dead turn on the course and immediately turned hard left, which cut right across his front wheel, which decked him and left him and his moped sprawled ignominiously across the highway. The two rear outriders stopped and I also stopped at a distance, but the leading outriders signalled to just go on; at the end of the ride, after going up a single-lane one-way street, I inquired about the man's condition. I was told that they had taken his licence and fined him heavily, but I was also told that he had been very lucky because if they had not been in such a rush, they would have taken his bike as well.

The trip was worthwhile, and I had been treated with total respect before I left, including an invitation to the council chambers, where they presented me with a gold souvenir of my visit. More importantly, I had seen the twists and turns of the TT course, and I had even seen a half-rotten dog at the side of the road on part of the circuit, which Richard and I were taking odds on still being there on the day of the race. I had even got to swim in the Mediterranean Sea, having gotten within 10 yards on my previous attempt, but the most important thing was that I could make my final preparation with a good knowledge of my destination, and with any luck it might even be a little cooler when I returned.

When I got back to the UK, it was time to work out my final choice of saddles and handlebars that I could use for the World Championships, to conform to the new regulations that would prevent riders from even starting to emulate Moser with a very prone position and chest support. I thought the regulations were a good idea to prevent things from getting out of hand. It was the UCI's job to regulate the sport, and they had given plenty of advance notice since their revised regulations came into force on 7th May. There was no problem for me to ride within the regulations, but the main difficulty I had was moving my saddle far enough back, because Old Faithful and Mark II were both built to accommodate a saddle position that was just behind the bracket line. Now I would have to either adapt a saddle or mess about with frame dimensions.

In the end, I managed to get my saddle just over 4cm behind the bracket line without resorting to metal-bashing this close to the championships, and with the rest of the bike conforming completely, I took a risk on the saddle getting through. I won the British Championships at Leicester again, and I managed to pin down Ian Emmerson, who was vice president of the UCI, as well as being president of the BCF (British Cycling Federation) about my bike, but I was not able to get an opinion about my riding style. Also at Leicester I talked to a couple of older riders and we had a good discussion about whether I should be riding the Commonwealth Games instead, since they were on at the same time. It had been a decision that I had had to make, but I was more influenced by European sniggers, as I tried to explain nineteenth-century military oppression of Third World countries, and how they celebrate this with the Games, than I was by Rule Britannia. The look of sheer incredulity that the Hour Record-holder would even consider attending such a gathering in preference to the World Championships made my decision immediate and absolute. The reality was that, of the 70-plus nations in the Commonwealth, only a small handful had any potential in cycling at all, as the others lacked the infrastructure and wealth needed to support a mechanical sport like mine.

With all that sorted out, I headed off to the World Championships. I was part of a very small team, a lot of riders having chosen to ride the Commonwealth Games because, ironically, a lot of the sport's funding was dependent on results there, as much as at the World Championships. There was Chris and me for pursuit, along with three or four other riders.

My hopes of getting slightly cooler weather were dashed, as the temperature just rose and rose to the point where it was 36°C at night, and to compound matters, there were only two hotels in Palermo that did not have air conditioning, and Doug (Dailey) had managed to get us booked into one of them. The situation was so bad that each of us had a fan at the end of our beds blowing down our bodies and bottles of water lined up to replace the sweat that we were constantly outputting, even when lying completely still. It was so bad that if an arm was tucked in beside your body, a puddle of sweat would gather there in a matter of minutes.

Eventually, Chris had enough of it and changed hotels, along with his coach Peter Keen. I might have done the same, but it meant that I would be alone, so I stayed put in the hope that the exceptional heat would pass. We knew it was exceptional, because even the local papers in Sicily were talking about African heat, and that was what it was, as we were not far from the Sahara Desert, and the wind was blowing it northwards to us.

I got used to it a bit, and pretty soon it was the day before the pursuit ride. Sandy had to get all the bikes ready, but most importantly the ones that we would be using the next morning for the qualifying round. For me, there was only one bike in the equation, and that was Old Faithful, as my Mark II machine was left at home because of the difficulty I had in moving the saddle back to meet the new regulation. Sandy was team manager as well as mechanic, and he had already been to the managers' meeting with the UCI, where my name had been mentioned specifically in a tone of hostility. I had also heard independently that the Belgian and US representatives were close to walking out in disgust at the UCI's contempt for protocol.

The faint plume of smoke rising from the summit of Mount Etna was a sign of the tremendous pressure building up under the surface, and the sight of it should have made me think about the present situation with the UCI. Sandy was tuned in, even though he was not a federation president, and he asked the UCI if they would check my bike right away, to be sure it was OK. It was not OK. While the officials measured and measured, they picked up on my known weakness – the point of the saddle that would allow me to comply – and they refused to allow me to use it, as they said it had not been produced to these dimensions by the manufacturer.

Sandy and I had a problem, and the only thing we could do was to find a commercial saddle that would slide far enough back to conform to the new regulations. Sandy went out hunting and came back with a saddle from a boy's bike, which he had been offered, and this finally took the tip to the 50mm behind the bracket line. On final inspection, the entire bike could no longer be stopped by the present regulations. This had taken up a good part of Sandy's day, and thankfully Chris's bike was quick and straightforward. The only thing left to do was to touch up the frame with white spray paint, which I had cycled into town for.

We cycled back to the hotel that evening, in the knowledge that at least there would be no problem with the bike the next day, and I slept as soundly as I could do, despite the ever-present heat. Sandy and I did not have much contact on a daily basis with the UCI, as our own British Cycling Federation President Ian Emmerson was not resident with the team but with the UCI instead, since he was its vice president. We had seen him, though, since he popped in to wish us good luck one day while we were at dinner. It was always a question in my mind how far he would risk his career with the UCI to defend a conflict of interest for the BCF membership. It did not matter much to me anyhow, as I never had much opportunity to seek his advice. Luckily the president of the US federation was a cyclist and a hands-on type of guy who insisted on spending time with the team, and I was always slightly jealous of the US riders for having a president who would stand up for them, with no political obligation to the UCI. He was someone who was actually among the riders and had a good insight into what was going on at the more expensive hotels, where our political masters were resident – clear of us 'practising' cyclists.

On the morning of the qualifying round, I woke as on any other – soaked in sweat with a slight headache. With water and a light breakfast, it soon cleared before I headed down to the track in good time for a light warm-up and to deal with any eventuality. As soon as I arrived, Sandy broke it to me that a new rule had been made up and that I would have to use different handlebars. I could not believe it, and at first I thought it was a joke, because if it was true, then surely Ian Emmerson would have helped in the UCI decision, and as my federation president, he would have phoned our hotel to let us know the evening before.

This he had not done, but it was still true, even though the rule was unwritten and unconstitutional. Not only was it unconstitutional, it was downright sneaky to change rules in the dark of night and conspire to keep them secret until the last moment from the only intended victim. The rule was then delivered to me verbally in French and then Italian, with all sorts of arm movements and gestures, which I did not quite get, but when I asked for the written rule, I was told there wasn't one.

This was an hour before my start time, and Sandy said that I might as well conform to their wishes, and Chris offered to lend me a pair of tri-bars, although there would be no time to adjust them properly. I only knew two modes in these situations, and those are either fight or flight, and in those short minutes I had snapped totally into fight mode. Sandy tried again to get me to just go with it, but by now I was invisibly seething. I responded with the statement that 'the hell I will,' and continued with a philosophical point of view that 'even God cannot give or take away my ultimate right – the right to go down fighting.'

That was my view and I stuck to it. I expected no help from either Ian Emmerson, my president or the BCF, since they had Chris to win the title, but I thought that some foreign countries would strongly object to the misuse of constitutional power, which they did. For the immediate moment I had more to think about as I could not be stopped unless I violated this new unwritten regulation during my ride. The bike conformed completely and they could not change those rules, because all the riders would be disqualified, so I could not be stopped from taking the start line.

For my ride, there were six or more officials at the trackside with red flags and walkie-talkies, and as soon as I started, they were looking for my hand touching my chest or shoulder. There was only one problem, and that was that normally my hand never does that unless I hit a bump, and the officials were half raising their flags but half holding back as they were unsure what to do. In the end, after 3km of the 4km ride, it was Hein Verbruggen on the start-finish line who took control of the situation and stood right out on the middle of the track, waving me to stop.

At this point I had had a gutful of 'fascist dictatorship' as I saw it, and I aimed right at Mr Verbruggen, who jumped aside in time to avoid collision, and at that moment I would not have swerved a millimetre to avoid a 35mph man-to-man impact. Despite the red flags and calls to stop, I carried on and I simply aimed at anyone who stood out on the track. I managed to secure a 4km time of 4-31, which despite the slight distractions, was third-fastest qualifier – the same sort of position I had won the championship from the year before.

I was, of course, disqualified and that was the end of my pursuit series, and now I would be thinking about the TT championship to be held at the course in Catania that I had seen already, but in the meantime there was a lot of press interest in what had happened. The press in Italy tore the UCI apart, and the leading newspaper, *Gazetta Dello Sport*, described them as 'Mafia' on the front page. The saga took up much more space than the end result itself, and Chris's victory was overshadowed to a large degree by the whole debacle. To add insult to injury, I was brought down further by a young boy's act as I tried to cross the six-lane highway as I left the track. I stood at the kerb, dazed and subdued by the morning's events, when the boy – no more than eleven – grabbed my hand and said, 'Bree, Bree, Bree!' as he gesticulated with his free hand to allow myself to be led before he immediately used his bare palm to force his way through the horn-blaring lines of traffic. Not only had my hopes and plans been destroyed in a few hours, but I had been helped across the road in my twenties! How much worse could it get, I wondered, as I bowled back to my team hotel?

After I had time to reflect on what had happened, I decided that I would use the handlebars that Chris had offered me, and with over a week to play with, I hoped that I would have time to adjust them and get used to the slightly different pedalling style that the position forced me to use. I had brought a set of tri-bars of my own, and had hoped to spend some time on them with a mind to future use, but they had nowhere near the range of adjustment that Chris's bars did, although they had a much longer reach, which was the way I was hoping to go with time to work on it.

I found TT preparation difficult because of the heat, and because I was totally unmotivated and emotionally drained by this stage, and all that I felt like doing was collapsing in a corner and closing my eyes to the world. The sleepless, sweat-soaked nights continued and my emotional indifference to everything that interacted with my senses deepened to the point where the TT was just one more race I had to endure before I could escape this never-ending nightmare.

On the day of the time trial, the lift and motivation I should have had on the big day were totally absent. I was propelled by a sense of duty that I must try my hardest, but I just wanted it over with so that I could move on to my next engagement in Sardinia before finally reaching the refuge of my own house. As a result of exhaustion and emotional deadness, it was as though I was not even there – it was like everything was going on around me, yet I was somehow not part of it or even part of the body I was existing within. I did not even laugh when the UCI checked my bike to the millimetre with a plumb line on a cobbled street.

The start of the TT was a long drag up the main street, and by the top end, I was already gasping for air and was suffering from extreme heat build-up. The car thermometer told us it was 42°C in the shade, which I could believe, because there was no cooling effect from the flow of air over my body at all, and it seemed that the faster I cut through the air, the more the intense heat would sear my exposed skin.

I was sporting a bright red one-piece aero helmet, with Specialized emblazoned right across it, and a medal place would have given me a good cash bonus by prearranged contract. In less than five minutes after starting, my head was on the verge of being hard-boiled and in an instant, I snapped and ripped it off, with the poetic parting phrase, 'Fuck you!' as I saw it career towards a large window through my sweat-blurred squint. Luckily it had a grille and that was the last I saw of the helmet until a boy came to me after the finish and said, 'You dropped your helmet, Mr Obree.' I remember the rest of the ride as a downhill struggle against heat exhaustion.

An overwhelming stench halfway through was a distraction from my self-imposed punishment as I instantly knew I was in Dead Dog Alley. Richard had been right – the fly-blown carcass was still there, and in 42° heat, the aroma was even more intense than before. I rode to the end, knowing I was on a really poor ride, but my belief in not giving up drove me on to the finish.

The result was as bad as I thought it might be, and I did not even make the top twenty. At least the whole thing was over and done with, and I could swiftly move on to Sardinia, where I was joining a lot of other well-known riders to take part in a criterium and a track meeting. It was not all bad, as someone who had been at the time-trial start area recounted to me that when the UCI officials had passed in an open-top car, they had been booed by the crowd as a result of the direct reporting of my disqualification by the Italian press.

There was a lot of talk at that time of suing the UCI over what had happened – not for the rule that they made up, but the unconstitutional way in which it was instituted and applied. For me, I could not take any more navel-gazing about 'what ifs' or litigation that could not happen and I just wanted to get on my way to Sardinia and a step nearer to going home. There was no time wasted in departing and there was one last supper together that evening before everyone would head off the next day. It was perhaps a little awkward as Chris and I were at the same table along with a few others. Chris had been so successful as his victory in the time trial now made him double champion, while my perform-ance had been so poor. My feeling of humbleness and humiliation was lifted temporarily by a little boy who came to our table looking for my signature on his jersey. I duly obliged and then the boy looked over to Chris and just walked away. That got me through the meal, but my sense of failure was deeply ingrained and was only destined to get worse as time went on.

I had to transport all my Worlds baggage to Sardinia as I was going directly via Rome. There, I bade farewell to the team and I took my own flight to Sardinia. I managed to avoid a huge excess baggage fee by surreptitiously poking my finger under the zipper of my fully laden bike bag and taking about 25kg off the real total, as was my normal practice. As I waited for my flight, it hit me that I was totally alone in a strange country and that I was an outsider, even within my own sport. The more time I had on my own, the more depressed I became about everything, although I had an approach to be part of a team, Le Groupement, to think about for the 1995 season.

When I arrived in Sardinia, I was taken to a hotel where most of the riders would be staying. It was a modern hotel with two wings – one was traditional and the one where I would be staying was space-age, where everything was glass or mirrors and everything was elec-tronically controlled. The place was deserted and every time I came and went there was no-one at reception, but music would play automati-cally and the mirrored elevator would take me to the floor where my crystalline chamber was situated. It was beautiful, but it was devoid of humanity and with its view of the semi-arid landscape, I felt as though I was disconnected from the human race. I was depressed before I came, but staying in this isolated and cold environment only made me sink deeper into my own self-made void.

I was there two days before the other riders, and when they did come I hardly saw them. At the riders' meeting before the track meeting to take place the evening after, one of the pros said that they were all going out for a ride in the morning, if I wanted to come. My gut feeling was that it was a leap into the unknown and that I should stay fresh for the track meeting, but my intense loneliness forced me to haul my jaded carcass downstairs for the ride. It was not an intense ride overall, and we only went out for three hours or so, but when the track meeting came round that night, I was almost in a stupor.

I had both Old Faithful and a regular track bike as I would be riding a few events. Most of the other riders were Italian and had no problem understanding the announcer, but for me it was a magical mystery tour from the off, as I had no idea how many events I would be riding, what events they were or how long they would be. The other riders would point to which bike I had to use as I heard my name on the tannoy, and I had also mastered the question 'quanti giri?' which meant 'how many laps?' which would give me some idea what I was stepping up for. The bunch races were the most confusing, as I would have to wait for something to happen before I could be sure of what race I was in, but to be honest, I do not think that the public were that bothered about who won what. Most of the big hitters of Italian cycling were there, including Ciapucci, Fondriest, Berzin, Bugno, Casagrandi etc, and seeing them all ride together on the track was what mattered more than anything.

The main event for me was a pursuit ride against Berzin and by the time it came round, I was absolutely stuffed. Because it was a bumpy outdoor track, Berzin decided he would just use his standard bike, whereas for me, Old Faithful was part of the show, and because I was so physically exhausted, I wore my fast helmet that I had thrown away the week before and my lightest wheels and tyres. In the end, though, the result was inevitable, but at least I had pegged the losing margin to a minimum. The result did not seem to matter much to anyone, and when it was all over, we were whisked back to the hotel for the riders' meeting about the circuit race the next afternoon.

It was an all-pro affair, and as such it was longer than the average circuit race in Britain, and I was fearful before the start that unless I raced clever, I could end up embarrassing myself because of how jaded and sluggish I felt. My fears were unfounded as I discovered on the start line, one of the riders who spoke some English explained that I must not go too fast and that after some famous riders attacked and came back, I must follow his wheel and attack, but not serious – just to show ourselves to the public. The whole race was at a steady pace and I finished well in the group, and everyone was happy with the way it went.

After a good evening of post-race festivities at the hotel, and another night in the space-age room, I headed back home via Rome airport, where my excess baggage caught up with me and took a huge chunk out of my visa. It was a mundane arrival as opposed to the year before, but pretty soon I would be off again to a race called the 'Kilometre de Mestre' which is a 1km time-trial where the riders compete twice side by side on opposite sides of the road. It is adjacent to Venice, and the whole event is organised and partly sponsored by Mr Cohen, manager of the local bank. I arrived on the Friday evening before the race on Sunday afternoon, and on the Saturday morning, a diminutive, friendly and outgoing man who spoke very good English introduced himself as Sandro, and said that Mr Cohen had arranged for him to show me the best of Venice before bringing me back for the evening meal. I saw most things there were to see, while being forbidden to spend any money, and I had been educated by Sandro as I went along as he seemed to know almost everything about the history of Venice.

When we returned to the hotel I was told that my wife was going to phone and that I should take it in my room. Anne broke it to me that my brother had been killed in a car crash. He had fallen asleep at the wheel and had died instantly on colliding with a truck. He worked in the South of England and was on the last leg of his journey north to see us. He had woken on a previous occasion on hitting the rumble strip, and his attitude to near-death was completely nonchalant, which no-one could comprehend but me, since we had shared the same child-hood. Nonetheless, while it was news that I could never be prepared for, on first hearing it had no emotional impact whatsoever, and that evening I felt no different to any other, except for the feeling of guilt that I was unemotional.

Mr Cohen arranged that I go to dinner with a local rider and his wife, rather than meditate alone in the hotel. It was quite strained because no-one really knew what to say, and for me, I felt an obliga-tion despite understanding the gravity of what I had heard. I could not stop thinking over and over about the loss and my life without Gordon, yet I remained unfeeling. I felt an urgency to get home, but it was impossible to change flights, and Mr Cohen asked me if I could ride just one leg of the 1km race so that the crowd could see the world hour record-holder in the flesh.

On the ride, my mind was elsewhere, as by now, I was desperate to get home to my parents as much as anything. As soon as I finished and made my way from the huge crowds, I packed and got ready to go to the airport for my flight home. Once I was seated comfortably in the aircraft, the relative solitude allowed my emotion to at least come to the surface and I started crying uncontrollably beneath my pulled-down skipped hat.

The next few weeks through the funeral and the start of the grieving process were tough, although I had not cried again since that time on the flight. I did a lot of reflecting about our lives and I felt guilty that I had not spent more time with Gordon in his adult life. There was a time when he had moved out of my parents' house to a small flat in the town, and I hardly ever visited, despite his proximity. I can see now that it was at the time when I had been involved in crime with Gordon Stead, and thinking that I could only be a burden to my brother, I could not conceive the idea that he could possibly want a person like me to come round. I spent a lot of my time in isolation and shame and I did not realise that my brother hardly ever came to see me because he did not like coming to the house for his own reasons. His death also made me feel like a sole survivor because we had been 'brothers-in-arms' at school, and because Gordon, Matthew and I used to go on tours together. I was the only one left to enjoy the memory of our trips.

I did not have long to come to terms with it when cycling commitments came along again. I had agreed to ride the six-day race at Bordeaux with Tony Doyle and I did not want to break my contract. The organisers had phoned to see if I was all right for it, and I explained that my form had dipped a bit, and after the Worlds it had been average at best anyway. Bordeaux was the last place I had seen my brother alive, because of our commitments, and it was poignant returning to the place where we had been together just a few months earlier.

I had seen plenty of the six-day circuit already, but I had not been a participant, and I had always wondered what it would be like to be part of the strange and insular world of the six-day circuit. Generally I was all right to ride the race mentally, except that I do not think that my concentration was as good as it could be. When I first arrived I was pretty apprehensive about it, because the majority of the racing takes the form of the Madison, which involves one partner being in the race at all times, while the other partner rides slowly on the higher part of the track. The riders switch places every time they converge.

My apprehension was based on fifteen or more teams switching places in the race constantly and the sharpness and skill needed just to avoid causing a stack-up. I had ridden one Madison at Herne Hill, in London, which is a bigger and much wider track, and that seemed to give me plenty of excitement – and near misses. It was not just the thought of causing a huge stack-up that bothered me, but also the fact that I was partnered with Tony Doyle, who was one of the world's very top riders at six-day racing, and who had also been world champion at pursuit in the '80s – the same Tony Doyle who had pulled my jersey all those years ago when I still had hairy legs. Because I was partnered with Tony, I wanted to race at a reasonable standard, but more than anything else, I did not want to do anything that would get us disqualified or withdrawn from the race through a loss of concentration.

Everything went fine at the six-day and I managed to stay upright, even though there were a few other fallers, but at the end I was absolutely exhausted. I could not believe that some of the riders were setting off for the start of the next six-day, and the masseur suggested that they probably used a caffeine suppository just to get there without falling asleep at the wheel. A statement that brought me right back to my brother. Not that that had been the first time, as a German motor pacer was the near-double of him from a distance, and the first time I saw him, I just froze while I came back to reality. In my confused state, I almost called out to him.

We ended up thirteenth and that was the last appearance of the year. It was not my last trip abroad, as I had agreed to open Martin and Miriam's shop in Arizona, whilst making a holiday out of it, and at some time before Christmas, I would have to go to a team meeting and launch of the Le Groupement team in France. Before that I was asked to an evening for Specialized dealers, and while I was there, I heard that the five times Tour de France winner, Miguel Indurain, had beaten my hour record by less than half a kilometre. At that point, I wondered what the outcome would have been if I had had more time to prepare, or if I had not had to do the two-thirds distance beforehand – maybe I could have done 53-plus km too.

I did not have long to wait before these ideas were truly academic, as Tony Rominger took the record to over 55km in two steps. When I did go to the USA in December, I was neither world champion nor hour record-holder, and it was now that the World Championship debacle, losing my record and the death of my brother started to tell on me – in mood and outlook on life. When I was leaving the USA, I got a message as I was waiting to board the plane that I must phone Frank Quinn, who was now my agent – a professional agent based in Dublin. The message was that I would have to board the next flight to Paris instead, as the Le Groupement team meeting was on the eve of Christmas Eve. It had been arranged that Robert Millar, also one of the Le Groupement riders, would pick me up at the airport and we would drive down to the south of France in time for the team meal.

With a delay for Robert at the airport and the long drive, we ended up getting there an hour or so late. There was no food left and the attitude of the team manager and director was that they should go hungry and that will teach them to be late. None of the other riders properly acknowledged us – or me in particular, rather – and the only riders who were friendly were the non-French, apart from Luc Leblanc.

I would have gone hungry indeed if I had not had my usual emergency supply of cornflakes and skimmed milk with me. The next day, we were taken to a garage showroom, where we spent the whole day checking out clothes and getting photos taken in the freezing cold. During this time, the director made a quick remark about me, and the self-centred French riders, who were assembling for a group photo, sniggered to themselves. By the end of the day I realised that I felt completely uncomfortable in this company.

Robert and I left together with our bundle of clothes and he gave me a lift to the ferry, and then onwards to Heathrow to be back in time to be at home for Christmas Day. On the way he explained that there would be 'medical backup' in the team, and that £2,000 would come out of the contract to pay for it. He explained that the real cost would be £8,000 and the team was making up the difference. I said that I was happy to train and race the way I have always done, and that I would not need the 'medical backup', and to pass it back to the director.

I was due to fly out to a training camp in the French Alps on 1st January, and the week at home was when my depression caught up with me, to the point where everything seemed so pointless and such a terrible effort. I was all packed, ready to go the next morning, when I had a couple of New Year drinks. In my depressive torture, I had to have more to try and escape the blackness. Soon I had become nearly intoxicated and started saying how I was an abject failure and how I hated myself and that there was no point in being alive. My diatribe only got worse, to the point where Anne had to phone her mum and my sister. It was my comments about how much of a failure I was, how much I hated myself and the suggestion that I should kill myself that concerned them most. I was thick with a bad cold anyway, but it was my present state of mind that convinced them that I should not be on that flight in the morning.

The last minutes of 1994 ended with my wallowing in self-hatred, despair and sadness over everything I had lost – my position, my title, my hour record, and most importantly, my brother. The start of 1995 began the same way, and although it was impossible for me to see it in my state of mind at that time, the only way for me to go now was up.

fourteen: here comes superman!

Early morning on New Year's Day 1995, I woke up with a hangover and a worsening cold as I set about the business of getting ready to leave for my new life, as a matter of duty. It took everything I had mentally to try and force myself on, but Anne being a staff nurse could see obviously that it was unwise to go in inhospitable conditions with inhospitable company with such a bad cold and in my particular frame of mind. She insisted that I stay home, but with my own ability to force myself out there on a knife-edge, I did not have much resistance to offer anyhow.

We tried to contact the Le Groupement office directly, but there was no response and we tried phoning Guy Mollet, the team manager, directly, to no avail. It was not until 2nd January that I managed to make contact, and without even asking what the problem was, he said right away 'You are off the team. Goodbye', and with that, my future on the peloton was not to be. Mostly I was glad, partly because I was in such a poor frame of mind, and partly because I had had bad vibes early on after being treated so poorly. Later I wondered if it was my refusal of 'medical backup', my non-appearance at the ski camp or the team's finances that caused the greatest problem, not that it mattered now, as I was back to being the 'Lone Ranger' of professional cycling.

Now I had nothing much left to go forward with, for as well as losing my crouch position I had a bare skin suit as well as a bare trophy cabinet, but at least that was about to change. I had an appearance invitation to Dortmund to ride Old Faithful again after breaking the track record the year before. I had been whispered some good advice the year before by the organiser, Mr Clausmeyer: that I should not break it by too much as I might have to come back next year. Unfortunately I did not heed his advice and this time I missed my record by a few seconds. While I was there I got talking to Mr Clausmeyer about how I was not sponsored, and he said he could sponsor me to some degree but because the sponsor, DiE Continental – an insurance firm – only sponsored the amateur team they could not give me much financially, but he could give me enough fast Continental tyres to see me through the season as well as loads of clothing. He understood that when I got a serious sponsor I would change over, but in the meantime I accepted the arrangement as it would save the embarrassment of riding in plain clothing.

After that it was back to the Scottish winter, and for me January and February were bleak months, as I lurched into depression, pointlessness and unmotivated ways. The events of New Year's Eve repeated themselves a couple of times as I tried to escape the black weight bearing down on my mind at any given opportunity.

In February, my sense of pointlessness made me consider giving up cycling altogether, but eventually when I decided that I would carry on, my motivation started to grow as my depression seemed to disperse. I had been invited to Tony Doyle's training camp in Lanzarote, and although I was not in good shape when I got there, being around keen club cyclists helped me come out of my darkened bubble.

When I got back, I took stock of what I had to do to get back into serious competition, and the first priority was to find a tri-bar position that I could adapt to and race on. I reckoned that somewhere in between maximum possible adjustment, and the minimum – where the arms are tucked in close and tight – there would be my perfect position, and all I had to do was find it. The tight, tucked-in position was not for me at all, so I went to the other extreme and found that, with my arms as high up and stretched out as possible, I could really get the best out of myself. The more I rode it, the more I was convinced that it was as good as my old tuck position and eventually I had it refined to my exact adjustment.

Now I was enthused and there was no going back, and in March I was even getting excited about the season to come with my new position. I managed to emulate the position on my standard track bike, and on the road it felt really good, so I arranged to ride the Good Friday track meeting at Herne Hill in London, where I would ride a bunch race and also as eight-station pursuit, where the riders are stationed at equal gaps around the track and start at the same time.

Rob Hayles was the main threat and was stationed on the far side of the track from me. When I started I realised that I was not on the form that I hoped to be, compared to the other riders. It was an embarrassing end for me, as Rob caught and eliminated me from the race. It was not the debut of my new position that I had hoped for, and I think a lot of riders treated it as a joke. Certainly, there were plenty of would-be comedians in the track centre that day, and I had no choice but to go along with the jibes after a performance like mine.

Doug Dailey, though, was not one of them, and after saying how he enjoyed watching my new style – with almost a straight face – he asked me if I would like to ride the pursuit event at the Athens World Cup in just four weeks' time. My immediate rush to the affirmative let him know that I was back with serious intention. The World Cup series was a new addition to the track-racing calendar, and each nation had to get a certain amount of points at each discipline in order to have riders in the World Championships. The fact that Doug trusted me with this task was a great lift to my confidence, and for once I was glad that the selection process still had an element of subjective judgement.

I also told Richard from Specialized that I intended to turn it around and that I was due to ride in Athens. He had witnessed my sluggish performance, and I said that if he did not want to sponsor me at this time, then I would totally understand, but he said that if Doug was willing to give me a lifeline, then so would Specialized. The end result was that despite my dreadful ride, I came away feeling good and thinking that, pretty soon, I would be able to look back at my performance with humour too.

The next day, I rode in another meeting at Manchester velodrome, which had newly been completed. The result in the pursuit was just as bad as before, but this time I treated it as training to get faster. I found that my handlebars needed adjusting too, and I was keen to get home to continue the process of improvement in both equipment and form.

Apart from getting the same handlebar set-up on Old Faithful and Mark II, I did a lot to turn around my huge deficit in velocity. Where I had been so depressed and unable to train before, now I had bound-less energy and motivation to train and fiddle with bikes. When I left with Old Faithful to go to Athens as part of the British team, I knew I was a lot quicker than I had been, but how much quicker I could not be sure. When it came time for my event, I was very nervous, not just for myself, but also because Doug had stuck his neck out a bit in selecting me after my Herne Hill ride, and I was desperate to repay his faith with a win.

The World Cup pursuit is only two rides, in order to push along the schedule. Qualifying was vital, as only the two fastest ride a final directly, and thankfully after an all-out effort I was in that final with a rider called Muller, whom I had not heard much of in pursuit events. In the final I managed to build up a lead over Muller, and in the end it was the British national anthem that was played. The very best riders were absent but, looking back to a month earlier, it did not matter – a win was a win, and my finishing time was reasonable.

After my comeback to winning ways, Doug asked me if I would like to ride the World Cup races in Australia and Japan that would be coming up shortly. I immediately said yes, but what Doug forgot to mention was that I would not be travelling with the British team, as I *was* the British team. I would be travelling on my own to Australia, where he had arranged for a 'friend of the Federation' to help me in the event, but in Japan I would be on my own. Doug had seen me doing everything on my own before, and I had been a solo traveller to European tracks many times before, so neither of us really saw a problem with it.

I had quite a bit of time at home while the Federation organised the flight tickets and everything. I headed to Manchester a day early to do some track training with Doug before departing on my latest venture, via London, Sydney and finally Adelaide, where the track is. I got as far as the check-in at Heathrow Airport, only to be asked, 'Where is your visa?' A lot of frantic phone calls took place and the only solution was to get to London's Australia House first thing in the morning, get the visa, and get a new flight with my credit card.

To expedite matters, I checked all my gear in the luggage store except my bike and a spare T-shirt. I headed straight into London on my racing wheels, with no brakes, found a cheap hotel near Australia House, and first thing in the morning I formed the start of the queue. I quickly got my visa and set out to buy the next available flight. The Federation had faxed the Australians to let them know that the British team would be arriving a day late, and when I arrived, I was dead beat, but luckily it was late evening in Australia, so I could go straight to bed.

I was racing the next morning and this time the competition was more classy, as Philippe Ermanault and some other big hitters were taking part. I had a good warm-up, and I made no mistake with the qualifying round, by going directly into the final as fastest rider. The final with Philippe was quite a close-run affair, but I edged him out in the latter stages to win my second World Cup event. It was a new Australian record in the process, and one of Australia's largest newspapers had a large picture of me in full flight, with the headline 'Superman' above it. The position had started to be known as that in the press, because of the arms straight out in front.

I had a few days to kill before the entire show would fly to Tokyo, and my friend Tony, who had been part of my Friday night drinking binges, and his Australian wife Toni, drove over from Melbourne, where they now lived, and my time was filled with catching up with my old friends.

When I bade farewell to Tony and Toni, I caught the flight to Tokyo that most of the riders were on, and from this moment I was on my own and I would have to be my own manager and mechanic, as well as rider.

I headed down to the Tokyo Dome track the day before my ride, to check it out. When I arrived, I was greeted by humble youths bowing politely and repeatedly, and asking 'very please, Mr Bree', while gesticulating that they would like an autograph. When I had dealt with them, I saw the track, and I had never seen the like in Europe. It was made completely of steel and was jacked up to the exact angle by a ring of hydraulic ramps underneath the outer rim. The track was huge compared to the normal indoor track, and was wide enough to hold a car race. It was part of the kierin racing circuit – a sprint-type event where eight or ten riders are led out by a motor pacer who swings off at two or three laps to go when the action really begins. Most Japanese professionals are kierin riders and because of the 370 tracks in Japan, kierin racing is second only to horse racing in how much revenue it derives from betting.

Impressive as it was and fun to ride on, the part that mattered to me as a pursuiter was the bottom part of the track at the black line and how well the shortest line can be held on the curves. On those grounds, it was satisfactory, but I would not like to fall off on it, as the surface was like the super-grippy type that they put on bad corners on the road. There was just one last factor, which passed most riders by, and that was the higher air pressure inside than outside. This was created by air pumps to hold up the dome ceiling, which was made of weatherproof canvas. It was a small difference, but it had a noticeable effect on velocity.

The next day I came back to ride the qualifying ride, which once again was vital to getting into the final. Fortunately the problem of riding around with no schedule to guide me did not take place, as I had become friendly with Lee and Max Vertongen, who helped me out with lap times. Now being favourite to win had a big advantage, because it meant that I was last rider up, and the schedule given up by Max – father of Lee, both New Zealanders – meant that I knew whether or not I was on the pace to qualify as I was riding. Lee was also riding the event, but this did not deter Max from helping the lone Brit. Where Moser wanted to emulate my old style, Lee was the first rider who wanted to copy my new style and a couple of rides round the track on my bike convinced him to take it on.

After qualifying fastest in the morning, I left my bike at the velodrome and walked the half-mile back to the hotel to relax, before riding the final against Philippe in the afternoon. I took in some lunch and lay down with my stereo and my next conscious moment was waking up and looking up, realising I was due on the line in less than 15 minutes. At this moment I was Superman, as I got changed quicker than he does, and I flew down the stairs and ran up the street with the sleep still in my eyes and limbs. I fetched my bike and arrived in the velodrome to the sound of my name over the tannoy. The French team could see that I had slept in, as I must have had a sleepy look, and they beckoned me to their stand, which was right behind the British one, to a static warm-up bike. I was just swinging my leg over it, when I was hailed to the line. Within a minute or so, I was facing the countdown. At this point, I was rubbing my face and saying to myself, 'Wake up! This is the final!' The ride felt as sluggish as my walk to the starting gate, and I went three or four seconds slower than in qualifying, and Philippe beat me by a reasonable margin. When it was over, we both went back to our stands and I went over to shake Philippe's hand over the low fence, and he shrugged his shoulders with his palms forward in an almost apologetic way. I had always suspected that Philippe was a good sport, but I took this as confirmation. While we were attempting communication in pidgin French and English, his team behind gave me snoozing gesticulations in a fun-taking (yet friendly) sort of way.

If my sleeping-in entertained them, they were in for an even better treat from the Japanese team pursuit squad. Pursuiting events are not normally a Japanese forte, but their team was on the line and ready to give it their best. They shot off the line at sprint pace, sustained it as long as they could, which was about two laps, and then just got slower and slower. In the end, their heads were bobbing up and down, and when they were finished, they were so done that they just collapsed on their backs in front of my stand. The best was yet to come, as one of the men managed a gasping request to their coach, who pulled out a pack of cigarettes and gave them one each.

I would be riding the British Championships at Manchester not long after my return, and apart from riding to London and back for my visa, I had not managed any time-trial type events, but with the track being so large, there was no problem for me to put in a good effort during the open session the day after the pursuit. In the evening, I went out to Tokyo with three other riders, and we ended up at the fairground, which was well stocked with good rides. The following morning, I was on my way back to British soil.

It had been a good trip, but it was good to be back and not just to spend time with my family, but also to do some structured and consistent training, as well as to carry out some minor adjustments to my position, which was still evolving. With the British Championships coming up, I wanted to be on the best form possible, so that there would be no room for criticism over my selection for the World Championships in Colombia.

Martin had spare time on his hands and offered to come to the championships with me, and when we headed off it was a heat wave. The heat just went on and on and we had to open the hotel windows wide to keep cool enough. That was how I liked it when it came to pursuiting, because the warmer the air, the easier it is to go fast. On the qualifying ride, I was partnered with Bryan Steel, and there were a lot of whispers going round that he was going really quick. I was riding to a 4-30 schedule and would try to raise on it, and with three laps to go Doug was shouting to really go for it, but since I was up on my schedule, I knew that I would qualify easily.

When I looked up at the result screen, I realised what all the fuss was about – I was close to my own world record pace, and if I had really gone out for it, I could have broken it. I cannot remember who I had in the quarter-final, but I beat him easily. The next day I was riding the semi-final with Matt Illingworth, who had always been on the British team, and I knew him well. When he asked me if I would not catch him and eliminate him from the series, I agreed. If I eliminated him, then he would be relegated to fourth place, and the loser from the other semi-final – no matter how slow – would receive the bronze medal and I though it fair that there should be a ride-off so that the best man would win it.

When it came to the ride-off, I slowed up to stay behind Matt in the last kilometre, even though he was going flat out as he agreed, and in the end I got a time less than a second outside my world record from 1993, and I was kicking myself for being so sporting. The final was my chance to crack out for it full on, but when it came round, the efforts of the series had blunted my pure speed, and I just missed the record again. At least I was British Champion for the third time, and my times sent a signal round the world that I really was a favourite for the World Championship once again. I felt unstoppable, and now I really could look back at my Easter ride with a smile.

Martin and I left the track that evening and camped out on the journey back, which was our original intention when we left, since the weather was so fine. I realised that I would have to commence my period of absolute dedication to the championships pretty soon, and because of that I arranged to go on a short tour around the island of Arran, meeting up with another couple of cyclists on the island. It was only a few days later that we set off for it, and my intentions for our trip were clear – this was going to be an absolute blow-out. It had to be the absolute opposite of dedication to fulfil my strange sporting interpretation of yin and yang, which means opposites like hot and cold or pleasure and pain. My interpretation was that the stronger I make the blow-out as one opposite, then the stronger the dedication can be afterwards as the other opposite, that would help me in the Worlds.

The debauchery started before we even got to the ferry, as I had started drinking before I got there. The whole weekend for me involved extreme drunkenness as we camped down the coast – a short stagger from the nearest pub. Cigarettes were smoked on top of the alcohol, which is a shocking state of affairs for an athlete, but then, if this was yin, it was all in a good cause to strengthen my yang for the World Championships.

When I got back I was drained, but I immediately set out on my Worlds campaign and everything that did not conform to my idea of total and utter dedication was excluded, such as alcohol, caffeine, cakes and late nights. Basically, my plan consisted of training, good food, and rest. I also had to go to Manchester a few times to train with the squad on the track, and on one of the trips we were given our inoculations for Colombia. Most of them were not major, but the yellow fever one would knock us back quite a bit and could take the edge off our speed for a little while.

It did not affect me too badly, but it did take an edge off my top speed, and with a World Cup coming up shortly in Manchester, I wanted to work at getting it back as quickly as possible. Most of the top riders would be there except for my main rival – and reigning champion – Chris Boardman, who had had the misfortune of smashing his ankle in a crash at the Tour de France. The British team was riding the World Cup as a last competitive meeting before we would head out to Colorado for our pre-Colombia adjustment to the altitude that we would be racing at.

At the meeting in Manchester, I knew I had the measure of all the top riders who showed up, and in qualifying, I put in a reasonable ride of 4-24, which earned me my place in the final. My opponent, as it turned out, was not any of the riders I had expected to challenge me, but an Italian rider called Colinelli, who eclipsed my qualifying time to challenge me head-on. I had never seen or heard of this rider, but I hoped I could beat him because my parents and my sister Yvonne had come to see me in action. There was almost nothing between us for most of the ride, but in the end I was beaten by less than a second. One thing for sure was that he had given me something to think about, and another thing was that we were bound to cross swords again come the Worlds.

There was more for me to think about for the moment, as the whole team had to get our bikes into boxes and get ready for long-haul travel. Our destination was Boulder in Colorado, where we would be staying at Mike and Tina Hayes' house, at 5,000 feet, for a week or so before heading to Breckenridge in the mountains at 9,000 feet. It was a huge house, which was large enough to accommodate the whole track squad and team officials.

We had been advised that it might be better to take it easier for a few days when first going to altitude, so the first thing I did was unpack my bike and static trainer and set in about an absolute full-on training session at the rear porch of the house – in full view of my reclining team-mates, who had taken the advice to heart. After a couple of concerned comments about being careful not to overdo it, I told them I would be back soon, as I was leaving to find a hill for my big gear, before it got too dark. Contrary to initial fears I felt no ill effect apart from the aches and tiredness of training, and I continued on my path of total dedication, with no respect for altitude. A week or so later, it was time for a step up in altitude and we set out on the drive up to Breckenridge. The road went up all the way, and when we arrived we were truly in the mountains, as the large house we were staying in looked out to some tremendous scenery and the off-season ski town that would be our home for another two weeks.

It was the same step up in altitude again, and this time I noticed it in climbing up the stairs after I arrived. I was undeterred from my relentless quest for maximum form, and I set in about the static trainer right away. The next day I was desperate to ride to the summit of Hosier Pass, which tops out at over 12,000 feet, as part of my aerobic training. It was a breathtaking ride, both through lack of oxygen and the Rocky Mountain scenery. Descending from altitude was amazing too, because the thin air allowed me to glide down the pass at amazing speeds in my Superman position.

After a week or so, Matt Illingworth told me there was a group going out for 50 miles or so over Vail Pass, if I wanted to join them. A longer run fitted into my training plan, and 50 miles would be the most I would want to do. I took some food in my pockets, and extra water to be ready for any eventuality, and when we headed out, it transpired that the ride could be nearer 80 miles. On the first climb of the day, I found myself beside Chris Newton at the front of the group of eight, and being half-wheeled by him. The speed went up and up as I countered his challenge, the rest of the group warned me not to mess with Chris in the hills, as Chris just stared ahead.

The rest of the group told us to steady the tempo, and my challenger was subdued for the time being, and all the way to Vail, where we stopped at a café. The first thing we met on our departure was Vail Pass, and from the first incline, my challenger (a road rider) set about his task of domination, and in no time, half of the group were outpaced and out the back, and before we were even halfway up the pass, it was just us. The battle intensified and after I took it on from the front I managed to crank up a pace that he could not follow, and as I rounded the summit with Chris a little way behind, it was Geoff Shergold, who was our temporary manager, who I saw standing there with a wry smile. I did not realise I had gone a step too far and my seniority should have told me that matching him would have been enough, and the result was a quiet friction between us, after the coach seeing my display of authority and the lads tipping his 'King of Hill' crown to the side with a few subtle jibes.

One thing for sure after that ride was that I could hardly walk for a day or two, which I hid well, and that night I was glad of an early bed.

That was a luxury that Geoff did not have since his room was the sitting room, and his bed was the sofa, and he could not retire until the last bum had left it. I suspected that he paid for it in backache, but I cannot be sure, since he seemed the type that would suffer a lot before moaning about it.

Another thing I had to think about now was that young Mr Newton certainly knew how to pull a practical joke, and from now on I would be careful where I left my toothbrush. Yvonne McGregor, who held the women's hour record and was seeking pursuit glory in the women's event, was not so careful about her camera and left it sitting on the sideboard. Mr Newton took the opportunity of adding a few rather vulgar shots to her photographic diary, with some help from the lads. I heard from Yvonne after our return home that it inspired a strange comment or two from the staff at her local chemist.

The team went out a couple of times to the local pubs, and most of us had a few drinks since it was still three weeks or so before we would be competing. My yang had not weakened and I drank only diet Coke, and Yvonne McGregor went one better by not going at all. Some of the team went on to a nightclub, and one of them had to get bailed out of the police cells in the early hours of the morning, after urinating in a public place, to the entertainment of the entire household. The fun had to end sometime and on September 11th, we set out on the long journey to central Colombia. I remember that date because it was my 30th birthday and it passed off without any congratulations or good wishes of any kind. Waiting endlessly in a humid Miami Airport lounge did not seem fitting for the occasion.

When we finally got to Bogotá Airport, I was so tired I honestly thought that I might faint, and then we were delayed from leaving the airport because there had been a shooting outside. Everything had a military look about it as we were taken to our hotel, where we stayed overnight before heading out to Boyaca. We were travelling by mini-bus on our six-hour journey, and it was an immediate introduction to the Colombian style of driving. When overtaking, oncoming traffic was no impediment, as the overtaker would expect both lines of traffic to move over a little while he drove right up the middle. The concept of a safe distance from the driver in front was non-existent and on multi-lane highways it was a bit like being in a moving parking lot.

Our hotel in Boyaca was still not finished, but it was comfortable, and the town itself was relatively small, around 20,000 or so people, but there was a sizable population near by, in local towns and villages. There was a local velodrome which we could use at set times, as the sessions were allocated to different nations at different times, and the level of demand meant that we would be sharing with the Australians.

The track was only 6 or 7 miles away, and we would just cycle to and from it, which was not as straightforward as it sounds because we would have to ensure that we had an armed police outrider with us for the entire journey each way. The Colombian government had requested that we use them because of the proximity of rebel territory, but after a while we just dispensed with it unless one was ready to leave with us right away.

There were so many things that were memorable from that time, but the main one was our official welcome to Boyaca. Each team was welcomed to Colombia in different parts of the district, and when we arrived at ours it was mobbed with people, and there was a bandstand with a band and an MC in the crisp open air. The band played for us and we were all introduced individually. The band played again, there was a bit of razzmatazz, we were all presented with specially prepared gifts, and then they asked that one of us would step forward to sing our national anthem. At this point, Sandy, myself and Gordon Johnson (the team manager, who is also Scottish) all looked at each other because none of us knew the words, apart from the title. The net closed in on the other three as the huge crowd waited, and suddenly Chris Lillywhite, a Chelsea supporter, stepped forward to the microphone for a powerful rendition. When we left we were pulled and jostled, and the crowd were cheering, screaming and baying for autographs as we clambered into our people carrier. As we drove through the crowd and headed away I felt as though I had seen the re-birth of Beatlemania.

After a few sessions at the track my times were looking good considering it was quite bumpy, but then toothache I had before I left Scotland came back and worsened gradually, to the point where I had to take the antibiotics I had been prescribed by my dentist for such an occurrence. They thought it was an abscess and gave me antibiotics for my trip, but they had no effect and it got so bad that I could not sleep for the pain, part of my face and neck were numb, I had problems moving my right arm, and more importantly I was now riding at a pace that would struggle to qualify for the Scottish championships.

I was in such pain that I had no choice but to ask Pedro, our interpreter, if he knew a dentist. He had already been trying to sell us emeralds with his armed sidekick, and he seemed to have no problems with contacts. It was now only one week to the championships and the pain was now so unbearable that even my bigoted imagination of what a South American dentist would be like could no longer prevent me from getting it dealt with 'el pronto'.

I went with Pedro and his sidekick to another town where we mounted a set of stairs to what appeared to be a modern and professional dental surgery where the white coat-clad dentists were brother and sister. I was privileged to receive immediate attention from the brother, and when he saw my teeth he looked shocked, but when I explained about the abscess and the antibiotics he almost hit the roof in a fervent diatribe about European dentistry, which needed no interpretation from Pedro. I said that my wife had contacted the dentist at home and that I was to have the longest molar in my right hand lower jaw pulled out. He managed to say in his pidgin English that in Colombia we save teeth. He also explained through Pedro that his shock was at all the mercury in my teeth, and that this practice had been banned in Colombia for eleven years.

He set about my root treatment and an hour later I felt as though a miracle had happened, as I came off the chair completely and utterly cured. My pain, bodily stiffness and heavy tiredness were dispelled to the extent that it was as if I'd never had them. I would have to get the tooth treated again and filled with mercury-free white enamel, but right now I wanted to get straight down to the track and try out my newfound energy.

When I arrived at the track I still had time for a pursuit effort on our session, and Doug was a bit surprised to see me as he thought I would be convalescing from an extraction or worse. When I set about the ride I felt like I really was Superman, and I went over half a minute quicker to finish with a world class time and even the Australian coach, who hid well his occasional monitoring of my times, could not subdue his look of surprise at my turnaround. Now I could rest easy at night because I had my raw speed back, and with only two training rides before I would take on the world again, I was back in a strong position.

All I had to do now was relax on my bike between training sessions and keep my legs turning over. On one ride I was with Yvonne McGregor when the strangest thing happened. We had stopped for a Coke at a shack on a hilly back road when we saw two cyclists coming up the hill to the shack. Yvonne burst out, 'That's Jeannie Longo and her husband, let's join them when they pass!' When we caught up with them, I went to the front to speak to Jeannie (probably the greatest cyclist ever) and we got talking about the hour record. She said she would like to attack Yvonne's record and started asking my thoughts on the best tracks and the likes. After a bit of prevaricating I suggested she should ask Yvonne herself. I swung over to introduce the two women, who had never met, and Jeannie was so embarrassed that Yvonne had been behind her all the time.

The championship was held in Bogotá so we made the long journey back a couple of days before the opening rides, and the first thing I set about doing was to check out the track. We had only been in our hotel for one night when we headed down there. It was less than a kilometre, but we would use our road bikes to get back and forth. On the way out I followed Sandy in a large group of cyclists who were cycling out to the hotel, which was a hub of activity for the championships. I was some way down the road when I realised that the group had diverged and that I had followed them blindly in a dream. My attempt to find my own way back was futile as I seemed to go round in circles, and to compound matters I had taken Old Faithful for a reason I cannot remember, and could not for the life of me remember the name of our hotel so all I could ask for in my pidgin Spanish was for a big hotel. This went on for hours until I was hopelessly lost in my bare skin suit and a bike with no brakes.

I was starting to panic a little: it seemed so hopeless as the only item I had on my person was my plastic hotel key as well as the fact that there had been those shootings when we arrived. Now I was homing in on people who looked the least bit official and asking them in my best Spanish, while showing them my plastic hotel key, and wracking my brain for the name of the hotel. I struck lucky as I bumped into a gentleman from the British Embassy, and in no time at all he had worked out which hotel it was and he kindly drove me to the front entrance. Doug was pacing about at the front doors wondering what had happened to me during the four hours I had been missing.

Strangely enough my total loss of direction continued, as I looked for the breakfast room the next morning – the same breakfast room I had been to twice before. Some of the riders had been just ahead of me, but when I arrived at the foyer I could not find them as I opened doors to broom cupboards and conference rooms. I had a minor panic attack as I felt a cold sweat and tight breathing come on while I seemed hopelessly lost in the hotel foyer. I had to ask a foreign rider where the breakfast room was and he looked at me as if I was crazy.

Later that morning I had finally arrived at my ultimate destination, on form and on time. This was the very reason for my season, and my yang and I had a game plan that I had not yet revealed to Doug or Sandy. I wanted to do a ride that was not my fastest in the qualifying, but that would be quick enough to get into the top four riders so that I could save my best for the second ride.

My ranking meant that I would be amongst the last riders to go and that would allow me to judge the minimum pace that I would need, and I could judge that one ride by the schedule times that Doug would be showing me from the trackside. Colinelli went flat out and was fastest, and I qualified third, which was ideal, after all you do not get medals for qualifying fastest.

Round two was the quarter-final and if I did the ride I wanted, then I could give myself a tactical advantage for the final the following day. The rules are clear that the fastest winner will ride against the slowest winner in the semi-final and the format is that the ride-off will take place first which means that not only would I earn myself an easier opponent, but I would also have an extra seven or eight minutes' recovery time. That does not seem much, but as there was only to be one hour between the semi finals and finals then any advantage in the first ride could be the tiny difference that wins or loses the gold medal in the final.

My tactic worked and Colinelli was slower than his mega-fast qualifying ride, whereas I rode full on with fresher legs and won that vital fastest winner spot by just half a second, and even with the slight advantage I had won with the use of tactics I knew that at my absolute best there would be almost nothing between Colinelli and me. My rival in the semi-final would be Philippe Ermanault and although there was not much between us, it was enough for me to safely ride to a schedule and enough that I could go away only thinking about the final and make the groove in my mind which would automatically follow in the ride, as I had done for the final in '93. Colinelli on the other hand would be facing the Australian rider Stuart O'Grady who had gone very quickly, and there was no way of safely guessing what his maximum capability was.

That night, as with the night before, there was no relaxation. I started to visualise the final with Colinelli as I had done on the eve of absolute success or failure with Philippe. The track here was outdoors and because it was a 333-metre track the ride would be twelve laps, which mentally I broke down into quarters so that the distance seemed less. I could count one, two, three as each quarter came round and I had the last quarter broken into laps so that I could imagine that the end of each lap was the race finish and I would ride it like it was the last lap until the next one, and after that one it really was the last lap and death or glory would mean just that.

I imagined the rhythm of my legs that I would need for victory, and hyperventilating and being blown out physically before the halfway point in the thin air of Bogotá. My impression was realistic, because some riders had received oxygen at the trackside already, as they were lying there gasping to regain control of their breathing, and I had experienced the same feeling on my hard ride that day. I spent ages on and off the static bike trying to loosen my legs up and I used the technique of making the final seem so much further away in time by thinking about all the things that would happen before it would come round – getting up, washing, having breakfast, travelling to the track and getting changed – in order to relax enough to sleep.

In the morning my every waking thought was of the final, and again I was imagining going round and round the track and seeing the laps go down the way that I had planned. We went to the track really early so that I could focus totally while doing loads of gentle warm-up, and before I knew it, I was on the start line and looking across the track at Philippe. My whole plan was for a single-pace ride that would save me going to the limit before the final, but Philippe went a little quicker in the first half than I expected, and I had to raise on my schedule in a controlled way to be certain not to be a victim of complacency. It was a hard ride, but not as hard as the one I was about to see Colinelli do. Stuart O'Grady started really fast and Colinelli had no option but to respond early by going well above his schedule. He was given a hard time most of the way before his dominance won out in the end. As he sat on the trackside gasping for a breath, I knew he had worked to his limit for his place in the final.

The first part of my plan had gone well and now the next event in my life would be the ultimate test that would leave me feeling relieved, unburdened and acceptable, or an abject failure. I stayed on my static trainer the whole time between rides, with my bike facing into a corner so that no-one could catch my eye. I had my personal stereo on and

Doug and Sandy knew enough about riders – especially me – to leave me alone in contemplation. The music I was listening to was '60s music, but there was one song on the tape that I played over and over as it had special sentimental impact on me, and I was drawn to it at that time.

When my brother and I were small we had gone to the Grand Bazaar at the town hall in Newmilns, and with our combined pocket money we bought an old suitcase record player. We had made our way through the back streets to the forest, where we used the wind-up facility to play the two records that we got with it. One of them was 'Hole In My Bucket' by Ken Dodd, which we quickly turned into a Frisbee, but the other was 'Jennifer Juniper' by Donovan, which we listened to over and over together in the safety of the forest.

That song was the one I listened to and it made me think of Gordon and all the times we spent together, and also brought out my feelings of loathing for that town. I had not been thinking about Gordon unusually much on the trip until now, but that also unleashed a whole lot of emotions that were incredibly powerful, and when the moment came to step up to the starting gate I was not only in the mindset that I would rather die than fail here, I was also deeply in that mood. I also felt like a little cat that was trapped in a corner by a bunch of snarling dogs that had no choice but to fight to the death, tooth and claw.

As I got the countdown I focused on the groove that I would switch on to as soon as I started. I almost took a glance over to Colinelli but reminded myself in time that this was about me, just me. My motivation was such that the countdown could not come quickly enough, and for the first half of the race, I rode past my ability as planned. I had asked Sandy and Doug not to give me checks on Colinelli until then, and when they did, they said we were neck and neck. I rode the next three laps like it was the last quarter, and my lungs by now were heaving in and out like bellows, but with the thin air it felt like I was breathing nothing.

When I reached my first false finish, I could not have gone on, if it were not for the circumstances, but the 'finish' was just one lap, and with the power of the groove I went for that 'finish', and when I passed I went just one more lap to the next 'finish'. All the while my body was racked in pain, and I was losing my ability to think or focus. When I got to the genuine one-lap-to-go, I just managed to focus on the signal from Sandy that I was level and at that point I was already in hell, but my frame of mind kicked in and I set out for total self-destruction. When I reached the line, I could barely see it.

My effort had paid off as I had opened up a winning gap on my rival, who may have been relying on a conventional effort in his ride. When I came to a stop, it was payback time, as my body ached all over, and even as I got my breath back my lungs were on fire. The victory did not make much impact on me emotionally, except that it gave me a strong feeling of job satisfaction and relief that it was done with. It did give me a great deal of pleasure, though, that Hein Verbruggen – who had disqualified me the year before – had sat and watched me ride to victory and that he would reluctantly have to present me with a gold medal.

After the ceremony there was the usual mayhem with reporters and the public wanting my time, but since I had done my ride I was happy to make myself accessible. That victory was not the end of my championship, as in six days' time I would be taking the line in the Time Trial Championship. We spent another couple of days in Bogotá because the rest of the team had races to ride, and it was good being World Champion and just coming and going with no pressure now that I knew my way to the hotel.

When we got back to Boyaca, where the time trial would be, I had to start focusing on it and trying to recover as much as possible from my pursuit efforts. It was hard to do a sustained aerobic session because I still had a bad cough that worsened afterwards, and I also felt physically drained right up to the ride. Something that touched me deeply at that time was the opening ceremony where the children from all the local schools marched in groups with immaculate school uniforms and banners depicting scenes of violence with crosses across them that could be understood in any language. Some of them depicted death and blood, while others showed embroidered images of masked guerrillas with machine guns and I realised that that had been my only image of Colombia before I came here and saw decent people trying to live decent lives. That was just before the championships and that night I did a session on the static trainer and felt not bad, and my cough had died away to almost nothing. I was not so nervous about the time trial and I did not spend as much mental energy thinking about the next day's ride because it was not so polarised into success or failure, and I knew I could ride to oblivion in the distance and just wait and see what came of it.

On the morning of the championship, I felt really lethargic, especially when warming up. I mentioned to Sandy how I felt and he said that if I stopped in the ride I would be walking back, because the result of my ride might be essential for Britain to have a place in the time trial at the Olympics the following year. When I started, my worst fears were confirmed, as I was just not getting on my usual pace. I had ridden the time trial course before I left for the pursuit, and at that time I felt so strong, but now I was a shadow of my former self, and I was powerless to lift myself, no matter how hard I tried – it just was not there, not that day.

I kept hoping I would ride myself into it and get stronger as the ride progressed, and as I saw the last climb coming up to the town centre, I gave it absolutely everything I had, which was already nothing. I was completely and utterly exhausted, but from somewhere I found the strength to give it good pace to the line, where I was ready to collapse. When I got to the line, it was not the line, and I was directed up the steepest hill of the day, which just went on and on. I had been badly misinformed about where the finish was and when I had heaved and hauled my carcass to the real line, I had never felt so exhausted in a long time. The net result was that I was nineteenth, while the cut-off for qualifying Britain to have a rider in the Olympics was top twenty. It was a terrible ride from start to finish, but I was still World Champion and I had done my duty.

That was my World Championship participation over, but I would be staying on for a few days more, while the road riders took part in the Road Race Championships. The evening before the race, Sandy said that, according to Pedro, the British team should come to the opening ceremony of the Championships. He explained that he was busy with bikes, Gordon was busy with massage and Doug and Dave Smith (the road coach) were busy with riders, and so maybe I could go with Pedro since I was a free man – just in case a British face was required.

I set off with Pedro, who introduced his girlfriend, who was pregnant. We went to the opening ceremony, which was in another town and it was excellent, with fireworks and Colombian music, and since the festivities seemed to go on all night, the three of us went to a bar, which seemed to be slightly upmarket. After speaking to the man at the door, we got in and even got seats. He introduced me to a couple of his friends, one of whom was an architect who could speak pidgin English. He asked if I wanted a beer, and as I was about to refuse, I realised that my block of total dedication was over, and accepted the offer. We had a few beers and then a huge row erupted between Pedro and his girlfriend, who turned out to be sixteen and an ex-pupil of his, since he is a teacher. She stormed out, closely followed by Pedro.

I stayed and had a whole lot more beer with Pedro's friends, who I was getting on with very well, between my improving Spanish and his architect friend's English. It was not long before the entire bar was joining in on a World Championship celebration and everyone wanted to get an autograph or a photograph taken, as well as wanting to buy me a beer. The end result was dancing on tables and the like, and when it all had to end, Pedro's architect friend gave me his car keys and said that he would collect his car tomorrow. I pointed out that not only could I not drive, but I was barely able to stand. He eventually bowed to wisdom, and being intoxicated himself, he kindly gave me a lift, which was a better idea – after all, at least he could drive.

A couple of days later, we embarked on our long journey home, and when I looked back on the whole experience, it was overwhelming – the amount of life that had happened. More than anything, I had won my champion's jersey, and once again I had endorsed it with beer stains. There would be more celebrating when I got back, and over the winter I would start thinking about my next major campaign – the Olympics in Atlanta.

fifteen: search for olympic gold

Frank Quinn had phoned me while I was still in Colombia to let me know that I had a main sponsor for the season to come, a Scottish company called Scotoil. It was a company that specialised in providing services to the oil industry, and was headed by Iain Davidson, who was a keen cyclist himself. Frank met Anne and me at our local airport not long after my return from Colombia, and we drove north to Aberdeen, where we met Iain, saw round the company headquarters and held a press conference.

It was a relief to know that my death or glory effort in the final had earned me a solid, reliable sponsorship for my time right through the Olympics to come in '96, in Atlanta. Now I could look forward to having nothing in my way, as I would train and ride as favourite for the gold medal in my event. It was also a very amicable sponsorship, in that Iain had no objection to me having all my regular side sponsorships, like Specialized or shoe deals, although Scotoil was my overall sponsor. He also had no objection to my picking up jersey sponsorship in the off-season track and time trial events, which were about to commence. In this situation, I would wear a jersey for a one-off sponsor and continue to wear the Scotoil name on my shorts.

My first European appearances were taking place right away and my first trip was a double, as I would be riding the Kilometre de Mestre near Venice on the Sunday and a pursuit match against Chris Boardman the following evening in Paris. I travelled to Italy on my own, as I already knew Sandro, Mr Cohen and a few other people. I was riding my Mark II bike, which I had won the World Championships on, just two weeks earlier. It was a little poignant coming back to this race and the reminder of the fact that it was the first anniversary of my brother's death, but it did not take away from my focus, and I managed second place behind Mario Chipolini. This time it was so much fun being high up on the makeshift stage in the street, with Mario and Maurizio Fondriest, the beautiful girls presenting the prizes, the flowers and the huge bottles of champagne to spray into the huge and enthusiastic crowd.

I did not have long to savour it before rushing to pack my bags and head out to Paris, where I would be racing Chris the following night. I could not prevent my mood dropping down a notch now that I was on the cold, inhospitable streets of Paris, as my intuition had assured me it was since my earliest visits, a feeling reinforced by every trip I made here. The urban warmth of Mestre made the polarisation a lot more stark than it would have been had I come directly from Glasgow, but nonetheless I was in a good enough frame of mind to step up to the line and take on Chris with a top-class performance.

There was a near-capacity crowd at the velodrome, and to add to the tension, the ride was being shown live on French TV as well as in most of Europe on Eurosport, and Chris and I would have to be ready on the line for an exact time. I lined up in my new Scotoil skin suit, my World Champion rainbow colours round my chest, my World Championship bike and with my current form, I was pretty confident of a favourable outcome. The only thing that detracted from my image was a small spanner jammed between the nose of my saddle and the seat pin, which was an emergency repair after my bike had been damaged in baggage handling. The seat clamp had been weakened already by the necessary adjustments to conform to the UCI's saddle rules the year before.

I knew I could not afford any complacency and I wanted to start hard from the gun and take command of the race from an early stage. I readied myself on the countdown for a huge starting effort to get the bike rolling, but I only managed two knee-straining efforts before I came crashing ignominiously to the ground. I was only yards from the starting gate, and as soon as I got to my feet I knew exactly what had gone wrong – the entire bottom section of my bike had broken off. As I stood in the full glare of a live European audience, I felt no emotion or feeling about the situation. I though to myself, 'That is a bit unfortunate', and although I was completely calm, I realised that there was a lot of panic and reaction around me, and as the shoulder-held cameras pointed squarely at me, I reacted – as I often do – in a manner that I thought would be expected of me. I started waving my fists about a bit and kicking the bike a bit, while trying not to laugh or smile as I set about my tantrum act. I continued to feel totally indifferent to the seriousness of the situation, as it almost seemed to be happening to somebody else.

The director of the track series asked me to fetch my back-up bike, and when I explained I had none as I had come directly from another race, he was not altogether pleased. We had missed our slot on live TV, but the restart was due in an hour or so, and in that time we would have to try and borrow a bike from one of the foreign teams that were competing. Frank was there, but he could not speak any foreign languages, and he busied himself in trying to appease the irate director instead.

I sought out a bike on my own and the first port of call was the French team, which Philippe Ermanault was in, but the manager of the team said point-blank that the answer would be 'non'. I asked about at a few other teams, and either they had no bike to lend or they were using them in their immediate rides. Finally it was the good old Italians who helped me out with one of their team pursuit bikes, despite the fact that they would be using them right after my ride with Chris. The bike ironically belonged to a Mr Colinelli, but because he was riding right after me, I could not adjust his seat height.

Thanks to the Italians I had a bike to ride just minutes before our rematch. I would have to ride it as it came – no practice ride and no adjustment. When we started, I had to perch on the point of the saddle, as it was too high, and gearing was way lower than I was used to. I rode at least ten seconds slower than I would have liked, and Chris could have humiliated me easily, but chose to pull his punches and make do with just winning the race. There was a bad atmosphere all round and I was glad to get back to my hotel and close the door on the whole thing.

I arrived home the next day and threw my wreckage into the garage and enjoyed a week at home before I headed out to my next race. It was a 50km time trail, and it was held in Les Herbier in the west of France, and I knew it well because I had ridden it the year before and finished fourth. It was a rolling course through mainly minor roads, and there would be no problem with traffic, as the entire route would be closed off except to official vehicles. The Chrono Les Herbier was a festival for the provincial town of no more than 8,000 people, and it took the total resources of Les Herbier and some of the outlying towns to organise and stage such a major event. From my experience of the previous year, the largest part of the festival would take part after the race in a couple of oversized beer tents, where food and wine would be liberally consumed. This was of no concern to me, though, as I was here purely to ride well in the race.

On the afternoon of the race, I was ready with the time-trial bike I had used in Colorado and Colombia, and I felt not bad with my form. I was a little nervous from the pressure I put on myself to do a good ride, and on the start line, I was mentally built up to really go for it. At the halfway point, I thought I had put in a good effort, but at three-quarter distance, it all went wrong, as the handlebar stem I had built myself snapped as I pulled on the bars on a hilly section. I came crashing to the ground and bruised my face, while the following car almost ran over me when I suddenly became a static heap on the road.

It was an embarrassing end following the incident at Paris, but again I had an emotional blackout and I did not feel untoward at all, and certainly not angry or frustrated. When I got to the finish, I explained that I had a mechanical problem, but I did not see the organiser at that time, or the driver who would be taking me back to Paris first thing the next morning. There was talk of another rider driving the 500km or so back to Paris, who would give me a lift, but by 10 o'clock that night, I had not seen anybody at the hotel and I reckoned the organiser had been a little annoyed by what had happened and had not gone out of his way to arrange my transport. Everybody that mattered was at the celebration, including my driver from last year, who could hear a bottle being corked at 1,000 metres, and by 11.30 I was deciding whether to go it alone to be sure of getting to Paris for my early morning flight.

I asked the bar lady if there were any trains to Paris, and she told me there was a midnight TGV but I would have to go to the next town. Having seen or heard nothing of the organiser or anyone else, I felt pretty abandoned, and my survival instinct kicked in. I used the last of my francs to take a taxi to meet the 12 p.m. train, but when I went to the ticket desk she explained that this was Sunday, so the next train would be at 6.30 a.m. I bought a ticket with my credit card, and set about half-dozing in one of the metal station seats, only to be ejected at midnight when the station closed.

I looked about me, and every house and hotel was totally closed and darkened, so I decided I would sneak round to the platform and half-doze there until the train came in the morning. I put my emergency jacket on and ate my emergency cornflakes, but in no time I was very uncomfortable and shivering with the cold. My exertion in the afternoon, my smack to the head and a lack of substantial food had left me totally drained, and my overwhelming desire to lie down and sleep, as well as escape the frosty night, stoked my interest in a parked train on the platform.

I saw that the carriages had electric doors and I forced them open with all the force I could muster from my tired arms and legs. Once me and my bike bag were inside, they flopped shut behind me and I lay down with my jacket and slept across the seats in the relative warmth of the carriage. I woke up to the sound of locomotive engines and a shunting feeling through the carriage. It only took seconds before I was wide awake and pulling the doors apart to escape an uncharted mystery tour of the French railway network.

It was lucky I had been woken, because the train set off towards its destination and the TGV was due shortly. I had been warned that my bike bag would not be allowed, but I was in no mood for adhering to rules and regulations and I reckoned that the technique I had used in Madrid to board this same train would work again. I got to Paris and managed to catch my flight on time. I was soon home and catching up on my lost calories and lost sleep, and at least that was the last time-trial appearance I would have that year.

A few weeks later, I had an appearance at Ghent, Belgium, but this time it was on the track, and I was riding standard races, and thankfully nothing fell apart on my bike this time. I also met the organiser of the Chrono Les Herbier, and he had been OK about the handlebar situation, but was a little insulted that I had panicked and taken the train. I also rode the Eddy Merckx Grand Prix again and I put in a good effort within a darkening cloud of indifference to achieve an unimpressive seventeenth place.

The rest of the year was spent as off-season, and it was not long before I had descended into full-blown yin, with alcohol being the main intoxicant at that time, and as usual there would be no such thing as moderation. It was always the case that if I drank a little, then I would seek out more and more at all costs until complete oblivion was achieved. And on the way I would tell everyone about me – how I was a complete failure, that I hated myself and that they would be better off without me, despite being the current World Champion. The next day I would always excuse it away as the drink talking, and carry on regardless.

The winter months were difficult in training terms, as my ingrained indifference turned more to passionless demotivation and I had to really push myself out to go through the motions of training. My next foreign trip was to be Tony's best man in Victoria, Australia on New Year's Day, and on this occasion, my yin reached its ultimate point between the stag night, nights out and the wedding itself. It had been my standard practice in previous years that at the stroke of midnight I would suddenly switch into yang and dedication, and stick to it for fear of perpetually delaying the moment for the lack of a strong enough defining time or date. Here there was no exception other than the fact that New Year would be nine hours old by the time it came round in Britain, and as the night went on, I decided to work on British time. Intoxicated as I clearly was at the end of the reception, I returned to my room in the motel and – unable to resist the compulsion – I opened the bottle of duty-free I had purchased, and set about the business of ending up paralytic.

On the first of January, I was on the other side of the hill in terms of attitude, and I refused cake, alcohol and all the things that contravened utter dedication. I even made my first serious training ride of my campaign and with a whopper of a hangover, I was really not sure if I would make it back in the searing Australian heat with a lack of water and an over-ambitious distance in the deserted back roads of this inland area.

On my return, I forced myself to train hard that winter and spring, although sometimes it was difficult as everything seemed so pointless. At those times I would remind myself that this was for the Olympic Gold Medal, but although I understood the importance in thinking terms, I never felt any passion about it. Sometimes it felt like I had to do this because I was so useless I could not do anything else, and that old feeling of detachment from society crept back into my psychology before the start of the season of '96. It was not just cycling that was affected, as almost everything in life seemed completely pointless at times, and in total I felt like I was on a nauseating roller-coaster ride that would never end. At times, in that early season, the world seemed so bleak and pointless and when I pushed myself out for a training ride it was after as much procrastination as possible. I would be totally unable to push my legs round at anything more than a touring pace, and sometimes I would be compelled to think about suicide, despite my logic telling me that everything was okay.

My depression twisted reality to the point where if I did win the gold medal, then life would still be so pointless. At one point during that early season, my sense of pointlessness and isolation, mixed with self-hatred, became so powerful that I was reduced to near-walking pace as suicide seemed the only answer. I looked about in the forest areas for foxglove digitalis, which I knew was deadly poisonous, but I could not find any and carried on back to the house. With the passage of time, my ability to train returned, and for the time of year, my form could be described as reasonable.

My first campaign of the season was a World Cup event in Cuba. It was still early season, and only Doug, Yvonne and myself would be going directly via Miami and Mexico, and the sprinters would meet us there from their racing ventures in Trinidad. Cuba was an ideal place to cycle, as the wide roads were almost devoid of motorised transport. Any vehicles that could be seen were mainly 1950s vintage and were driven slowly to conserve fuel. The town we were staying in was very strange because it seemed to consist wholly of suburbs, and the only inkling of a town centre was a half-stocked mini-market and a pizza shop. It was famous for one thing, though, and that was the spot along the nearby seafront, where Ernest Hemingway wrote *The Old Man and the Sea*.

In the pursuit event itself I was second to a Spanish rider called Martinez, whom I had lapped in my quarter-final ride in Colombia just six or seven months earlier. I found it difficult to get fired up for the ride at all, and I seemed totally oblivious to any emotion I might have had about it at that time. I listened to '60s music, including my 'Jennifer Juniper' song that had fired me up so well in Colombia, but this time the music only served to make me feel even more sad, and my long stare became worse over the next couple of days – the type of stare that fixes on one point, while your mind turns it into a black hole which consumes your entire consciousness.

When it was time to go home, I knew I was on a downer again, but I could not snap out of it or talk myself round. After all, how could I when it was not self-generated – it was just there? When we reached Miami, I was hauled into immigration, which quite clearly meant that I would miss my onward flight, and Doug and the other riders had no choice but to go on without me. Doug already knew what the trouble was, as I had confided in him at a low point, about how my true identity was as a criminal. It was my criminal record that prevented me from crossing customs in order to reach my flight to Britain, and it would be an unspecified time before I would have any chance. I was forced to sit in a room full of other detainees for an inordinate amount of time in unbearable heat, and when I went up to ask about my case, I was rebuffed in a manner that could start a prison riot. Between the expletives, he said that if I did not shut the f*** up, the US government would have me in handcuffs.

A few hours later, I was told that I would have to wait in the duty-free lounge until the next day, when my entry would be considered, or I could stay in the airport hotel at this side of customs at my own expense. I chose the latter, but I was so depressed that I was driven towards the lounge bar, where I proceeded to try and wash away the insidious, suffocating blackness that I was immersed in with alcohol and tobacco. To be honest, anything that might make me feel better, had it been available – lighter fuel, glue, hash, cocaine – would have been acceptable to me; anything to add just a speck of colour to the grey and black pointless world that was my vision of reality.

Eventually, a little before closing time, I was the only person left in the bar. The bar staff clamped down on my continuous consumption of beer, and since I was the last punter, they asked me what my problem was. It was not long before the key, well-used words were spoken, like 'failure, hate myself, pointless, kill myself' came to the fore. Someone spoke to me for ages, which was nice, because it distracted me from my feeling of total loneliness and isolation, at least. Eventually I went to my room to stare at one spot on the wall and allow myself to be sucked into the void once again, and now and then smoke cigars while contemplating how it would be better for everybody if I were dead. After a while, a knock on the door and an enquiring voice about my safety distracted me from my dark place. After that, I must have fallen asleep.

The next day I was told that I was able to catch the next flight, and I made my way home to continue with my isolated, torturous and never-ending training programme. Things picked up a little, and training became a little easier, which was fortunate since my next race would be the Athens World Cup race, where my mood was a little better than in Cuba. My result was worse, though, as I failed to get a place on the podium with fourth, and my lack of dominance was starting to show.

Next on the agenda was the British Championships for pursuit, and a defeat here would be embarrassing as well as a threat to my place in the Olympics, and it would also let the world see that I was unable to prepare properly in the run-up. At the Championships, I was using the pursuit rides as a try-out for an all-carbon bike built by Chris Field at Hotta Design. It was a beautiful machine that had my exact handlebar and seat positions and was kitted out with a pair of Specialized wheels from Richard, as well as the exact gearing. I took Old Faithful with me as well, so that if anything unexpected happened, then I could still step up to the line and continue with the race series.

I had a chance of a tryout in open session, and it seemed to be up to the job, but on the starting effort, where tremendous forces twist the handlebars and frame, a thunderous cracking noise came from the front end that could be heard by the entire crowd, who were seated in quiet expectation at that point. I instantly sat down so that I would no longer be straining the front end, and carried on regardless to qualify fastest by a slight margin. In the next ride, I used Old Faithful and got through to the semi-final with no problems, but my times on exactly the same set-up as a year before were five or six seconds slower and I was only getting away with it because I had previously had a huge margin over my British peer group.

The cracking sound turned out to be caused by a minor problem, and I used the bike again in one of the last two rides. My fastest time in the series was 4-26, which was a full five seconds slower than the previous year, but the foremost thing in my mind was that I had gotten away with it. I left the championship with quite a bad chesty cough, and I hoped I could prevent it from getting any worse, because I was due to ride the British 25-miles TT Championship in one week.

We had another World Cup event at this time near Milan. In my memory, it seems as though we spent an inordinate amount of time there, going back and forth by bike from training rides on the track. My moment of truth took place in the late evening, under darkness, with powerful spotlights around the large outdoor track. I did not qualify in the top two, and I had to ride against Martinez for third and fourth places. This time I got the better of Martinez for a place on the podium, behind the winner – Markov of Russia – and Philippe Ermanault, who took silver.

Despite the ever-narrowing language barrier between us, Philippe and I talked about the dilemma that a lot of people in a lot of sports were talking about – there was no test for cheating with EPO (a hormone stimulant), and it seemed to a lot of people that the choice was lose or cheat, because the other riders could be cheating too. For me, it was irrelevant, since I had made my stance clear at Christmas '94. Philippe was no supporter of drug-taking either, and he felt angry about the situation.

At a stretch, I was able to shrug off my result as reasonable and late that night, when I got back, I was shattered. As it was past midnight, everyone else was in bed. When I went to bed myself, it took me a moment or two to realise that something was badly wrong. Something was indeed wrong, very wrong – someone had deliberately urinated in my bed. I instantly knew who it was, and for the first time in years, I felt anger as the incident took me right back to that deserted cellar in my childhood. I flew out the door to his room, with nothing but extreme violence in my mind and a locking knife in my hand, but as I marched up the corridor, past the rooms of foreign riders, enough sanity returned to stop me going any further. Rather than disturb the sleep of all the riders who were to ride the next day, I slept on the floor as best I could, between seething with anger and discomfort. In the morning, there was a narrow avoidance of violence with the intervention of other riders, but I made it clear that I would make it known to team directors that he was a disruptive bad apple. There had been a barrage of 'practical joking' since I had ridden with the bunch over Vail Pass in Colombia, some of which could be described as sabotage or vandalism. I could only fathom out the motive for this latest attack as dislike or jealousy, but either way, it had gone well beyond the point of practical joking, and I could not think of it in any way except as a disgusting act of malice.

In the meantime, my cough rapidly became a full-blown chesty cold, and with just days before the 25 Championship, it was at its peak, and it looked unlikely that I would be able to ride. Not having had very good results and wanting to repay my sponsor's faith in me, I was desperate to ride the one event I knew I could shine at, and at the same time I could start to show that I was worth my place in the Olympic TT.

I travelled south on the Friday for the Sunday event, with the hope that I would recover sufficiently to ride, otherwise I would have no choice but to spectate. The evening before the race, I did a light ride on the static trainer, and as I seemed to feel not bad I decided there and then that I would ride the next morning. It was an early start, but it was a perfect day for time trialling. I was the most motivated I had been in a long time, I was focused on the start line in a way that persevered throughout the ride, and the end result was good. I finished with a time of 48-55, which was just short of the championship record, and it was a two-minute denial of gold to Chris Newton, which pleased me no end.

Things were looking better, but not for long, as within a week I would be laid out in bed with what I thought was a rather pernicious virus that would pass within a week or so. I could hardly move, think, speak or eat and I could not bear to look at direct light. I persevered in the hope that it would disappear any day soon, and I could return to the Olympic build-up, but in the meantime I could only get vertical by sliding out of bed and making use of furniture, and the stairs were off-limits, as I did not possess enough energy to tackle them. In all, I was effectively bedridden for three weeks, and when the turning point finally came, I was nine pounds lighter than my racing weight and a good part of my form had evaporated.

During that time I did not call a doctor, since I constantly thought recovery was just round the corner, and the effect of antibiotics on my form in 1993 discouraged me from seeking out the ubiquitous cure-all, as the dentist in Colombia had described European attitudes to the indiscriminate use of the drugs. I cannot remember much from that time, and I believe I was mentally as well as physically subdued. I cannot remember wanting to get out of bed or eating anything without enormous effort. There was no music or TV during that time – just stone-quiet darkness.

When I came out of it, whatever it was, I had to push myself even harder than I had done already in the season, because I was so far behind. It was decided that I should stay with my parents so that I could treat it like training camp, where I could just train and rest, with no distractions. When I say 'it was decided', I mean that like most times during my life, I let everyone else decide where I would go, and the only input needed from me was 'whatever'. My parents thought it would be best, my wife was too polite to counter and say that I should train at home and I accepted the outcome like a child.

After a little while, when my form was not picking up as rapidly as I would like, in order to be on the pace for the Games, my parents were questioning whether I should bother going if my form might not be at its best. I reckoned I would keep training, and if I was below par, I would go anyway, as I might find a lot of form at the training camp before going to the Games proper. My efforts at that time were longer aerobic training on the road and short intense efforts on the static trainer for four minutes at a time, and I could see how well I was performing in comparison to real life, because I always took a mental note of my exact achievable pace on it before some of my fastest-ever rides. It told me I was a long way short of medal-winning form just before I was due to fly out, and the thing that seemed to let me down most was my inability to go to the 'red zone' and hold it without caving in mentally. The problem was that the whole thing seemed like such an incredibly mammoth effort, compared to how it used to be, but more than anything I had no drive and no passion whatsoever.

The first stop for the team was Tallahassee in Florida, where we would spend quite a bit of time at the British training camp, and this is where I hoped my form would take a big leap forward. I had the Hotta equivalent of my TT bike, with a full carbon construction, much like the pursuit bike, and as soon as we had the chance, I went out to do a time-trial effort on the long straight roads of Florida. Louis Passfield, the physiotherapist, helped to measure heat build-up and fluid-loss over set distances. I had as much fun in the humid Florida heat as I had done in Sicily for the World Championships, and at this stage I had absolutely no Olympic ambition at all – just duty.

In some of the time-trial efforts, I could only produce a standby effort, as my eyes would form a thousand-mile stare as I was riding. On the long straight highways it was so tempting to just ride on and on to exhaustion and fall over. Sometimes I would do a pursuit effort, but again I could muster no fire or passion to drive me through the effort before I sloped back to my room, where I spent almost all of my time. I had brought a university textbook on biology, which I read now and then, and the rest of the time I just slept or stared.

I thought that Tallahassee must be one of the loneliest, most depressing places I had ever been to, and for me it probably was. Then we all went to Atlanta, Georgia – and boy, did it make Tallahassee look like a party! I was in the centre of the world's media, public attention, and was fulfilling what would be the dream of a lifetime for most sports people, yet I felt more lonely, more cut off from the world, more point-less and more depressed than I had done for a long, long time. Everyone around me seemed to be so tuned in and part of the whole Olympic dream, and I felt like I was so out of place as the only person who was not connected – I was a total and utter alien here, and in the world as a whole. I was not that well connected to the body I was inhabiting, even so I tried to push myself in training, because I knew that I had to do well to justify my existence to myself.

I spent part of my monotonous days going to the track or doing some time-trial training that Doug would help to time, and attempting to make an effort was incredibly difficult, as a sort of invisible weight hung on me and made every physical and mental activity an uphill fight against lethargy. During other parts of the day, I would wander round the village, where among the crowds of fellow competitors I would feel even more lonely than ever, and the need to be alone and isolated would drive me back to the small room I was sharing with Shaun Wallace, who is also a well-known cycling innovator. Shaun was not very often in the room during the day, and I would have peace to disappear into a deep stare at the ceiling. I got on well with Shaun, but my isolation and the amount of effort it seemed to take to converse with people at that time drove me to seek solitude.

I did not sleep very much in this state of mind, and I got my solitude by cycling about the deserted village at 3 or 4 a.m., and usually I would stop somewhere and just try to work out what the point of anything was. Sometimes during the day I would walk round to the British team relaxation club, where there were pinball machines and the like, and the athletes could have a beer and some nibbles, which I never accepted. The more people that came in, though, the more necessary it became for me to depart because more people round about me only increased my feeling of alienation and loneliness. I felt much worse, ironically, being round about the British Olympic Team than I did with the general mass of foreigners, because feeling totally cut off, alienated and lonely within my own national team made me feel so much more worthless. If there was what I heard referred to as team spirit, then not a hint of it filtered down to me through my almost impervious shell of black depression.

The official opening ceremony was a distraction from the mental pain of moment-to-moment living. Doug said that he was not going to go to the ceremony as the last one he attended in Munich 1972 would do him, and on an athletic level he could not recommend it to any rider. We all decided to go anyway, since most of us had relatives who were staying at home who would be watching on TV, as the team came out of the tunnel. In my case, Anne would be coming to the Games, but my parents said they would watch on TV if they could stay up late enough. We all had to wear the team attire, as supplied for the opening ceremony, and with the pervasive heat and humidity, it was almost impossible to stop sweating, but to counter the loss of fluids officials kept coming round with bottles of water.

All the teams had to decamp in a huge stadium, while the actual opening ceremony took place, then when it was all over, the teams would be called to be ready to make their way to the tunnel. There seemed to be some confusion as to what team was up next or a mix-up with the timing, but the net result was that the British team had to make a run for it en masse down the long, winding corridor to the neighbouring stadium, to the tunnel of a billion eyes. Most of us grabbed our water with us, as we had been advised to do, on account of the long evening to follow.

We had been told that we would have to be prepared for a long night, but I did not expect it to be as long as it was. Once we were in the centre of the stadium, there was no way out until the end, except by special request. After all the water I had drunk, and several hours having passed in the stadium centre, the call of nature was overwhelming to the point of extreme discomfort. At this point I had isolated two reasonable options – the first of which was to put my hand up in the air and shout, 'Please, Mr Samaranch, can I go to the toilet?' or, alternatively, I could pee into my empty bottle under the cloak of baggy clothing. I chose the second option, whilst hiding behind a couple of other athletes, which was not as straightforward as it seems, since the centre (where we were) was criss-crossed with roving cameras on wires that constantly whizzed by while filming from above. The presentation went on so long that even some of the females among us were forced to use the technique, and by the end of the night, almost every bottle had been used and left in yellowy piles on the grass.

The last part of the evening was the lighting of a McDonalds advert by Muhammad Ali, and at that point I thought that I ought to take my second – and last – photograph of the Olympic Games. Doug had been right about the ceremony, and it took ages for everyone to be bussed back and forth to the village. I really could not be bothered with any of it anymore, and I thought I would just lie down on the pavement until someone offered me a lift back – and if they did not, then to hell with it. I boarded an almost empty last bus and got into bed by about 4 a.m., which would not help the athletes who were due to be competing the next day.

I immediately slipped back into my previous frame of mind, except as the next few days passed, everything intensified to the point that I detested myself and everything seemed completely and utterly pointless. At that time, I truly believed that I was a burden on everybody, and that the world really would be better off without me. I realised that I had two beautiful little boys and a loving wife, who would be deeply affected by what I planned to do, but I knew that living with a terrible person like me would be worse, and that I must do what was best for everybody. Besides, I did not think I could stand to be alive any longer with my self-hatred and pointlessness.

I went to the window and climbed out so that I was clinging on with my buttocks, and as I was considering my moment of freedom, I thought about writing a note to explain how necessary it was, but I could not express in words the reality as I saw it, or the depth of my feelings. I left it and climbed back out of the window and onto my buttocks again, as I pondered the effectiveness of four floors, and thought about what would happen if I was only crippled. I was mulling it over, when I heard Shaun saying, 'What the hell are you doing out there?' Instantly I snapped back into my façade and said, 'I was just taking some air,' as I climbed back into the room. Strange as it seemed to Shaun at the time, he did not persist with it beyond my initial explanation, and after that point, I became more confused about life, and my nocturnal wanderings continued on and off until the fateful day arrived when I would have to reach deep down inside myself for a ride that would again justify my existence, prevent me from failing my sponsors and provide emotional and spiritual survival.

When that morning came, I had never been so despondent and unable to motivate myself at an event, and the Olympic rings meant nothing to me at all. I was virtually dead as an athlete, and as I tried to warm up for my ride, I knew that I was facing my nemesis, but I had no fight in me to prevent it. When I was led out for my ride, I bit back the almost unbearable need to cry, scream and laugh at the same time, as I knew that I would rather be anywhere else on the planet – or under the planet – than be here right now.

I forced my legs round as hard as I could for as long as I could, but a humiliating ride was inevitable and my pace was at least twelve seconds slower than it should have been. I had decided to use Old Faithful because I did not want to humiliate the Hotta machine – or myself – and when the final rider, Colinelli, had ridden, I failed to make the top ten. I was desperate to hide away alone, well away from that cauldron of judgmental thoughts and the sea of invasive stares picking away at the last threads of my defenceless self-esteem. I had already escaped in the largest part by hiding inside my head, where no emotion could hurt me, as I had done as a child, and it would be a long, long time before I would be able to come out of my hiding place.

Anne was there after my ride, as well as Richard from Specialized. I made a quick exit from the velodrome, and from my safe haven, I felt no emotion at all, or rather, if I did feel emotion I was insulated from it. The aftermath was difficult, because trying to talk to people was such a physical and mental drain. Richard was visibly disappointed at my not being able to pull out a death-or-glory ride to get a good result, but he did his best to give the impression that he was happy that I had done my best.

Anne stayed for another couple of days, but because of the shortage of accommodation she flew out before my own departure time. I was supposed to be staying on for the time trial, but because of my lack of form, or perhaps because of my poor frame of mind, Doug proposed that I forget about it and set off home early. It was an idea that I quickly agreed with, and a day or so after Anne left, I too was on my way home.

Before I left, I joined the other riders who had finished their rides, on a last night out. Once I started drinking, I was compelled to drown the sadness and depression and to carry on regardless in an effort to drown the hidden pain in my mind, with ever more vigorous consumption. At one point in the evening, I remember shimmying up a large flagpole to fetch down an Olympic flag as a souvenir, but I also remember hitting the ground with quite a bump and having a rather sore arm the next day.

The relief was short-lived, and the need for more alcohol soon returned, and since we were heading to a beer hall just outside the village, I would have plenty of opportunity. Sooner or later, I was thrown out and I made my way to the village centre, where Ziggy Marley was playing live. I remember sharing a discreet can with some other athletes, and on the buggy ride back, as I was becoming too sober again for mental comfort a Russian rider offered me a drink from his water bottle and, to my surprise, it was almost pure alcohol. I coughed my way through the equivalent of a couple of shots and finally staggered back to my bed to look forward to departing that place the next day.

When I arrived home, I still had a sore arm, a sense of despair and pointlessness and the remnants of a career. There was only one positive thing that came out of the Olympics for me, and that was the fact that most of the pursuit gold medals had been won on my Superman position, and that emulation is a great form of compliment.

The black place I was in before the Olympics did not let go, the inability to train properly continued. Every day I thought, 'I have to get out of this rut', and every day it was the same. Every day I felt like I was choking back tears, as I tried to push myself as I knew I should be able to, but I could do nothing to change things. There was no reason for the bleak pointlessness, but trying to convince myself that all I had to do was get fast would only end up being countered by my depressive thinking, which would have me asking myself, 'What is the point of being successful? What is the point of being wealthy? What is the point of being alive?'

This situation went on and on, and in the end I had no form for the World Championships in Manchester, and my racing season was effectively at a close. That was not my last race, though, as I received an invitation from Lee and Max Vertongen to come over to New Zealand for a racing/holiday trip over the festive season. By then, my mental blackness had turned to a lighter shade of grey for no explicable reason, and by then I was wondering how I could have let myself be in such a bad frame of mind before.

I was able to push myself to get the best form that I could before heading south to the New Zealand summer. My form up to then had evaporated away, and the best I could hope for was to build it up to the point of being reasonable. Not long after I arrived, I found myself in a pursuit match with Lee, who was in the middle of his season and preparing for his national championships in a few weeks' time. He was obviously on top form, but he had the grace to beat me in a manner that was not humiliating.

I also found myself in a few bunch races, and thankfully I avoided humiliation by ensuring I was on the right wheel at the right time. There was also plenty of time for relaxing in the Antipodean sun, but despite that my mood took a nosedive during the trip, and I remember lying on the bed in the middle of the day, wondering how I could feel this bad when, really, everything round about me was so good. That was not the first time in my life that I thought there must be something wrong with me, but this time I thought it in earnest. I unconsciously manipulated events so that I could obtain my usual medicine, and a couple of occasions of total inebriation were to follow. We travelled to Lake Taipo, where Max had a holiday home and a boat, and by this time I was feeling fine again, and after a couple of days there, I really felt more than fine. One evening, after a day in the boat, I felt so alive that I woke everyone up at 3 a.m. to tell them to get up, as it was such a beautiful night. It seemed the right thing to do at the time, but in retrospect I believe it might have been a little over the top.

I gave Lee some handlebars that I had made, since he was also using the Superman position. I had started playing around with the production of handlebars as a business, since I had it in my mind that my time in top level cycling was over, as I could not cut it any more. I was starting production of tri-bars that would allow a full Superman position on a standard bike, without slippage or flexing in both aluminium and carbon fibre. It was a small-scale operation that took place from a small workshop in my mother-in-law's property, where I was the sole proprietor and worker.

When Lee got set up in his correct position, he was desperate to test it out in a big way by attacking the New Zealand hour record at the outdoor wooden track at Wanganui, which was only a two-hour drive from Palmerston North, where he and Max lived. He was not sure about it, though, but I knew from riding with him that he was on terrific form and I urged him to go as soon as possible. The weather was fine and calm that day, and with a phone call over to the caretaker of the track, he was all set for an attempt that evening.

All the officials had been organised at short notice, and after a short delay for various reasons, he finally set off on a schedule of 50km, which I had urged him to do. At the halfway point, he was well up on the mark, but darkness was closing in fast, and two or three available cars were driven to the track centre, so that the headlights could guide him through his last section of torture. It was pitch black at the end, and he had to guess his way through the unlit parts, but despite that, he finished well over 50km to take not only the New Zealand record, but that of the entire southern hemisphere. He had also taken my unofficial outdoor sea-level world record that I had set at Herne Hill three years earlier. For me, I got a great deal of pleasure out of helping and witnessing such an incredible performance by a great athlete pushing himself way beyond the boundaries of normal hard effort. Perhaps it was because I was the only one there who could actually feel the beauty of what had been done, and only I could empathise with every pain-drenched pedal-stroke that he refused to surrender to. Either way, witnessing the pain and the pleasure from the outside left me quite emotional and, in a small way, slightly inspired.

Lee and I raced again at Invercargill, in the very south of the south island, where the next stop from the beach is the Antarctic, and we could feel its proximity in temperature as we arrived. The track there was an old-style, very large tarmac oval, where we took part in several hard races. The top Australian riders were also there for the racing festival, but thanks to my slightly improved form, I was able to hold my own, while Lee won a race or two, which was fitting for the form that he had.

Unfortunately, my feeling of being so alive and on a high was only a temporary inversion, and during our time back at Palmerston North, I drank the best part of Joss's gin (Max's partner) and smoked a joint or two that was offered by one of Lee's friends, in a vain attempt at reclaiming what had been so good. Soon it was all over, and I was back in the Scottish winter in our nice house with my family. Looking back on it, I had a great time, even if I did leave behind a quiet reputation of being slightly mad.

Now that I was home, I was forced to try and take stock of everything and try to decide what exactly I was going to do. It was a new year and a new season ahead, and I would either have everything to play for or everything to dread, depending on which way I would be able to think about my possibilities. Either way, I would have several months of thinking before I need turn a pedal in anger.

sixteen: darkness and dawn

I spent the winter of '97 burying myself in setting up the production of superman tri-bars in readiness to exploit the demand that would surely exist after so many successes on that position around the world. I was really hoping to carve a future for myself in the engineering business by supplying to a niche market. At the same time my training had taken a real nose-dive because I had no sponsors and no hope, as I saw it, of muscling back into the money-making end of the sport – I was completely disenchanted with it and I only rode when I felt like it.

No sooner had I amassed a pile of component parts for my full-reach handlebars than the UCI acted to outlaw the riding style by applying rules to limit the reach that a handlebar can have. Pretty soon the time-trial governing body in Britain had followed suit and almost overnight most of the potential buyers had been taken out of the equation. Since professional cycling was out of reach, I was left with the handlebar business as my only potential income in the short term. As time went by, I did sell a few pairs of the bars but I would have to redirect my energy into producing bars that conformed to standard dimensions that had a clear advantage over rival handlebars already available on the market.

I knew that my carbon fibre handlebars were lighter, classier and had a better mounting clamp than the others, but the main problem was actually getting to the customers. I also produced bar-ends for mountain bikes in carbon that were lighter than any on the market and I sent a set of these and a set of handlebars to *Cycling Weekly* for their 'new products' page. They got a reasonable write-up but very few orders came of it. I thought that my image as the 'washing machine man' and my bike falling apart on live TV had seriously undermined my credibility.

About this time I also started to get involved with the promotion company, Red, to publicise the forthcoming Pru-Tour which was sponored by Prudential and was Britain's largest stage-race, covering most of the country. If it had not been for the Pru-Tour promotion then I would have had almost no earnings at all to justify myself as a father and a husband, since my handlebar venture was not exactly on the way to setting me up as a captain of industry.

After being so gung-ho about how my business would be so successful, and being boundless in energy and ideas and sometimes working all night without the need for a break, I now felt like such a failure and had no drive at all. Before I was due to make my first journey to promote the Pru-Tour, I realised I had a track meeting to ride in Dundee in under three weeks' time. I had agreed to ride before my fall from enthusiasm and I had a verbal contract that I was loath to break, though it was tempting. I knew my form was poor, but some of the promotion had already been based on my presence at the event and morally I knew I had no choice but to institute a policy of damage limitation and train as best I could until the meeting.

I managed to get my form up to mediocre despite my continuing mental block about hard training. In my frame of mind at that time the intensity of world-class training seemed like nothing short of bloodless self-mutilation, and with a pervading cloud of apathy and pointlessness hanging over me it was impossible to sustain any hard effort. Luckily for me my Kiwi friend, Lee, was coming over to stay with us to get in some races in the British season and he would be here in time for the Dundee meeting. This was good because with Lee here to make the Scottish riders look silly he would distract attention from me. My plan was foiled as Lee had a stomach upset on arrival and I had to go it alone, which led to a large embarrassment as I got lapped in the pursuit and beaten into second place in the Scottish 15km Championship.

At that point I decided that I would never ride again and that I would make handlebars or whatever. It was the 'whatever' that kept me awake at night, and it was also responsible for an awful lot of introspection that only served to fuel my sense of worthlessness. That summer of '97 I felt like an abject failure – my handlebar business had still come to nothing. I was unqualified at anything else but cycling and now I was a failure at that too. In my mind I saw myself as someone who had achieved something, made some money, and had hit the ground again as a useless ex-criminal who could not even provide for his family any more.

I went to the first appearance of the Pru-Tour promotion and did quite well at speaking, despite the black weight hanging on me. The next few appearances were not to be that way as the lure of my alcoholic medicine was too tempting and I got pretty drunk at the hotels the night before, and sometimes even more so with a pre-organised carry-out in my room. On one occasion I got really drunk in the hotel and told all the staff of Red that I hated myself and I wanted to die. The worst occasion was when I had to meet them at a hotel in Birmingham. I set off by train and being in a mood where I could barely face up to my Pru-Tour obligation, I bought four cans of German beer at Glasgow Central for later on that night, but when the departure of the train was delayed, I decided that I would have a beer or two at the bar in the station. I knew it was perhaps a bad idea, but with the way my world seemed to me at that time, any resistance that logic had to offer was futile and my alcoholic escape had started much earlier than was either planned or wise. It goes without saying that the German beers did not remain unopened, but as my medicine went down something was not working and my desire to no longer exist became stronger.

I was driven to seek escape at the buffet car over and over until the black demon was driven out from my thinking. This I successfully managed, but only when the ability for any cohesive thinking was extinguished. I staggered my way through the centre of Birmingham, stopping to ask for directions at any available pubs and consuming more alcohol for good measure. All the while I convinced myself that I could pass myself off as sober when I arrived by saying some words to myself that sounded pretty coherent to me. The world was no longer black – it was completely blurred and spinning instead, but it was still a better world than the one I had left behind in the land of sobriety. When I finally arrived late at the hotel and delivered welcoming words in my well-practised, sober voice to Liz and Wendy of Red, it was instantly noticeable that I had a serious problem with alcohol. It was just as obvious that I had a serious emotional problem when I asked Liz for one of her cigarettes and proceeded to tell them once again how pointless it all was and how much I hated myself. I was very lucky, and thankful, that they were the compassionate sort and allowed me to carry on and try and be professional the next day at the public presentation.

Thankfully, that was my lowest point that summer, and after those incidents the team were careful to try to keep me clear of alcohol at the hotels. I felt better for it physically, and since the dark clouds around me seemed to have cleared I had no driving need for alcohol or substances anyhow. On previous occasions where I had been peacefully paralytic, it has been incredibly difficult to pose for photographs while feeling like a fake, and physically exhausted and hung-over the next day. It was even more difficult trying to produce a long and impassioned speech cohesively and to mingle with important people without them noticing the powerful smell of alcohol on my breath.

One of the last and best trips I made to promote the Pru-Tour was to Medway in Kent, and the plan was to fly down first thing in the morning and return that some evening. I was feeling good and I decided that I would cycle the 20 miles to the airport, lock my bike, and cycle back in the evening. Everything went to plan except that I had to run to make it on time for my 6.30 a.m. flight. I accepted the complimentary drinks on the flight because I always find being publicly in the open such a nervous-making thing that a couple of drinks on the flight might make me more relaxed, I thought. The alcohol did that, but since I had no dark cloud to expel there was no need for further beverage that day. Everything went fine, but when I arrived at Glasgow airport with my cycling gear on once again I got a shock to discover that my bike was gone from the railings out front.

In an instant I realised that it could not have been stolen in plain view of so many security people and that they themselves must have cut through the U-lock and taken it away for security reasons. On asking, I was directed to the information desk where the head of security came and explained to me that they had been hailing for the owner of the bike all day and in the end they had to remove it because of the bomb risk it posed. He led me to a room right behind the check-in desks and right below the Tap and Spike pub, which was busy, and there they had placed their bomb risk for safe keeping. I thanked them, shook my head in disbelief, and cycled home with the thought of how lucky it was that I was not a real terrorist.

Towards the end of the summer I started feeling really positive and decided to make a comeback. I had been in contact with Joe Beer, who is a sports physiologist, and he suggested I should take notes of heart rates and the like, which I did, distracting though it was to my own system which was based on feel factor and a well-used static trainer which I could gauge myself on from previous efforts. Joe's methods were good in as much as they told me the same things that I could feel already by being tuned in to my body and its recovery. I trained hard, using my tried and tested methods, and kept an eye on Joe's measurements while I was doing it. For the first time in well over a year I was training with passion and really wanted to get out there and give it my best in a race. With the return of good attitude came an amazingly quick comeback to form and I could have kicked myself for having allowed myself to be so negative for so long. Now I was in a new reality that I had been deprived of all summer by the black, all-consuming fog that had engulfed me and completely obscured my vision of hope and truth.

I raced a 10-mile TT in England and was narrowly beaten by Johnny Clay, who was the 10-mile champion, but I was not downhearted because I had been slowed by a tractor at the turn and I had not yet reached my previous top average speed on my all-truthful static bike. A few weeks later, and still with total motivation, I rode the same TT course and went thirty seconds quicker to come within seven seconds of my own 10-mile record on the new position for UCI events. No one could say I was a fake after doing that ride on a standard position, and to drive the point home I would be riding the same bike in the British Time Trial Championship the day after, where the bikes would be scrutinised for conformity. It was a hard undulating ride and, although my legs were a little tired from the day before, I won it by a handful of seconds from Stuart Dangerfield, who would later go on to beat my 10-mile record.

I had come out of the darkness and into the light, and now I had my mind set on pursuit or even team-pursuit for the World Championships in Perth, Australia, in a month or so. I contacted Doug, who invited me down to Manchester to train with the squad and to have a go at qualifying for the individual pursuit place by going under 4-30. I had lost count of how many times I had gone quicker than that in my career and although my new form was recent and I had not done any specific training, I reckoned I had the measure of it.

The first time I tried it I was off the pace from the start and swung off after just six laps. I stayed and trained to be part of the team-pursuit should I be called upon to ride in an emergency. I spent a couple more sessions at Manchester and each time it was the same story in the pursuit despite the fact that I was going not bad in the team-pursuit rides. The end result was that Doug asked me to travel to Australia with the team in case illness or a crash took out one of the team members. I went in the hope that I could get a ride to rest a pair of legs for a later round, but as it transpired I was completely surplus to requirements.

It was a foreign rider who pointed out to me how out of place I looked just sitting there all warmed up in my skin suit with nowhere to go. The phrase 'how the mighty have fallen' came to my lips but was never uttered. My positivity and form had risen out of nothing like a desert orchid and now the icy wind of new truth would cause it to wither and die. The death had been slowly coming till now, but in the end it was quick. Self-analysis became my prime purpose between waking and sleeping and the deeper I peered into the pool of life, the darker and murkier it appeared.

We were in Australia for quite some time but in the course of just two weeks I had gone from being on a real high to being on a complete and utter low like I had been at the Olympic Games. I was so desolate that in the end I was drinking cans of beer on the sly to dull down my misery, and at that time it was also the third anniversary of my brother's death and I found it impossible to avoid the thoughts that took me right back to our unhappy childhood together.

The night before the team's flight home I had several beers alone at the lakeside, which was nearby, and such was my self-destructive mood and desperation to escape life that I even bought a packet of cigarettes and smoked half of them before throwing the other half in the lake when I thought about how disgusted Gordon would be if only he were looking down from a higher place. I pondered whether I should just swim out and drown so that it would all be over and I would not have to live with my defective head any more. The idea that Gordon's death was not altogether an accident seemed to set a precedent for me but I thought about Anne, my children and my parents and I realised that they would not understand that they would be better off without a person like me. In a way I felt a bit imprisoned by them because for me, alone at that time, the decision would have been easy to make.

In the end I went back and hid under a duvet and hoped that daylight would come late to my eyes. The next morning I was struggling to find the mental energy to deal with the packing process as every little action seemed like a huge task. I went out and bought some more beer to help me through the day, and when we got to the airport I bought some duty-free vodka to take home. On the flight there was conversation and people trying to be friendly, which was like torture to me as I had to think what they would like to hear in response, and the energy needed to do that from the black place was painful to try and find.

I took advantage of the free drinks on the flight to make life seem more manageable, but after a while in such close proximity to other people I lost control and opened my duty free on the quiet. I knew it was a stupid thing to and it was not long before I was pretty intoxicated, but the struggle to respond was an easier one than it had been. At this point I hid behind a book, but at a certain juncture in the flight I found myself in a really black place and I rewrote a poem which I had been working on earlier:

TIME RELENTLESS

On winter days dark and dull,
Of wind and rain and shrieking gull,
Grey puddles lament with angry cry,
The passing clouds that scurry by,
And hearing waves crash to shore,
To caress the ocean depths no more,
And rocks and mountains on the land,
With time and tide are turned to sand,
And cold winds whistle, wail and whine,
As if to mourn their passing time,
But who will grieve with heartfelt tears,
Our own wasted months and years?
Not drinking mates nor friends we know,
Not even those with fondness so,
That love should live and ride the hearse,
That takes us to lie 'neath silent verse.

I passed it to some of the team in a hope that somehow they would understand me. Most of them thought it was interesting but perhaps a little depressing. A short while after that, I told the entire team, including officials, that I was going to kill every one of them. If I could not stab them or whatever, I would grow a virus and poison them. That certainly broke the façade of normality that I had been trying to hide behind, and it became obvious to everyone that I was both drunk and out of control.

We stopped at Bangkok airport where a Russian rider was thrown off the flight for drunkenness. The flight staff were keen to dole out the same penalty to me since it is an offence to be drunk on an aircraft. It was only the verbal and partially physical restraint of Marshall Thomas, a coach with the team, to get me to keep my head down and act sober, as well as his pleading of my case to the flight crew, that allowed me to fly on to London. It was a good thing he did, since the frame of mind I was in at that moment was such that I had decided if I got thrown out of the plane then things would have reached such a low point that I would simply take my life – I would dole out the treatment that I thought I deserved.

When I got to London I bade farewell to the team and excused away my behaviour as the result of drinking. When I got to Glasgow it was quite late and, partly because I could not face any more travelling and mainly because I desperately needed to be totally alone, I stayed overnight in a travel lodge. I truly wanted to be at home with my wife and kids, but I could not bear to have anyone talking to me no matter how much I loved them. I made sure I had a more than adequate carry-out and took my medicine alone before heading home the next morning.

When I got back I was determined that my career was truly over and a few weeks later, in an outburst of self-destruction and unprovoked anger, I destroyed my Mark II bike that I had won the World Championships on and my time-trial bike, which was less than one year old. When I was finished with them, the pieces were so small that both bikes could fit into a bin-bag. Old Faithful had a lucky escape by the mere fact of her absence from the workshop. Destroying my favourite tapes and CDs appeased my need for self-harm and punishing myself for no clear reason other than an intense feeling of self-hatred.

Things continued that way for quite a while, with alcohol abuse being quite common, and then things turned around and I started training for the Christmas '10' with a view to riding for Scotland at the Commonwealth Games. At that time, when I was training and feeling positive about riding, alcohol had absolutely no appeal whatsoever and dedication was the order of the day. Again my form would have to make a Phoenix-like rise from the ashes in less than six or seven weeks.

With total drive and energy for every ride it did just that, and in the 10-mile event I almost broke my own Scottish record and I set an off-season British record that stands to the present day. After that I did long training rides in the early months of 1998 in the hope of getting a grant from the Sports Council to allow me to get by financially while I dedicated myself to the task. I remained positive through these long winter months despite the fact that I had no sponsorship to speak of, knowing that even the lowest level of grant that had been spoken about would see me through financially. I also knew that even if I won three gold medals at the games, there would be no financial return to compensate for my investment in time or for the money that I could earn in other ways during that time. Without a modest grant I would have to risk everything on world championship success to make my season viable.

For the first time in a long while I would be competing for just national and personal pride as well as for the sheer hell of it. Then, eventually, my grant award came through and when I saw it I honestly thought that two digits must have been left out. Then I thought, 'Martin – this is one of Martin's pranks'. It was no prank though, and the total living expenditure of my grant for Commonwealth Games living expenses was £460. I was pretty dumped, to say the least, to think that over the year I was worth less than £10 per week. I had a lot of thinking to do and I did not make immediate decisions since my form was so good that my gut reaction was to carry on regardless.

The more I thought about it, the more I could not help thinking about those with a good salary who would be soaking up the praise for good management of their funds if I won the medals I hoped to, and then I realised that even if I did win them then they would make little difference to my cycling CV since mentioning Commonwealth Games medals would be an afterthought to my other achievements. My dedication and positivity gradually ebbed away and after my first race of the season, the Ayr-to-Girvan time trial, I lost my motivation completely and decided that, once and for all, cycling as a sport should be jettisoned from my life. It was ironic that the first race I won in my life at seventeen was also the race that I won in closing my career at the age of thirty-two. It was a decision that Anne totally supported and she was not slow to openly voice her disdain at the grant offer, which she would describe, when she was polite about it, as nothing less than an insult.

As I crossed the finish line at Girvan it was the moment that my career as an international racing cyclist ended. Not having cycling in my life left a sudden hole in my hopes of earning money for my family and at that point I had to think about reigniting my handlebar dreams, which had faded due to a lack of commercial response and business experience on my part. Initially I set out my plans with incredible vigour, but as time wore on things started to seem hopeless again and everything became a huge effort. I was trying to stay positive and hopeful but I could not hold back the blanket of suffocating mist that choked the worth out of everything that I knew.

Before long, in the summer of '98, I was reaching for my alcoholic medicine yet again, but I needed more than that to lift me out of the black mist even just for a brief moment. I knew that acetylene would have an even greater power over my unseen enemy, but it was unpleasant to smell and taste. I was so desperate at that time, though, and by holding my nose I could avoid most of the stench and just half a breath would allow me to fly over the black mist for what seemed like an eternity to see the sunlight once again in its true brightness. This became a more and more regular need on my part, and on one occasion I stayed in the workshop all night with beer and my friend, acetylene, to fight off my dark oppressor, depression. I had not drunk that much but in the end I had to come down, and on this occasion I had reached the point where I could no longer free myself and the world about me became more and more bleak. In the end I started crying uncontrollably for no singular reason and it was my father-in-law, Steve, who found me. I could not stop and I told him how useless everything was between bouts, and I could not understand what was happening to me as I tried in vain to pull myself together.

Eventually, Anne came over and I regained composure in Steve's kitchen. I said that I must have something wrong with me and that I must be a depressive or something like that, which I sometimes thought when I was younger. Anne said that she had been concerned about me for a long time and that she had arranged to see Martin's doctor friend privately in Glasgow to see what he thought. The doctor agreed to see us at short notice, but because psychiatry was not his speciality he could only give a general opinion. By this time I seemed quite calm and, as I have done throughout my life, I hid behind my façade that is quite impenetrable to all but those who are closest to me. The consensus was that it was just a blip and that I should avoid alcohol in future.

The doctor's opinion was certainly correct in regard to the consumption of alcohol, but he did not see the connection between cause and effect. To me it seemed that I drank and abused substances when I felt so really bad that I would do anything to either escape it or make it more bearable, but to the outside world it seemed that I felt emotionally really bad whenever I drank alcohol. I came away with the feeling that something was destroying me from inside in intense and unbearable intervals in a way that no one else could see. I felt misunderstood and isolated because no one could see me as anything but a binge-drinking alcoholic, who only had to give up drink in order to be just fine.

My deep depression continued and so did my gas-propelled vacations from the black zone. One night it got out of hand as I was now inhaling enough to almost pass out to get the relief that I sought so badly. I did pass out on one occasion and when I came to the bottles were on top of my legs. I was so anaesthetised by the gas that I managed to get them off of my legs on my own but it did not take me long to realise that my left leg was crushed so badly that I could not move it. My right leg did not escape unscathed either, but somehow I managed to make it to my feet to try and pretend that nothing had happened. I was in extreme pain and, like a toddler, I had to hold on to objects and surfaces in order to move around. When Anne came she saw the vomit I had left as a result of the gas and we went immediately to the hospital, where I stayed for about a week before hobbling home on crutches, which I needed for some time. I was lucky in that I did not break any bones, but my muscles had been so badly crushed that even after a couple of months and some physiotherapy I was still walking with a limp.

Not long after that Anne came up with an idea which I was not that enthusiastic about, but then, at that time, I was not that enthusiastic about anything, including breathing. Sooner or later the world became brighter again and pretty soon I was cracking into our plan like a whirlwind. We were going to open a coffee shop with a large play area for kids and now there was no end to my enthusiasm as I set about building a 3-metre by 7-metre, two-storey climbing frame with some of the materials I had bought for handlebar production. My enthusiasm led us to buy far too much catering equipment, toys and bouncy castles for the realistic size of our operation. I was thinking huge and had us looking at closed-down supermarkets and warehouses. All that business with depression and alcohol seemed well behind me now, and I thought to myself that all I had to do was just give myself a good shake.

The planning department brought us back down to earth and every place we looked at had an almost insurmountable obstacle to overcome before permission would be considered. In the course of our project we heard so many horror stories where people had fulfilled the initial obligations of the planning department only to be told 'no' on previously unmentioned grounds, like not being in keeping with the surrounding environment. Our plan was still on but we were very wary about having to risk everything before we could get approval. What held us back was not the risk involved in business, but the risk of not being in business at the whim of unelected civil servants. At that time I felt a sense of purpose while trying to set up our business, but as things dragged on I felt like I was in limbo – neither a cyclist nor a businessman.

After more than a year we were still in the position where we would have to commit to a long lease before we would be sure that we would be allowed to use the premises. On top of that we saw Mr Singh, a local businessman, being turned down on whimsical grounds after committing almost £1 million for premises that most local people thought would be perfect for a similar project to our own. Our plan was not completely dead but we had so little trust now that we were incredibly wary about throwing the dice. We even considered going abroad, but in the end we decided that the upheaval would be too much.

As the difficulties of getting into business seemed to mount and time went by, my enthusiasm waned and my sense of failure and depression resurfaced. At this time an ideal building we were looking at on the Beach Park at Irvine turned out to be unsuitable for children since that area turned out to be quite heavily contaminated by toxic waste from old chemical works. Our business idea was effectively dead and my mood suffered as a result.

Anne saw through my façade and one day, when she was driving, she told me not to take it the wrong way but she had made an appointment for me to see the doctor. I admitted life was a strain for me at the moment and agreed. When the time came the doctor recommended that I see a counsellor and this was arranged to be a once-a-week session. Seeing the counsellor did not make me feel any better. In fact it made me feel more depressed than before, which apparently is quite normal because the counsellor helps bring issues to the surface that have long since been suppressed. I explained to the counsellor that I quite often had thoughts of suicide. I reassured him that I had no intention of acting on them, but that those thoughts were never far away.

During the time of counselling I was due to fly out to Switzerland to ride the Tony Rominger Classic road race. I was to ride in a group alongside Eddy Merkx, Miguel Indurain, Francesco Moser and other famous cyclists. For me it was not to be a serious race and it would be a good day out. When I set off for the airport it was a particularly bad time for me and it was a struggle to converse with people or even to be in their company. It was hard just to be awake and alive in a world that was so intolerably dismal that morning. When I got to Glasgow airport I downed two pints at the Tap and Spike – the pub that had sheltered my 'bike bomb'.

At London I felt no better and would have ended it there and then if I had had the means – such was my overriding desire to be dead. Instead, I sought out more drink on the grounds that if I must be alive then alcohol, or any substance for that matter, would dull me. When I got to Geneva I had gone way beyond black. I was quite intoxicated but not drunk, wandering about the arrivals area of the airport with dark glasses and a skipped hat and my headphones on full volume. My old feelings of failure, worthlessness and abject self-hatred had fully returned. At one point I was crying into my bike bag when a woman from the airport staff approached to see if I was all right. I rebuffed her as politely as possible but her approach startled me into the next phase – action.

I wrote a note to Anne, my boys and everybody, apologising for being such a useless person. I said that I hated myself but I loved them all, and argued that they really would be better off without a person like me in their lives. All the while I was shaking and tears were running down my face. I put the note inside my passport and put it in my pocket. Then I went to an airport chemist and, not knowing what the most lethal pills were, I asked for aspirins and managed to buy three large boxes of them on the excuse of being on a long vacation and needing to stock up. When I came away from that chemist I was afraid that I might survive so I asked an airport worker if there were any other chemists in the building and he directed me to another. There I was able to buy four more boxes with the same storyline, which gave me 112 pills in total.

I took my seven boxes and went to the bar where I consumed two or three of them from under the barstool, washing them down with several beers. The strange thing, thinking about it now, was that at that time I felt a total calmness in the knowledge that I was sure to die with 112 pills. I continued drinking and swallowing, and made my move by throwing my passport, with my note still inside it, to a member of staff at the upstairs check-in desk. Then I dashed downstairs and out into the darkness, abandoning my luggage in the airport.

When I got outside I started to feel incredibly thirsty, but rather than going inside again and risk being stopped, I bent down and drank from a puddle in the car park. There I set about the business of consuming the remaining boxes of pills with the aid of puddle water. A couple of times I could not help boaking up and although I managed to keep a lot of it in my bloated cheeks, which I swallowed again for fear of living, I still lost some of the pills.

Impatient to be dead I started to walk in the direction where I thought the River Rhone went under a high bridge and my plan now was to jump off there before the pills even had a chance to work. I walked and walked and I remember I had a cigarette that I had scrounged from the barman at the airport. I had no light, though, and tried to stop the traffic for a flame, but it took me jumping in front of a car before I was successful. I walked on, thinking that the pill plan was not working whilst my thirst was now becoming unbearable. I saw a restaurant and walked into the bar where I asked how far the bridge was and ordered a beer. The barman was confused about the bridge question and when I had finished the beer I ordered another before realising that I had left my money at the airport. I thanked him and walked away without paying. There was a bit of noise behind me but I kept on walking.

By this point I had covered miles and although I felt a bit wobbly I was very much alive. I found myself in a side road with a chemist shop in front of me. My immediate thought was that there would be something stronger in there than aspirins and I set about finding a way to break in. I ended up on the roof with the skylight as the only port of entry. So I ripped it up and peered inside, only to be accosted by complete darkness. At that point I thought that it was a hell of a drop into the unknown with no way out and the police on their way. And someone had spotted me from a window, so I moved quickly on.

Some way further I stopped at a bench in despair. I took out my penknife and readied myself for the ultimate solution, but as I was wrestling with whether or not I had it in me to pull the blunt blade hard enough and deep enough, I realised there was an eight-storey block of flats in front of me. But when I got to the top it was impossible to reach an exit and even the service door was locked.

Out on the street again I realised that there were lots of parked cars – and cars have seatbelts. I tried loads of doors before I found one that was open. I pulled the belt to its full length, cut it, and set off to find a suitable tree.

In a split second I had been bundled to the ground with my arm up my back, a boot on my shoulders and one on top of my head. The pain of the tarmac on my face pleased me, since I deserved it and more. I was taken to the station where I faced question after question. Eventually a psychiatrist came and after a while I disclosed that I had swallowed some pills. I was kept in the questioning booth for hours and in the end I could not sit any more and adopted a foetal position on the floor.

After a while I started to vomit bloody mucus and shortly after that I was taken to hospital where my grip on life started to wane.

I cannot remember much about that night except that my friend Gerald was there, deeply upset and confused. I had tubes up every orifice and people kept slapping me and telling me that I must not fall asleep. The short of it all was that during the night my chances of survival were evens, and that had I been allowed to go unconscious then I may never have woken up. Gerald played a major role in that not happening.

After three days in hospital I was well enough to be transferred to the start of my new way of life in a mental institution. I had no choice since I had been sectioned by a Swiss psychiatrist and when I arrived at the institution, which was set in leafy and spacious grounds a little way from Geneva, the immensity of the situation began to hit home. I still felt so depressed and confused that I just lay down most of the time. When I saw other patients I would think that surely there must be a mistake and that I did not really belong here. I was relieved of my belt and laces and had a room of my own with grilles on the window and a plastic mirror. I would not be allowed to leave until Anne had secured, in writing, that I would be transferred directly to a similar institution in Britain. Not only that, but I would have to be escorted by a psychiatric nurse the whole way.

Anne arranged all of that and when I got to Scotland I commenced my first long-term stay in Ailsa Hospital, which is relatively close to where we lived. From a young age I had known Ailsa as a word associated only with ridicule. I had as much ignorance about mental illness as anyone else and when I was driven past the Victorian buildings to arrive at the modern Park Ward unit, I felt that I had reached an all-time low. The realisation that I, Graeme Obree, was about to be a patient at Ailsa was the defining point, and not that I, Graeme Obree, had tried so hard to kill himself on foreign soil – such was my acceptance of reality.

Park Ward had twenty-plus patients and it was quite a large unit. I had a secure room to myself for quite a while and during that time I did nothing much but hide under a duvet trying to close my eyes on the black uselessness in my mind. At some point I became desperately suicidal and searched for any means at hand but without success.

When I started coming out of my depression I got moved to a dorm of six beds where nothing much really happened. When I first got admitted I imagined that things would happen like group therapy or a lot of talking with professionals, but those things rarely happened and most of my days were spent hiding away, reading, or hanging out with other patients in the smoke room, which was a kind of group therapy I suppose. I spent over three months at Ailsa before being given day passes and finally a full discharge.

I attended a clinical psychologist weekly and she set about trying to find the aspects of my character that affect the way I interact with the world and other people in ways that would depress my mood. Unfortunately, this is not an immediate fix and my sessions continue to this day, and not without some further setbacks, like the time I decided to load up my bike and go and live in a forest. After a couple of days a semblance of responsibility re-entered my brain and I phoned Anne to say I would come back. Before I knew it Anne had come for me at the phonebox. The police were also involved since, unbeknown to me, a nationwide search had been initiated and I only avoided a newspaper appeal for my whereabouts by a few hours.

A short internment at Crosshouse Hospital followed and at that time my psychologist reminded me that hiding in a forest was what I used to do as a child. When I thought about it I knew she was right and that I had allowed myself to follow a conditioned response from childhood. She was also trying to encourage me to develop my sense of self-worth just for myself. Until then I had always valued myself on what I was about to achieve or do for other people, so that I would feel only as worthy as my next race result. The absence of bike racing or, more accurately, bike racing victories, probably exacerbated my mental perturbance and spiritual bankruptcy.

Even so, I still began to think that I had to make a comeback if I wanted to feel all right about myself again, and that is exactly what I proceeded to do, with a plan to break the hour record one more time. I won a couple of races in 2000, but got beaten into second place at the Scottish 25-mile Championship, despite doing a reasonable ride – especially considering that my training had been inconsistent due to my mood swings. The inevitable happened and I lost motivation, only to retrieve it again later in the year after another brush with the dark side. This time I got really fit, even though it was coming on for winter and I became obsessed with regaining that record. I did 10-mile tests on my local measured course and my times in the UCI riding position were fast, although my arms would ache the whole way round. I got a chance to ride on the velodrome at Manchester, with Doug giving me a hand,

and I learned about what gearing to use and how much more power I would need to produce a record pace.

I was getting really close to that magic figure and started thinking about going for it as soon as possible and possibly during a track meeting. I didn't have to scout around very long before Terry Palfreyman, a BCF (British Cycling Federation) official, stepped up and offered to organise the whole thing. The big day would be the 23rd of December 2000, and before the end of November there was news of busloads of supporters coming from all over the country to witness the ride. I started to feel that same old 'all-or-nothing' way, and as the days went by and I was still not hitting full power, I started to panic a bit.

The situation seemed simple – I would reduce my medication. I was on such a high and I was so much in control that nothing could go wrong. I had been under medication since 1999 and the two that I thought could be holding me back were the anti-depressants and the lithium carbonate (a mood stabiliser). I was on 1.2 grams of lithium per day, which can have serious side effects – so that and the anti-depressants had to go. Everything went fine for ten days or so and then suddenly I didn't care about the hour record any more. I slid from white to black in a couple of days and when I hit the bottom it was as bleak as it had ever been. I overdosed on the medication to try to restore my balance but when I managed to force myself out on my bike, because I knew I had to, it was all I could do to turn the pedals over in bottom gear. Mentally and physically I had become a shadow of my former self in just a few days.

After another Christmas in an institution I began to feel better and the thought of that record attempt started to come back again. But the question had been asked that if breaking the hour record twice already did not satisfy me in the present, why should a third time be so different for the future? When I really thought about it I had to admit that I had no answer to this. I realised within myself that I was driving myself to new and bigger achievements simply as a matter of self-justification. In the end I agreed that I would not seek to break the record for a third time. And this meant that I couldn't race at all, even at club level, because this would only escalate into wanting more and more speed success and then the ultimate prize.

Not having an end goal was difficult because I had no imaginary pillar of success to hide behind, which left me feeling naked and exposed emotionally. It was a hard time but somehow or other I would have to stop 'being my achievement' and start 'just being'. It was difficult 'just being' and there were terrible feelings of insecurity, unworthiness and depression. The drive to make a comeback was overpowering however, and I felt like a burden to my family with a lot of making up to do because of everything that had gone before. I dreamed of the money I could earn from the hour record and the invitation rides that would follow, and how this would help us realise our ideal of moving into a larger house where the boys could have a room each. What this meant, however, was that my motives for cycling, along with an increasing fear of failure, were being inspired by everything but what should have been the prime desire – to attack the record through passion for the sport alone, and to be driven by the dream of the achievement itself.

It got to the point where every ride seemed like bloodless self-mutilation, and without passion I could never reach the training levels I had managed in previous years. I carried on like this for some time, unwilling to let go what still seemed like my only hope of self-worth. At this time, now the winter of 2001, I was also dealing with problems at the bedsit in the property we rented out, and since my mood had ebbed to the point of hopelessness and despair, it took all the mental strength I possessed to deal with these problems and to hide how I was feeling from Anne and the boys.

On 17th December I went to sort out some things at the bedsit. I was in a particularly low frame of mind where I saw myself as useless and a burden to everyone, especially Anne and the boys. I had a midday appointment that day with my psychiatrist, but not wanting to cause concern or be a burden I put a front on everything and determined to defeat this black feeling on my own. Yet again I was driven to seek the help of what really is the depressive's worst enemy – alcohol. One of the tenants asked if I was okay and tried to contact Anne at home, but she was out at the time. The feel-good effect that I had so desperately sought never came and no amount of alcohol could help. I then remembered Anne had asked me to feed her horse, which was kept at a farm in Kilmaurs 7 miles away, so I proceeded to cycle there, buying more alcohol on the way.

I woke up in the early hours of the next morning in a white room. The nurse asked me if I knew why I was there, and I said no. Anne was there too, and she explained that I had hanged myself at the farm. I knew that she had asked me to feed the horse after I was finished at the bedsit, but had no recollection of cycling there, or anything else that happened after that. There are two possibilities for my memory loss. One is that I was in an alcoholic blackout, which is unlikely since I managed to cycle the 7 miles, and the other is that hypoxia (oxygen starvation) had caused amnesia. I tend to agree with the latter.

It was dark when it took place, and the location is very isolated. Normally nobody would have been there and it was only by chance that a fifteen-year-old girl called Lizzy Murphy had an impulse to visit her horse at an unusual time for her. After hearing me say hello and 'sounding unwell', she decided to check on me later as she was leaving. She found me hanging with zip ties around my neck and ran for her father, Brian. What she saw must have been a terrible sight and one for which I still feel guilty. Lizzy and her father saved me and called for an ambulance. It was reckoned that normally I would have died had it not been for my unusually large lung capacity – 6 litres compared to the average 2-3 litres – but if Lizzy had arrived a minute later then I certainly would have been dead.

Anne and her family and relatives prayed all night for me. The next day, to the complete surprise of the staff in intensive care, I was attempting to move about and breathe on my own. When I eventually looked in a mirror my eyes were as red as snooker balls.

There followed a long stay in the mental ward at Crosshouse Hospital and for the first two weeks my eyes remained blood red before returning to normal in the course of the months. During and since that time I have busied myself with this account. I have had other difficulties since, but writing this book has had a positive effect, and been another part of my ongoing therapy. My diagnosis seems to be more complex than just a case of manic-depressive illness. The professionals allow that as a condition, but they believe that 'personality disorder' may be closer to the mark, if not a contributory factor. In the meantime I will continue with therapy.

Christmas 2002 was the first Christmas I spent at home with my family for two years, and 2003 started with more hope than new years in the recent past ever had. Even though when I feel insecure, point-less or worthless my first instinct is to train for glory as a route to self-justification I must be careful not to fall back into my old ways. This will only perpetuate a cycle that has existed too long and instead of this I am better trying to deal directly with whatever makes me feel that way – if I have the courage to do so. If I ride it should only be driven by passion for the sport itself with no ulterior motives. I feel and hope that the era of extreme depression and hospitalisation may be over, though it goes without saying that the future is nobody's to tell.

There has been nothing too dramatic about the start of 2003, I am glad to say, except the beginning of having my book published and the possibility of a feature film of my life being made in the near future. The dramatisation will concentrate mainly on my racing career with just a passing mention of my mental illness. From now on I will try to live my life 'just being' – without the drive to go beyond the limits in the longest hour of them all, just to prove myself worthy of another day's existence.

appendix: extracts from
L'Equipe 19 July 1993

EDDY MERCKX, climbing off his bike, said: 'Never again'. Obree got on the track twice within 24 hours and the second time was the good one. Francesco Moser was relying on science. Obree is more empirical, a DIY man and his record is a slap in the face of conventional ideas. How many racers have been through the wind-tunnel since Moser? And now comes this unknown Scot beating the record in a posture my granny might have adopted on her bike! What if we had made a mistake from time immemorial about the best way to pedal?

AND OBREE CATCHES TIME UP

From our special correspondent in Hamar, Pierre Ballester:
There are no words in English or in French to tell this true story; no sentences to sum up this hour that has overtaken space; no derisory superlatives to celebrate the fight of one man alone against appearances and certainties. We would have liked to see Obree riding on forever – to dig an unforgettable groove in the wooden track of the Hamar velodrome.

When he got up at 8 o'clock on Saturday morning Graeme Obree had everything against him. Only 21 hours to recover after his disappointment of the day before (50.689 km), a restless night ('I woke up every two hours') and the weight of fate at the end of the track. 'It was in fact my last chance, because once the expedition was over and the officials had gone, it would have been difficult to have another try due to lack of cash.'

'Old Faithful', as he likes to call her, was built with his own hands last winter, bit by bit: it was a genuine piece of recycling due to lack of cash, but there was no lack of genius. The bearing of the drum of his washing machine supports the crank. A bit of metal found on the road-side where he trained is the shaft of the pedal. The handlebars come from a child's mountain-bike, a left-over from his old cycle shop's stock. And the rest, according to his fancy, was assembled, welded and artic-ulated like Pinocchio taking shape.

So, when he got up that morning, as he did a few stretching exer-cises against the wall of his room for his stiff legs, as he swallowed a bowl of corn flakes mechanically, he glanced tenderly at 'Old Faithful' as if to tell her: 'Come on, old girl, today we do it.'

An hour after waking up, after a short warm-up, Obree caressed the stem of his machine, let his blue eyes rest on the front wheel and took off as if he was never to be seen again – as if he was going to the moon without any oxygen, without knowing whether he would ever come back. Bye, bye Graeme.

Obree. It's the story of a guy who goes over 6.5 metres with a bamboo pole. 'The bike that I'd used the day before matched every detail of my machine, but it was a bike . . .'

Then, at 9.10. a.m., the starter broke the silence of a deserted velo-drome. Even the two ranks of chronometers that overlooked the scene hadn't seen fit to mark the time. There were 85 witnesses: the stadium warden and some lost tourists watching in disbelief, unaware that a beautiful story, a fabulous record, was taking place.

'Right from the warm-up period I knew that my legs were responding. It was just a matter of holding.' In fact, the first regis-tered times were encouraging. With a tear in her eyes, Jane, the wife of Vic Haines, his manager, was holding up a slate with a livid smile at each passage of his dizzy rounds. This time the sellotaped arrow was pointing upwards and the figures comparing with Moser's times were preceded by a '+'.

A few thousands faster at 5 km (5'47" 116 for Obree; 5'47" 160 for Moser), a few seconds faster at 10 km (11'32" 940 for Obree; 11'40" 760 for Moser). Faster and faster, so much so that the Norwegian announcer who stayed only to honour his contract, could not help declaring, 'Obree is 10 seconds faster than the *old* 20 km record.'

The astonishment was growing under the silent dome and at the halfway point Jean Bayliss, the white-haired English lady in charge of the timing, could not help exclaiming that time was going slower for this 'Flying Scotsman' who had become *her* Graeme, and who had gained 14 seconds on Moser, nine years earlier, and 2,200 m higher at 25 km.

'Tell me Graeme, what will you do tomorrow?'
Then and only then, faces became tense. Lying flat on his crooked tubes, pressing endlessly on his rusty pedals driving 52 by 12, i.e. two teeth less at the front than the day before, sticking to that damned black line as if it were the only lifeline to his personal Everest, it was impossible for Obree to maintain such violent effort.

He didn't maintain it. In fact, he increased it! At 30 km silent frenzy was tangible: 17 seconds faster than Moser; five more at 40 km!

'Ten kilometres, Graeme, just ten more!' Everybody round the track was shouting – Vic Haines; Alan Rochford, the sponsor of his club in Essex, the Leo Racing Club; Anne, his wife, tiny and energetic; Richard Hemmington, the English Director of the American wheel manufacturer Specialized; Theresa, his mother-in-law, 'my mascot'; David Taylor, *Cycling Weekly* journalist. And to hell with this damned British reserve, even Kelvin Trott, Obree's tight-suited patron, the boss of a recruitment agency for accountants, started shouting, no doubt the most serious swearing of his career.

That was it. There were about fifteen of them scattered in that oval cage, open-mouthed like sparrows. And the first release came when Graeme cycled for the 206th time past that cone marking km 51.151; Moser's record. The second release came some thirty seconds later when the gun put an end to the joyful suffering of this man, who cycled round two more times with his hands up savouring an intensely intimate happiness. 51.596.904 – such was the dry record of a new page in history.

'To keep the pace, that's all I was telling myself' he kept repeating when he came down to earth. And he sprayed the track with cheap sparkling rosé wine, another sign of his modesty.

Four photographers immortalised this surreal event and the two journalists were cracking daft, excited smiles. And France 2, the only TV company on the spot were smugly recording pictures which passed quickly, so quickly.

Obree got everything he had been dreaming of when this little bike he had had in his head came to greatness. After he had passed the magic 50 km, one of his pals asked him in a very British manner: 'Tell me, Graeme, what will you do tomorrow?'

TEMPS DE PASSAGE		
	MOSER	**OBREE**
5 km	5'47''16	5'47''11
10 km	11'40''76	11'32''94
15 km	17'30''46	17'22''15
20 km	23'21''59	23'11''43
25 km	29'14''85	29' 0''46
30 km	35' 7''47	34'50''75
35 km	41' 0''30	40'39''76
40 km	46'52''01	46'30''39
45 km	52'45''88	52'20''03
50 km	58'40''11	58'09''53
Heure	51 km 151 350	51 km 596 904

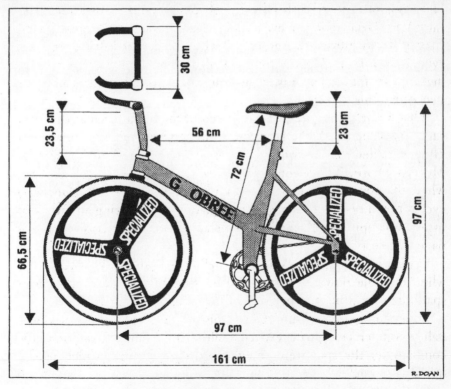

L'Equipe lists 'Old Faithful's' vital statistics below a table of
time splits for the record breaking run

REACTIONS

FRANCESCO MOSER: 'Of course I am very disappointed, but records are there to be beaten, as they say. What surprises me most is the fact that he attempted it for the first time and then beat it 22 hours later. I can't figure that out. As far as I am concerned I'll try again in January as I planned to long since. I'll go to Mexico like I did ten years ago.'

MIGUEL INDURAIN: 'The performance of this unknown Scot is extraordinary, especially as he went 450 metres further than Moser. It is a record that will need many hours of work to be beaten. At the moment I have not prepared anything. This winter we'll examine the possibility of doing it next year, but nothing is sure. For me it is a question of prestige. What counts is to beat the record not the record holder. To me beating Obree's record is as important as beating Moser's record.'

BERNARD HINAULT: 'That record had to be beaten one day. The problem is that the rules are not at all precise. Already when Moser had beaten the record his bike was not a conventional machine. So why not attempt it in a stretched-out position now? The rules are too vague for the two records to be compared. The only thing that counts is the number of kilometres covered, not how it was done. Nevertheless I admire what that guy has done.'

TONY ROMINGER: 'What that Scot did is great. I am sure, however, that at altitude one could gain still more, around 2 km extra. In the near future 53.5 km in an hour will be a possibility. If I work on it for one-and-a-half months I could reach 53.2 km at altitude. In any case, the first man to attempt it at altitude will smash the record. Nevertheless, what Obree did remains enormously surprising.'

JOSE-MIGUEL ECHAVARRI: 'It is perfect. Romantic ideas have won the day, scoffing at scientific research on the materials technology. I believe it is good to have this sort of thing from time to time. That's why I can only congratulate him most heartily.'

ALEX ZULLE: 'I did not know he was going to attempt it. I didn't even know that Scottish guy. It's really great what he has done, but I'm not personally worried. You have got to be an expert on the track to beat the record. I'll never do it. It's not my style.'

FRANCIS MOREAU: 'What is fantastic is that it's an unknown guy, unemployed, who built his own bike and managed to smash Moser's record. Sure it will open doors, it will give ideas to people. To me and to others.'

CHRIS BOARDMAN: 'I am really happy for Graeme. I was so disappointed for him on Friday. I am all the more happy with the performance he has just managed. It only increases my will to succeed.'

Pingeon understood

Talking for French-speaking Swiss Television, Roger Pingeon analysed Obree's record. Looking at the pictures in front of him and peering at the photograph from *Velo Magazine* on his knees, an idea occurred to him that could explain Obree's success.

'By turning the photo I realised that he had a special posture, as if he was standing on the pedals. In fact he is using this posture to its best advantage, with the minimal loss of force and without the normal disadvantage of the standing-up posture. He does not catch the wind as his head remains very low. Nearly all his body weight is pushing on the pedals, whereas normally it pushes on the seat. It allows him to gain two more teeth at the back and to achieve what only the tough guys can do in a normal sitting position.'

MAD, BRILLIANT AND HUMAN

From our special correspondent in Hamar:

Nothing at all could have predestined Graeme Obree to turn a new page in the history of cycling. Not his family, of modest means and more preoccupied with surviving the hard conditions of life in the West of Scotland than with satisfying the whims of their three children. Nor the cycling bug, which was never in evidence in the family environment. Nothing, except that inborn desire to create something out of nothing, to assemble bits of tubing and turn them into a living toy.

Born in Nuneaton, in England, in 1965 to a father who was a policeman and a mother who was a housewife, both originally Scottish, young Graeme grew up in Kilmarnock from the age of six after his father had been transferred. And it's in the shelter of his parents' small garden, together with a school pal, Gordon Stead, that the kid started playing with discarded bits of metal.

Bit by bit, with a hammer and a screwdriver, young Obree ended up working on the object of his dreams, his dreams of escaping. 'What I wanted was to be free, to go away on roads by myself, to discover things, and as my parents could not buy me a bike, I made one myself,' he explained recently.

'What I love most, is to build, to construct,' he added. 'That's why I started a course in mechanical engineering at Glasgow University although I wasn't able to complete the year because I couldn't pay for my studies.'

The right to dream

Obree probably did not know that the bike he was creating in his garage was his ideal. And that, with this bike, he was at last going to be able to take his revenge on his eternal rival Chris Boardman. Boardman was the favourite child of the British Federation, an Englishman from Liverpool, the Olympic pursuit champion in Barcelona. For him the whole range of computer logistical procedures were used to make him the flag-bearer of a proud nation.

Nevertheless it is Obree who became the 50-mile British champion at the end of June in Sandwich, the day before beating the 10-mile British record. It is Obree who last week arrived at Hamar rather than at the Bordeaux velodrome, as initially planned, for a first attempt to break the hour record, This attempt resulted in an unexpected outcome as it went through the prestigious limit set nine years earlier and two thousand meters higher by Francesco Moser (51.525 km against 51.151 km).

Obree lives with his instinct, his feeling, which dictates his way of life, his career as an amateur cyclist. He speaks of his 'body signals', his own remedies a long shot from any scientific data.

'He and Boardman are in every way at the opposite ends of the spectrum and his eccentric character takes him out of any category,' said David Taylor, the only British journalist present in Norway. 'Their rivalry is reminiscent of the rivalry between Sebastian Coe and Steve Ovett at their peak.'

So, if the latter follows a path dictated by a computer curve, the former relies solely on his impressions. It was a perfect scream to see him on Friday night in the corridor of his hotel arguing with anybody who would listen about his strategy for the next day. Everything improvised, terribly human. All this could very well disturb or scare the traditional cycling gurus he never accepted, with his 'abnormal' posture, with his body parallel to the ground, with his knees under his stomach, with his bottom at the very end of the saddle, with his preparation going against the grain of accepted ideas, with his machine lacking computer-designed composite materials. To prove that the fight between man and machine is no longer unequal. To believe that the dream can be attained.

Extracts translated by Jean Stassin and Rory Watson.